D1017524

Exploring Contemporary Male/Female Roles: A Facilitator's Guide

Exploring
Contemporary Male/Female Roles:
A Facilitator's Guide

Edited by
Clarke G. Carney
and
Sarah Lynne McMahon

UNIVERSITY ASSOCIATES, INC.
7596 Eads Avenue
La Jolla, California 92037

Copyright © 1977 by International Authors, B. V.

ISBN: 0-88390-135-8

Library of Congress Catalog Card Number 76-58237

Printed in the United States of America

Preface

In the past ten years, the conventional expectations of an increasing number of people have been shattered by hearing about alternative life styles. Most Americans who came to maturity prior to 1960 took for granted that adulthood meant getting a job, settling into a monogamous, till-death-do-us-part marriage, buying a home, and having children—the American Dream. Now our imaginations are titilated by myriad possibilities greeting us from the covers of popular magazines and television screens; our assumptions about what constitutes the right life style are being upset; and change seems to provide the most stable ingredient in our environment.

Almost daily we encounter descriptions and discussions of alternative sexual relationships. Short-term marriage contracts, cohabitation, group or serial marriage, communal life, and homosexual marriage are becoming alternatives to the traditional marital union. Unfortunately, descriptions of alternative sexual expressions often confuse sexual freedom and sex-role freedom. Thus, although sexual behaviors may change, rigid applications of sex-linked daily practices such as cooking, cleaning, and running errands still persist in many sexually open relationships.

Perhaps no area of change affects as many people or threatens as many varied relationships as basic assumptions about sex roles. Emerging feminism challenges not only legal statutes and economic practices based on traditional paternalism but also the content of sex roles within all relationships. Many activities within the home and in the vocational sphere are losing their sex typing. Even such biologically based roles as mothering and fathering are being neuterized to "parenting." Social scientists have suggested that many personality traits and behaviors are losing their long-held sexual identifications and are increasingly being seen as a function of the individual personality.

As we gaze into a future that holds a bewildering array of patterns, the very interfacing of our culture seems to be coming apart. Thus the individual must somehow create a design that fits him- or herself, but no one else. The potential for growth, creativity, and meaning in such a society seems limitless; the potential for incapacitating confusion, anomie, and a backlash into more rigid sex-role norms seems frightening and equally possible.

Our personal experiences and the recent social science literature indicate that sex-role concept is a central, controlling element of each person's self-image. Indeed, some of our assumptions about appropriate sex-role behaviors are so fundamental that we do not recognize their motivating force in our lives. We all have masculine and feminine characteristics: some that we develop and others that we suppress, some that we feel good about and others that we feel uncomfortable, guilty, or worried about.

Deciding between alternative life styles can be a momentous, scary decision for the young. Exploring new attitudes, feelings, and behaviors can be equally threatening to a person with years invested in a marriage, vocation, and mortgage. However, it seems to us that denying the value of undeveloped parts of ourselves and acting as though there are no options is self-defeating. Continuing stereotypic relationships that are not equal, not open, and not mutually self-enhancing can be defeating for a society. After all, both women and men need to cry, express anger, depend on other people, initiate activities, and love and be loved.

We can help individuals discover options when they feel they have none, provide a focal point for those who feel overwhelmed by too many alternatives, and furnish ways to change when people feel dissatisfied with their present lives. The structured experiences in this volume are intended to enable facilitators to help individuals reach these goals and achieve maximum growth—recognizing and integrating all aspects of one's personality to become more fully human.

Clarke G. Carney
February 1977   *Sarah Lynne McMahon*

Acknowledgments

This book is as much the product of a relationship as of a professional endeavor. The conception, the emphasis, and the content evolved over several years of interaction. As partners we planned programs, talked with students, led groups, and finally collaborated by mail. Our most original exercises emerged from afternoons spent with feet on the desk, good laughter, and numerous cups of coffee. Synthesizing two writing styles and personal/professional/political perspectives provided the greatest challenge to our work. Small matters such as who begins the group, who distributes the handouts, and who writes the letters were major issues or minor irritations at times. Perhaps our biggest accomplishments were working out patterns for dealing with our feelings, supporting each other through our ups and downs, and allowing for growth and change. Because of our experiences, we have become increasingly aware of how personal views of sex roles influence behavior and expectations. This awareness has taught us to value more highly the feminine and masculine parts of ourselves and each other.

We refer to the book as "our baby," and certainly the feelings of excitement, anxiety, and joy that accompany parenthood have also been ours. Fortunately, our baby has had an extended family to further its development. First, thanks go to John Steffen, who wisely suggested that we should meet each other. We appreciate friends like Christina Hunt, Bob Sinnett, Bill Ogg, Mike Lynch, and Dick Stranges, who gave us valuable feedback after they read the book and/or tried the structured experiences. We thank Carole Widick and Mike Cowan for adding a special dimension to the book through their article on developmental instruction. We are also indebted to Lillian Rice for typing the manuscript. We want to thank Rebecca Taff and the editorial staff at University Associates for their direction and contributions. Special thanks go to our spouses: to Myra for her support and encouragement and to Michal for the critical perspective of the humanist scholar.

We identified and acknowledged the creators and publishers of the structured experiences and instruments in this book when the authorship was known to us. We appreciate the authors' willingness to allow us to adapt their materials to our framework and regret not being able to acknowledge directly all those whose ideas and exercises have contributed significantly to the book.

Contents

Instruments

Readings

Appendix

Bibliography

Introduction

Leading a sex-role workshop sounds exciting and deceptively easy. "Let's get together and talk about our sexuality and how we feel about being men and women" has lured many unqualified persons into leading faddish groups. During the past decade, the proliferation of groups and the lack of adequately trained professionals to staff them has elicited justifiable criticism of the whole group movement. Qualified facilitators who adhere to the APA Guidelines for Psychologists Conducting Growth Groups (American Psychological Association, 1973) should maximize the growth potential for participants in any group situation and minimize the possible negative effects. In addition to group leadership experience, the facilitator needs a working knowledge of small-group dynamics, group-counseling theory, developmental instruction, and workshop goals and processes.

Helping participants integrate what they have learned is an important part of the process, if the learning is to last. Participants can be helped to set goals and establish plans for new or changed behaviors and to continue their experimenting.

If the total structured experience or the process is genuine and meaningful, participants will share very personal feelings, concerns, and perceptions. Occasionally, however, a participant may become distressed by the group experience, and the facilitator will need to offer individual or group counseling resources. If qualified to counsel, he or she may take participants as clients when other assistance is not available, or after the group terminates. If not qualified to counsel, he or she can help participants to find other assistance.

The activities in this guide, because they are focused on sex roles, require that the facilitator understand how sex roles and sexual stereotypes develop and how they function in our society. Equally

1

important, the facilitator should be aware of and reasonably comfortable with expressing his or her own feelings and attitudes toward masculinity, femininity, and the expression of sex roles.

Brown (1965) defines *social roles* as "norms that apply to categories of persons." As social roles applying to both men and women, *sex roles* play a powerful part in the development and socialization of each sex. For instance, girls and women are expected to be interpersonally oriented and nurturing; boys and men are expected to be achieving and instrumental. Each role includes a set of prescriptive rules; certain kinds of performance are expected. According to Brown, *stereotypes*, while not prescriptive, include "categorical expectancies." Men are seen as rational, cold, and unemotional; women as warm, emotional, and impressionable. The "drugstore cowboy" or the "jock" are images associated with the male stereotype; women are seen as incompetent, although good at the kind of detail involved in clerical work. They are "dumb blondes" or "sex kittens." These stereotypes are almost by definition negative. Although sex roles and sex-role stereotypes often play an important part in a person's life, more and more people are seeking freedom from negative aspects of societally determined roles and stereotypes.

PURPOSE OF THIS BOOK

This book is a collection of activities and readings intended as a resource for facilitators working with any group of individuals who may wish to clarify their sex-role identities and/or who are struggling with other people's sex-role expectations for them. It can be equally useful for working through a conflict that has come up in a different type of group—a conflict that can be traced to sex-role attitudes.

The activities are designed to be individually useful. Facilitators who work with a variety of groups in many settings—college campuses, churches or religious retreats, growth centers, community mental health centers, counseling centers, schools, and organizations—can choose those activities most suitable to the needs of their participants. The book can also be used for a self-contained, ongoing workshop with a specific male-female focus.

The structured experiences presented here are organized along two progressive, interconnecting developmental continuums: from introductory, getting-acquainted activities to integration and commitment activities; and from activities requiring little personal trust and risk taking on the part of participants to those demanding a great deal. Both continuums reflect the fact that attitudinal change occurs sequentially—newer and more complex forms of learning are built on previous experiences and learnings.

As stated in the article by Carole Widick and Mike Cowan in the Readings section (*How Developmental Theory Can Assist Facilitators to Select and Design Structured Experiences*), the goals and processes of structured experiences should be designed by the facilitator to meet participants at their own developmental levels. For participants who have only a rudimentary understanding of the sex-role socialization process, an appropriate learning goal might be a simple increase in awareness that new possibilities exist. For those who have some awareness, further expansion through exploration may be the most appropriate goal. There may also be individuals who have already had an opportunity for broad exploration. For them, integration and commitment within a range of alternatives may be the most appropriate goal.

When choosing structured experiences, it is important that the facilitator know the needs of the group. Involving the participants in the planning adds significantly to their feelings of ownership about the outcomes. Structured experiences can be used to meet individual or group needs that arise during an activity; the more spontaneous the activity is, the more effective it seems to be. Timing is crucial. Also, the facilitator's competency in selecting and preparing structured experiences with the appropriate complexity is reflected in how well the experience enhances personal growth and the growth of a group. The essential goal is to focus on the person and his or her experience rather than on specific content.

Stated in terms of a developmental continuum that recognizes individual variation, the general goals of the structured experiences in this guide are:

1. To develop an awareness of the social and psychological processes that affect sex-role socialization and sex-role stereotyping;
2. To gain a broader perspective on the functions of sex roles and sex bias in Western society;
3. To become aware of and more comfortable with the sex-role socialization process;
4. To become aware of and to explore personal attitudes, feelings, and behaviors that result from internalized sex-role norms;
5. To gain insight into the feelings and experiences of the other sex and the pros and cons of each sex role;

6. To become aware of and explore alternative methods for dealing with sex-role stereotyping in the participants' own lives;
7. To identify areas for personal growth and change;
8. To become acquainted with models of change in organizational settings around sex-role issues.

THE PARTICIPANTS

A sex-role workshop or selected structured experiences focusing on sex-role stereotypes are not forms of therapy, but rather developmental experiences to increase the individual's interpersonal skills and self-understanding. Ideally, participants should be relatively mature, healthy, effective, and willing to risk in order to learn. Individuals whose needs appear to be inappropriate should be referred to other more suitable activities, such as assertiveness training groups, consciousness-raising groups, or psychotherapy groups.

The more heterogeneous the group, the more care must be taken in dealing with differences among group members. Issues of religious preference, age, race, class, economic level, and education may account for different and conflicting norms within the group. If the facilitator feels that conflicts are not being dealt with, he or she may want to break the group into half and process the differences with an activity such as "Questions You've Always . . ." or use a group-on-group design. Issues of intimacy and confidentiality are important when people work together or deal with each other on a social basis. In a workshop setting, care should be taken to establish group guidelines about the amount of self-disclosure supported by the group structure. Because sex role and sex identity are usually central aspects of self-concept, facilitators should be sensitive to participants' reactions to experiential activities.

ROLE OF THE FACILITATOR

Ideally, the facilitator selects and directs activities to match the developmental levels of participants and guides participants in selecting personal goals without subtly or directly imposing any values or needs on the group. The facilitator serves as a model of effective interpersonal behavior by participating in activities when appropriate, by sharing experiences and feelings, and by accepting the "personhood" of others. By assuming a learning, participatory stance, the facilitator is open to new feedback, insight, and growth. However, the facilitator should not relinquish responsibility for the structure and dynamics of the group, as laissez faire leadership could result in unnecessary stress for participants. Open-ended discussions are appropriate after the group has developed cohesion and a working autonomy.

Perhaps the most essential function of the facilitator is to clarify the participants' expectations. It may be helpful for the facilitator to ask for the participants' expectations and then to share his or her own. The facilitator can state his or her qualifications, suggest to the participants how the activity fits their needs, and indicate that their individual rights will be protected and that they will not be subjected to unwarranted group pressure.

Because a male in charge reinforces the male-dominance patterns so prevalent in Western society, we recommend using female and male co-facilitators to check and balance each other while providing a greater breadth of experience for more varied group learning. Also, with facilitators of both sexes, each participant has a same-sex leader with whom to identify in the early stages of the group, which are often marked by challenges to the authority perceived to be vested in other-sex leaders.

Co-facilitators also perform an important modeling function as individuals and in their relationship. A male leader, for example, may express feelings, be sensitive, and display other nonstereotypic qualities. A female leader can counter the cultural expectations by being competent and assertive and by taking an equal leadership position. Issues of power, influence, and style and other conflicts offer opportunities for the facilitators to model an equal, open, nonsexual relationship between a man and a woman. Paying special attention to sharing tasks, the facilitators can take turns beginning the group, distributing supplies, setting up refreshments, or leading activities. A little imagination can turn routines such as moving chairs or cleaning up after a break into role-reversal activities.

If the facilitators differ in their status in terms of degrees, experience, or professional position, this inequality can be dealt with in the group by discussing how each facilitator feels and what perceptions the group members have about the situation. (If the male is in a more powerful position, see "The Mentor Connection" in the Bibliography.)

HOW TO USE THE STRUCTURED EXPERIENCES

Before conducting an activity, the facilitator should state its goals clearly to the group. However, explaining too much about what can or will happen may inhibit spontaneous reactions. Instructions for written responses should be read aloud to clarify any ambiguity. The most effective use of structured experiences is ensured when they follow a logical sequence, are conducted properly, and are processed well.

An attempt can be made to *involve* participants in the activities, encouraging each person to incorporate the learning in his or her own personal way. The facilitator can offer background material through lecturettes, handouts, or other materials for dissemination or viewing.

If used together in a workshop format, the structured experiences in this guide can be adapted to various time formats, including marathon and weekly sessions. We have found daily sessions of two to three hours over a two-week period very productive. To allow for optimal carry-over from one session to the next, sessions should not be scheduled more than one week apart.

Nearly all of the structured experiences in this guide are most effective with a group of no more than twelve and no fewer than six participants, evenly divided by sex. The physical setting should be selected to contribute to a relaxed, comfortable atmosphere, with ample space for group interaction and individual privacy; flexible, comfortable seating; and writing surfaces.

PROCESSING

The activities presented in this guide are all relatively simple and require no special expertise on the part of the facilitator. However, it is extremely important that the facilitator choose structured experiences with care and systematically integrate the cognitive and experiential learnings with the goals of each activity. As some of the activities can be expected to generate considerable emotional data, the facilitator must be especially concerned with the adequate *processing* of any experience, talking through the behavioral and feeling data that emerge. Processing the data generated by the activity is often more important than performing the activity, for it is during processing that much of the learning takes place. The processing phase of the total experience can be a powerful stimulus to personal behavior changes outside the group. Each participant must have a chance to talk about his or her feelings and perceptions of what happened. The effectiveness of the experience depends on this step.

When using nonverbal and fantasy experiences, it is important not to make assumptions about the thoughts and feelings of the participants. What seems positive to some participants may be negative to others, so participants must be helped to process the experience thoroughly.

Processing usually focuses on the experiences and perceptions of individuals and the interactions of the group during the activity. The facilitator must have the skill to ensure that the feelings that surface are adequately acknowledged and understood, in order to avoid a stressful, unresolved situation. Participants must be helped to generalize and evaluate their learnings.

Some possible topics are attitudes toward oneself and others, relationships with significant others, beliefs about people, purposes of learning and growing, changing behaviors back home, or setting goals. Some techniques that may be useful for integrating data are group-on-group, in which one small group observes another in process and reports its observations; one or more "experts" with observation sheets who share their reactions to the group interaction (the facilitator may share his or her opinions as an "expert"); instruments or questionnaires to consolidate learning; video tapes or films; lecturettes on theory; assigned readings; formation of dyads to feed information about verbal and nonverbal behavior back to fellow participants; and short fantasy trips or role playing.

INTRODUCTORY ACTIVITIES

During the beginning minutes of each group session, the facilitator may wish to state briefly the goals of the upcoming activities. A polished speech is not necessary and, indeed, might hinder establishing an informal atmosphere. However, the following points should probably be covered at the first meeting of a group:

1. Focusing specifically on sex roles has been made necessary by the changing pace of sexual identity in our society.

2. The purpose of the activities is to provide a safe and helpful means of self-exploration and self-enhancement in a group.

3. The facilitator is not a teacher, but, like the group members, is participating to learn. Participants are encouraged to give feedback about the structure of the workshop and the facilitator's performance.

4. The session is not meant to take the place of a therapy group. Individuals within the group will not be evaluated or "treated" by the group facilitator.

5. The purpose of any assessment instrument administered is to

understand the effects of the workshop, not to diagnose individuals.

6. Everyone is free to participate according to his or her own needs and competencies. Each participant has the right to say "no" to participating in any activity.

7. Although some individuals may desire to change their sex-role behaviors subsequent to this experience, the facilitator does not require or even expect that all participants will seek change; however, the facilitator is willing to help those who do wish to try out new ways of relating to others.

8. Honesty and respect for individual differences should be the guide for all interactions.

If assessment questionnaires (see the Instruments section) are to be used to chart changes as a result of an ongoing group or a workshop, they can be administered at the beginning of the first session, after the facilitator has made their purpose clear.

As a further assessment of the progress of an ongoing group, the facilitator may wish participants to keep personal journals (Pfeiffer & Jones, 1974) to heighten their awareness of the sequence of events and their emotional responses. These can be begun during the opening session. Reading the journals later will provide an awareness of and a reinforcement for the learnings that took place. Journal entries may be made in the group context or as part of a take-home assignment. If entries are to be made during group time, the facilitator must provide an adequate amount of quiet time.

A useful technique is for participants to record *objective* descriptions of the progress of the group on one side of a page and their own *subjective* reactions to the activities or sharing experiences on the other side. A typical entry might read:

We began by using a getting-acquainted activity where we made collages to describe ourselves and our sex roles.	I felt apprehensive at first because I felt there was nothing to tell except "housewife and mother." I thought of several silly ways to present myself, but did not feel free to share myself with the others in those ways.

Dyads may be formed during the course of the group to process the subjective material found in each other's journals. For example, during a two-hour session, ten minutes could be set aside for making journal entries and another ten minutes could be used to share these.

As part of the closing activities, the facilitator may wish to have participants review their subjective responses in order to gain a personal sense of what the group experience has meant for them. Journal entries may also be used at the end of a workshop to help participants formulate their goals for behavioral change.

In order to help group members become acquainted in a relatively nonthreatening way or to assess the feelings of a group at the beginning of each session, such activities as dyadic sharing of relevant personal data are useful (things I like about myself; why I am here; what kind of man/woman I am; etc.). Dyad partners can then introduce each other to the larger group or form foursomes. Participants may also introduce themselves by making montages or collages that represent themselves and showing them to other group members. Each participant can explain his or her collage; or the more risky option of having group members react to a collage, followed by the explanation, may be employed. Only a few minutes should be allowed for each explanation, or the activity will become too long.

Participants may be asked to share things they like about themselves with one another or to complete one of the following sentences:

One thing I like about my body is _____.
If I could be any food, I would be _____ because _____.
If I could dine with any woman (or man) living or dead, it would be _____ because _____.
One feeling I have right now about being in the group is _____ .
If I could make any change in the world I would _____ .
One thing I want the group to know about me that they can't tell by looking at me is _____.
My favorite play activity is _____.

At the close of an introductory activity or session, the focus can be shifted to sex roles through discussion of the following points:

To what extent were your perceptions of other individuals colored by their sex and their apparent sex role? Did your own perceptions color your experiences of others in any way?

Did you observe any difference between your nonverbal impressions of others and their verbal self-descriptions?

What characteristics of the other individuals in the group had the most significant impact on you during the getting-acquainted process?

At any point during a workshop the facilitator may ask group members to evaluate what has just taken place—to share what they did or did not like and why or what they wish had happened. The importance of giving and taking both negative and positive feedback should be stressed, and each person, including the facilitator, shares feedback without comments, questions, or interruptions.

Although feedback is not a part of the process for every structured experience, if feedback is to be used, the facilitator may wish to discuss the principles of feedback, give examples, and ask participants to look at their own verbal feedback behavior. Participants can be encouraged to focus on individual strengths to help establish a positive learning climate.

ROLE PLAYS

Several of the structured experiences in this book require participants to engage in a role play, which can be an especially effective learning strategy when the following guidelines are observed.

• *Preparation and Warm-Up.* Sometimes it is useful to allow participants to practice another role play before they begin the activity. For example, a group could be instructed to play a cluster of people waiting for an overdue bus on a cold evening.

• *Structure.* Roles should be *structured* sufficiently so that the participant can pursue the objectives of the activity and *unstructured* enough to allow for improvisation and creativity.

• *Acting.* Participants should be cautioned against unrealistic overacting.

• *Debriefing.* The longer and more impactful a role play, the greater the need for debriefing, i.e., allowing the participants to discuss their reactions to occupying a particular role.

INSTRUMENTS

The instruments in this book are intended to augment group processes in a variety of ways. The various questionnaires provide pre- or post-measures of participants' changes in attitude during the course of the workshop and are an accurate reflection of participant learnings. The Self-Assessment Questionnaire helps the participants determine their current decision-making and interpersonal communication skills. By reviewing these ratings, the individuals can determine their own goals prior to a group experience.

Participant responses on the Attitudes Toward Women Scale, Male-Female Role Questionnaire, and Androgyny Scale Exercise can be good starters for group discussions through comparisons of the responses obtained. Comparing male average scores with female average scores often adds interesting data.

If participants want clarification on the goals and requirements of any sex-role workshop, the "Agreement for a Workshop on Changing Relationships—Female and Male" may be used (see Instruments section) to present the ground rules. The agreement also acts as a contract between individuals and the group and serves as a valuable prelude to the idea of contracting for change in interpersonal relationships (presented more fully in the later structured experiences).

READINGS, BIBLIOGRAPHY, AND APPENDIX

The Readings section contains an article by Alice Jeghelian on sexism in our society and women's responses to it; Kingsley Widmer's introspective male view of sharing the domestic role and the academic limelight; Jeanne Marecek's presentation of research findings on androgyny and sociological trends in American society; Barbara Bunker and Edith Seashore's treatment of sex-role stereotypes in social and organizational settings; a discussion and some conclusions about androgyny by Sandra Bem; a description of stereotypic male behavior by Patrick Canavan and John Haskell; Joseph Pleck's examination of the male response to women's changing life styles; Florence Denmark's research findings on early socialization of men; and Roslyn Willett's study of women executives. Also included is a piece by Carole Widick and Michael Cowan on developmental theory, describing how the facilitator can adjust his or her style and presentation to fit the developmental needs of participants. The readings may be used as assigned reading for an ongoing group, as handouts, or as background information for the facilitator and a source for lecturettes.

In the Appendix are some guidelines to help participants gain the most from a topic-oriented group experience.

A brief Bibliography of books and periodicals on sex-role stereotyping follows the Appendix. No attempt has been made to present an exhaustive list of current publications. Rather, the idea is to provide resources (publishers, etc.) from whom such information can be obtained.

REFERENCES

American Psychological Association. Guidelines for psychologists conducting growth groups. *American Psychologist*, October 1973, p. 933.

Brown, R. *Social psychology*. New York: The Free Press, 1965, p. 154.

Personal journal: A self-evaluation. Structured Experience 74 in J. W. Pfeiffer & J. E. Jones (Eds.), *A handbook of structured experiences for human relations training* (Vol. III). La Jolla, Calif.: University Associates, 1974, pp. 109-111.

STRUCTURED EXPERIENCES

I Am a Man/Woman Who . . .:
A Values Auction

Goals

I. To become aware of the selective nature of sex-role attitudes and behaviors.

II. To gain insight into how individuals respond to and manage competitive situations.

Group Size

Six to twelve participants.

Time Required

One and one-half to two hours.

Materials

I. A list on newsprint of items to be auctioned.

II. Several sheets of blank paper and a pencil for each participant.

Process

I. Prior to the activity, the facilitator selects and posts on newsprint twenty to thirty items from the I Am a Man/Woman Who . . . Items List.

II. The facilitator distributes blank paper and a pencil to each participant and reads the following instructions:

13

"We will sell at public auction the list of items posted on newsprint. Each will go to the highest bidder. This is a once-in-a-lifetime chance to express who you are or what you'd like to be on the basis of what you buy. Bid on each item according to how important it is to you or how sympathetic you are to it. Your currency is based on your age, not your experience. To determine the amount you have to spend, multiply your present age by twelve. That amount gives you your age in months and that's your currency. Think before you buy. No refunds or exchanges are allowed."

The facilitator allows time for each participant to read the list posted on newsprint and to write down the items he or she wishes to bid on.

III. The facilitator begins to auction the items one at a time in a professional auctioneering manner to create a feeling of realism among participants.

IV. When all participants have spent their currency, the facilitator points out that the participants' attitudes toward sex roles may be revealed through their purchases and that by bidding on an item from the list they assigned a value to that item.

V. The facilitator leads the group in a discussion of the experience and what each participant has learned about him- or herself and about others by the purchases made. The facilitator may wish to ask the following questions:

How did it feel to bid on your items?

How did you feel bidding against men? against women?

Were you as assertive as you wanted to be?

Did you feel competitive? or did you hang back?

VI. Participants are told to complete the statement "I am a man/woman who . . ." on blank paper. (Fifteen minutes.)

VII. Participants share their statements with the group. Time is allowed for discussion of differences and similarities and what these mean in relation to sex-role expectations.

I AM A MAN/WOMAN WHO . . . ITEMS LIST*

1. To own forty acres of mountain wilderness.
2. To own the sports car of my choice (identify when bidding).
3. To cry freely.
4. To catch a touchdown pass at the Super Bowl.
5. To be the first U.S. woman astronaut.
6. To win an Olympic gold medal.
7. To be gentle and tender.
8. To be a public relations coordinator for the major oil companies.
9. To be in complete charge of my life.
10. To have Hugh Hefner's pad—and its contents.
11. To have boundless energy on four hours of sleep per night.
12. To have a marvelous figure that is centerfold material for either *Playboy* or *Cosmopolitan*.
13. To be exotic.
14. To be the author of the ultimate sex manual, *The Sensual College Student* or *The Joy of Sex* (your choice!).
15. To have an evening with Debbie Reynolds or Diana Ross or Jane Fonda (specify which when bidding).
16. To parent a genius.
17. To win a Nobel prize for peace.
18. To control the future of the Women's Movement.
19. To graduate magna cum laude from Harvard (specify field and degree when bidding).
20. To retire with a million at 40.
21. To have a gift certificate for one year of Primal Therapy—free.
22. To invent a cheap source of energy that any person or country can use.
23. To head the investigation of a political scandal (specify what kind).
24. To be the most original, exciting party giver in town.
25. To live out the sexual fantasies of your choice.
26. To discover an island and name it for yourself.
27. To have a live-in guru.

---

*To be interesting, the auction items must be current. Facilitators may want to add their own items or delete some that seem inappropriate for their group.

28. To be Woody Allen's analyst.
29. To write, direct, and produce an afternoon soap opera.
30. To found a commune on the ocean floor.
31. To be governor of _____.
32. To play opposite Robert Redford.
33. To be aesthetic-artistic-sensitive.
34. To be president of a prestigious university.
35. To be impulsive-spontaneous.
36. To have a 100-year-old Bonzai tree.
37. To be erotic-sensuous.
38. To possess an unlimited charge account at an "in" clothing store.
39. To express anger easily.
40. To be lead singer for a top rock group.
41. To have a happy family life.
42. To have an affair to remember during a European vacation.
43. To be Gloria Steinem.
44. To be the discoverer of the cure for cancer.
45. To be unconventional-independent.
46. To be one of Nader's top raiders.
47. To be the best comedian on TV.
48. To have inner peace.
49. To have an evening with Dustin Hoffman or Paul Newman or John Wayne (specify which when bidding).
50. To determine how the Federal income taxes/revenues will be spent for one year.
51. To be the author of the great American novel of the 1970s.

Where Was I Then?:
An Awareness Activity

Goals

I. To explore the relationship between developmental life stages and sex-linked attitudes and behaviors.

II. To become aware of the sex-role socialization processes that have affected participants.

Group Size

Six to twelve participants.

Materials

I. Newsprint and a felt-tipped marker for each participant.

II. Masking tape.

Time Required

Forty-five minutes to one hour.

Process

I. The facilitator explains that the purpose of this activity is to get in touch with one's personal history of sex-role socialization and to compare individual histories with group and social norms.

Developed by Clarke Carney and Donald Streufert.

II. Each individual is given newsprint and a felt-tipped marker.

III. The facilitator tells the participants to relax, think back, and jot down as best they can recall their thoughts and feelings about what it meant to be a man or a woman at the following points in their lives: prior to elementary school; elementary school; junior high; high school; and beyond high school. (Corresponding ages may be substituted for educational levels.) (Fifteen minutes.)

IV. The facilitator may process the data either by having individuals post their remembrances on the walls—males on one wall, females on another—or by having each participant state his or her recollections aloud and recording and posting them on newsprint according to the sex of the participant.

V. The facilitator leads the group in a discussion of similarities and differences between males and females evidenced by the separate listings.

Variations

I. The facilitator may wish to assign for discussion purposes one of the articles from the Readings section of this book or another reading related to sex-role and life-stage development.

II. In an ongoing group, the facilitator may assign the group as a whole to generate ten questions about sex roles applicable to different stages of a person's life. Each participant is then assigned to interview people outside the group who are at the given life stages. When the group reassembles, the results are posted on newsprint. The facilitator leads a discussion of the similarities across each age sample and the similarities and differences among the various samples. The facilitator may wish to point out how the interview results differ from or are similar to the results obtained from the group.

Peak Experience Lifeline:
Information Sharing

Goals

I. To share one's personal history.

II. To explore past events involving members of the same and the other sex.

Group Size

Six to twelve members.

Time Required

Thirty to forty minutes.

Materials

I. Newsprint or blank paper and a felt-tipped marker or pencil for each participant.

II. Masking tape.

Process

I. The facilitator introduces this activity as a means for participants to gain different perspectives on their lives.

II. The facilitator distributes the materials. Each participant is instructed to draw two identical, parallel lifelines and to mark on each line when he or she was born, started school, married, and graduated from high school or college. Participants are told to put stars on their lines to represent the present moment. On the first line, they list peak, outstanding experiences with members of the same sex (parent, sibling, relative, or friend). On the second line, the same is done for members of the other sex. (Note: Because experiences will be shared in the group, the facilitator should emphasize that participants write only the experiences they wish to share. No specific kinds of events need to be included—just what comes to mind.) (Ten minutes.)

III. Each participant posts his or her lifeline, and members of the group may move around the room to view one another's lifelines.

IV. The facilitator asks each person to describe how he or she felt about him- or herself at the time of each event and how he or she would feel re-experiencing the same events now.

V. The facilitator points out any differences in significant events for males and females and leads a discussion of how each sex reacts to its own or the other sex.

Variations

I. The facilitator may encourage the group to focus on similar experiences between men and women, between women, and between men.

II. The group may wish to discuss the kinds of experiences they find harmful/painful and the kinds they feel are positive.

Cocktail Party Mix:
A Role Play

Goals

I. To provide an opportunity to try different sex-role behaviors.

II. To generate feedback on how individuals respond to various sex-role stereotypes.

Group Size

Six to eight participants of both sexes. Several small groups can perform the role play simultaneously.

Time Required

Approximately one and one-half hours.

Materials

Strips of paper on which the Cocktail Party Mix Roles are printed (one set per group).

Process

I. Prior to the activity, the facilitator prepares and cuts into strips the three sets of Cocktail Party Mix Roles (Male, Female, and Either). (Colored paper may be used to distinguish among the three types.)

II. The facilitator introduces the activity by briefly summarizing the goals.

III. Roles are distributed and participants are instructed to read the descriptions they have received. The group members are asked to pretend for the next six or seven minutes that they are in their assigned roles at a cocktail party chatting with a group of acquaintances.

IV. At the end of the time allowed, the facilitator leads the group in a discussion of the group interaction. Discussion questions such as the following might be used by the facilitator:

How did you convey your sex role to the group?

How did you feel acting out this particular role?

How did the group seem to respond to your role and other roles?

How did you feel about other participants' behaviors?

V. After the debriefing discussion, the participants are instructed to turn in their role descriptions in exchange for a different role. Steps III and IV above are repeated.

VI. For the third round, the participants may choose to play whichever of the roles they like, including ones they may have played previously. They may select the role they feel most comfortable with (one they characteristically assume in such situations) or a role that would involve them in trying out new behaviors.

VII. After the third cocktail conversation, the facilitator leads the participants in sharing the reasons for selecting their roles.

Variation

A group-on-group design may be used in which an outer group observes an inner group and then shares their observations.

COCKTAIL PARTY MIX ROLES—FEMALE

---

1. *Seductive Woman.* You are proud of your fantastic figure. You dress dramatically to show it off and flirt overtly—no harm intended, of course.

---

2. *Hostess.* You are concerned about how the party is going. The guests are quite divergent in attitude and behavior, and you see your role as trying to avert any potentially embarrassing situations.

---

3. *Feminist.* You are an attractive woman but are dressed rather plainly and do not wear make-up. You are both sensitive to and aggressive about women being treated as sex objects.

---

4. *Better-Homes-and-Gardens Wife.* You are trying to live up to the feminine mystique. Your home, children, and your husband's career are your only preoccupations.

---

5. *Mother Earth.* You are an older woman who likes to give advice and explain how things are to younger people. You feel ambivalent about being out of competition for the sexual attention of men.

COCKTAIL PARTY MIX ROLES—MALE

----

1. *Dirty Old Man.* You drink a lot and talk loudly and lewdly. You compensate for a lack of action by telling sexy jokes and making sly double entendres.

----

2. *Male Chauvinist Pig.* You respect women who stay in their places. You believe that men should be men and women, women.

----

3. *Playboy on the Make.* You pride yourself on the coolness, sophistication, and subtlety of your seductions. The marital status of the woman is not a significant factor to you; only her social class and physical appearance really matter.

----

4. *Radical.* You are a vociferous sympathizer with the women's movement in word if not in deed. You jump to the defense of women's rights as human beings and confront women who are acting out a conventional role.

----

5. *Jock.* You have been a professional athlete who maintains a strong interest in sports. Although you are aware of the recent trend to integrate men's and women's sports, you have doubts about its benefits.

COCKTAIL PARTY MIX ROLES—EITHER

----

1. *Prude.* You don't believe in discussing sex at all. You consider sex a private and sacred subject and tend to speak in moralistic terms.

----

2. *Intellectual.* You deal with sexual topics on an impersonal level. You cover up your own feelings with remarks about the latest article you have read and findings in sociology and psychology.

----

3. *Centered.* You have had rich life experiences and appreciate the complexity of life events. You listen attentively to others and respond with your own feelings and opinions in a gentle, assertive manner.

----

4. *Happily Married.* You have been in a primary relationship for several years. During this time, you have negotiated a mutually supportive and equitable living arrangement and your conversations reflect your satisfaction with your life style.

Role Reversal:
A Meditation

Goals

I. To provide an opportunity to explore common sex-role stereotypes.

II. To increase understanding of sex-role attitudes and behaviors.

Group Size

Six to twelve participants.

Time Required

One-half to one hour.

Materials

One copy of "Woman—Which Includes Man, of Course: An Experience in Awareness" for the facilitator to read.

Process

I. The facilitator briefly states the goals of the activity.

II. The facilitator instructs participants to find comfortable spots in the room where they can relax.

III. The facilitator asks participants to close their eyes, relax their bodies and minds, and listen to the meditation.

IV. The facilitator reads "Woman—Which Includes Man,

of Course: An Experience in Awareness" in a slow, relaxed manner.

V. Participants are instructed to think about their feelings as they become aware of their surroundings, open their eyes, and re-form into a group.

VI. The facilitator leads the group in processing the data. He or she may wish to focus on the types of feelings an imaginary male may be likely to express and discuss how each participant relates these feelings to his or her own experiences.

WOMAN-
Which Includes Man,
Of Course

An Experience in Awareness

Theodora Wells

There is much concern today about the future of man, which means, of course, both men and women—generic Man. For a woman to take exception to this use of the term "man" is often seen as defensive hair-splitting by an "emotional female."

The following experience is an invitation to awareness in which you are asked to feel into, and stay with, your feelings through each step, letting them absorb you. If you start intellectualizing, try to turn it down and let your feelings again surface to your awareness.

Consider reversing the generic term Man. Think of the future of Woman which, of course, includes both women and men. Feel into that, sense its meaning to you—as a woman—as a man.

Think of it always being that way, every day of your life. Feel the everpresence of woman and feel the nonpresence of man. Absorb what it tells you about the importance and value of being woman—of being man.

Recall that everything you have ever read all your life uses only female pronouns—she, her—meaning both girls and boys, both women and men. Recall that most of the voices on radio and most of the faces on TV are women's—when important events are covered—on commercials—and on the late talk shows. Recall that you have no male senator representing you in Washington.

Feel into the fact that women are the leaders, the power-centers, the prime-movers. Man, whose natural role is husband and father, fulfills himself through nurturing children and making the home a refuge for woman. This is only natural to balance the biological role of woman who devotes her entire body to the race during pregnancy.

Then feel further into the obvious biological explanation for woman as the ideal—her genital construction. By design, female genitals are compact and internal, protected by her body. Male genitals are so exposed that he must be protected from outside attack to assure the perpetuation of the race. His vulnerability clearly requires sheltering.

Thus, by nature, males are more passive than females, and have a desire in sexual relations to be symbolically engulfed by the protective body of the woman. Males psychologically yearn for this protection, fully realizing their masculinity at this time—feeling exposed and vulnerable at other times. The male is not fully adult until he has overcome his infantile tendency to penis orgasm and has achieved the mature surrender of the testicle orgasm. He then feels himself a "whole man" when engulfed by the woman.

If the male denies these feelings, he is unconsciously rejecting his masculinity. Therapy is thus indicated to help him adjust to his own nature. Of course, therapy is administered by a woman, who has the education and wisdom to facilitate openness leading to the male's growth and self-actualization.

To help him feel into his defensive emotionality, he is invited to get in touch with the "child" in him. He remembers his sister's jeering at his primitive genitals that "flop around foolishly." She can run, climb and ride horseback unencumbered. Obviously, since she is free to move, she is encouraged to develop her body and mind in preparation for her active responsibilities of adult womanhood. The male vulnerability needs female protection, so he is taught the less active, caring, virtues of homemaking.

Because of his clitoris-envy, he learns to strap up his genitals, and learns to feel ashamed and unclean because of his nocturnal emissions. Instead, he is encouraged to keep his body lean and dream of getting married, waiting for the time of his fulfillment—when "his woman" gives him a girl-child to carry on the family name. He knows that if it is a boy-child he has failed somehow—but they can try again.

In getting to your feelings on being a woman—on being a man—stay with the sensing you are now experiencing. As the words begin to surface, say what you feel from inside you.

"What Are Little Girls/Boys Made Of?":
An Awareness Activity

Goals

I. To become more aware of female and male sex-role stereotypes.

II. To increase awareness of the values placed on certain personality traits.

Group Size

Six to twelve participants.

Time Required

Thirty minutes.

Materials

I. A pencil and blank paper for each group's recorder.

II. Newsprint and a felt-tipped marker.

Process

I. The facilitator divides the group in half—preferably by sex if the composition of the group allows—states the goals of the activity, and instructs each group to appoint a recorder.

II. The members of each group are instructed to think of all the opposite-sex characteristics they can in three to five minutes. Individuals should offer traits quickly without group discussion (in brainstorming style) as the recorder writes them down.

III. When five minutes has elapsed, each group should first react to its own list and then share its list with the other group.

IV. The facilitator places each list on newsprint to facilitate a comparison.

V. Some questions the facilitator may want to use in debriefing are:

Are there any overlaps between the lists?

Which list is more attractive? Has more positive connotations?

Would your ideal person be limited to one list or the other?

Where are you in relation to the lists of characteristics?

Where would you like to be?

Variation

This activity may be used effectively to precede a more individual, in-depth exploration of sex-role attitudes, particularly when a group needs more time to warm up.

Sex-Role Attitudes:
A Role Reversal

Goals

I. To explore sex-role attitudes and behaviors of members of the other sex.

II. To increase understanding of masculine and feminine aspects of sex-role attitudes and behaviors.

III. To learn to recognize stereotypes associated with male or female behavior in certain situations.

Group Size

Six to twelve people.

Time Required

One-half to one hour.

Process

I. The facilitator introduces the activity by briefly summarizing its goals.

II. The facilitator describes the scene to be enacted, in which the females will play typical male aggressors ("girly watchers" or hustlers in a bar) and males will play passive females.

III. The facilitator assigns role-specific behaviors for each group member. Females are to act like the stereotype of a male aggressor, whistling, nudging, or making suggestive remarks. Males may wish to portray the females as snobbish, giggling, etc. (If a group member resists any form of role reversal, the facilitator may want to assign him/her the role of group process observer.)

IV. Participants are allowed to enact their roles for about ten minutes; then group members sit in a circle for discussion.

V. The facilitator may wish to have the group members discuss how they felt in their roles: what characteristics emerged as sex-role attributes or stereotypes; what it was like to be seen as a member of the other sex; what they learned about themselves during the exercise; if they found the exercise to be easy or difficult; etc. Group members should be encouraged to share their reactions with each other.

VI. The facilitator guides the group in summarizing some of the more salient learnings that came from this activity.

Variations

I. Alternate scenarios, based on current problems and concerns of the members, may be generated within the group.

II. In a very large group, a group-on-group model may be employed in which half the group observes the other half and later comments about the performance and the stereotypical behavior observed. Then the observing group can have a chance at playing the roles.

III. The role-reversal scenario can be extended to include homework activities such as seeking a job usually considered to belong to a member of the other sex and role-reversal dates.

Female/Male — Pros and Cons:
Self-Disclosure

Goals

   I. To express ambivalent feelings about individual sex roles.

  II. To become more aware of others' feelings about sex roles.

Group Size

Six to twelve participants.

Time Required

Thirty minutes.

Materials

Blank paper and a pencil for each participant.

Process

   I. The facilitator states that there are disadvantages as well as advantages to any life situation and that each group member will now have an opportunity to express ambivalent feelings about his or her sex role.

  II. Each person is given blank paper and a pencil and is told to complete the sentence "Sometimes I wish I were a man (woman) because . . ." (Five minutes.)

 III. Making no comment on the previous activity, the leader gives the group members five minutes to complete another sentence "I am glad I am a woman (man) because . . ."

IV. Each member then reads his or her completed sentences to the group.

V. The facilitator initiates a sharing of the learnings, feelings, surprises, reactions, or questions that each participant felt at sharing his or her own comments and hearing the comments of others. The facilitator may wish to point out similarities and differences shared by the same sex or opposite sexes.

Early Messages: Female-Male Scripts

Goals

I. To become aware of the individual socialization process.

II. To gain insight into how that socialization process differs for women and for men and how it has affected participants' lives.

Group Size

Six to twelve participants.

Time Required

Forty minutes.

Process

I. The facilitator tells the group to sit or lie comfortably, relax, and think a few minutes about their earliest childhood experiences that made them realize there are differences between boys and girls. He or she may want to structure a brief fantasy to help participants improve their memories of early childhood experiences. Clues such as going to school for the first time or playing in the neighborhood could be provided.

II. The facilitator tells participants to think about the messages their experiences gave them about what it means to be male or female.

III. After a few minutes, each participant in turn shares with the group his or her experiences and their messages. The facilitator helps each participant make a general statement about his or her experience.

IV. Differences and similarities between male and female responses, as well as the effects of the scripts on growing up male or female, are suggested by the facilitator and discussed in the group.

Questions You've Always . . .:
An Awareness Activity

Goals

I. To identify areas of conflict and discomfort that are based on sex differences.

II. To increase understanding of and ease with members of the other sex.

III. To test assumptions about values, experiences, and attitudes held by the other sex.

Group Size

Ten to twenty participants.

Time Required

Seventy-five to ninety minutes.

Materials

Several sheets of blank paper and a pencil for each group's recorder.

Process

I. The facilitator divides the participants into two groups on the basis of sex. Each group is told to appoint a recorder, who is then given paper and a pencil to list questions the group would

38

like to ask members of the other sex. Each group is instructed to arrive at a general consensus on the questions, including a priority ranking in case all questions cannot be answered. The facilitator cautions the groups to ask questions that are within the experience of members of the other group, rather than rhetorical questions. The facilitator may wish to give samples of appropriate and inappropriate questions. (If there are two connecting rooms, the men should be asked to go into the other room.) (Ten minutes.)

II. The facilitator calls the two groups together and explains the procedure. The women's group is to read one question. Any man, or several men, can respond to the question. When all who wish to respond have done so, the process will be reversed, with the men asking one question and the women responding to that question. Either group may refuse to answer any question. The facilitator emphasizes that time will be provided for discussion after the question-and-answer step.

III. Starting with the women's group, the two groups take turns asking and responding until one group runs out of questions or time is called. (Participants are warned when there is time for one more question each.)

IV. Participants share their reactions to each others' responses, one question at a time.

V. The facilitator takes care to let strong feelings come to the surface and be worked through. Processing this experience is especially important during the discussion stage, as the groups may feel momentarily estranged. The facilitator may wish to ask such questions as:

How do you feel in the group now?

How did it feel to divide into separate groups?

How did it feel for the men to leave (to go second)?

Was any question or response particularly upsetting to anyone? (Fifteen to twenty minutes.)

VI. The facilitator leads the group in discussing the assumptions behind certain questions and the respondents' reactions to these questions.

Masculine/Feminine Show and Tell: Posturing

Goals

I. To share concepts of masculinity and femininity.

II. To become aware of how body language is associated with sex roles.

III. To gain an understanding of the influence culture has on group norms.

Group Size

Six to twelve participants.

Time Required

Thirty minutes.

Process

I. The facilitator tells participants that they are to work only from their *own* concepts of masculinity and femininity.

II. The facilitator instructs the group to think of the most feminine body position possible. When all participants have images in their minds, they place themselves in that position, moving as necessary to take the position.

III. While remaining in the position, each participant shares how he or she decided on that particular position and how it feels. The facilitator may note similarities among group members—e.g., whether most of the participants are seated or standing.

IV. The facilitator then instructs the participants to imagine the most masculine body position possible. Participants assume that position, and the sharing process is repeated.

V. The facilitator leads a discussion of differences between masculine and feminine positions, how people feel in each, and what each position says about a particular person's view of men and women. The facilitator may wish to point out the passive/active dichotomy of female/male cultural stereotypes.

Variation

This activity is also easily adapted to larger microlabs.

The Party:
Exploration of Sex-Role Behaviors

Goals

I. To explore the values and assumptions involved in the personal preference of women and men for male or female social groups.

II. To explore feelings relating to competition and cooperation with same-sex and opposite-sex individuals.

III. To provide feedback about behavior in mixed-sex groups.

Group Size

Six to twelve participants.

Time Required

About one hour, depending on length of discussion.

Materials

I. Four sheets of newsprint prepared and labeled by the facilitator.

II. Masking tape.

III. A 3" x 5" card and a pencil for each participant.

Developed by Carolyn E. Carder and used with her permission.

Process

I. Prior to the meeting, the facilitator prepares four sheets of newsprint labeled "Men I Know as Friends," "Men I Don't Know," "Women I Know as Friends," and "Women I Don't Know" and tapes each sheet on a separate wall.

II. The facilitator distributes 3" x 5" cards and a pencil to each participant and directs group members to imagine themselves arriving at a party without a companion. They are to decide which of the four posted groups they would join.

III. Participants are told to write on one side of their cards the group they would be *most likely* to join at the party; on the other side, they are to write the group they would be *least likely* to join.

IV. The facilitator tells the participants to stand next to the sign representing the group they would be *most likely* to join.

V. The participants in each group share their reasons for joining that group and the feelings each person might have if he or she were actually with the people chosen. (Ten minutes.)

VI. The facilitator tells participants to stand next to the sheet representing the group they would be *least likely* to join. The discussion process is repeated. (Ten minutes.)

VII. The facilitator reassembles the entire group to share reasons for and feelings about each person's choices. The facilitator points out similarities and differences, particularly those related to cooperation and competition. (The facilitator may wish to give a lecturette on the role of competition and cooperation in social situations.)

VIII. The facilitator states that opposite ends of the room represent the end points of a response continuum. He or she reads the statement "I tend to compete (or cooperate) with members of my own sex" and asks participants to stand at the points along the continuum that express their individual responses to the statement. After noting where they are in respect to other members of the group, participants share the reasons for their choices and the feelings elicited by the choices. Possible links with sex-role behaviors are noted by the facilitator.

IX. Participants then place themselves on the same continuum in response to the statement "I tend to compete (or cooperate) with members of the opposite sex." The processing for this step is the same as for step VIII.

X. The facilitator directs each participant to complete aloud the statement "When I'm in a competitive situation, I feel . . ." The facilitator then leads a discussion of alternate behaviors that could decrease negative feelings in such situations. He or she notes the links between competition and sex-linked behaviors, especially those pertaining to assertiveness in interpersonal relationships.

Variations

I. In step I, the four polar possibilities can be reduced to two by using poles that read "People of My Own Sex" and "People of the Opposite Sex." This would ensure sex-mixed groups for both continua.

II. As an alternative form of placement and processing, participants may place themselves on each continuum, making mental notes as to the reasons for their choices. Processing occurs after the placements on both continua.

Sex Roles in the Popular Media: A Group Collage

Goals

I. To explore the role of the media in perpetrating sex-role stereotypes.

II. To help participants become aware of sex-linked behaviors that affect performance in problem-solving groups.

Group Size

Any number of small groups of four to six individuals, balanced for sex.

Time Required

One and one-half hours.

Materials

Newsprint pads or oaktag, magazines, scissors, crayons, and glue for each team.

Process

I. The facilitator gives a brief lecturette on the role of the popular media—radio, television, magazines, newspapers—in the development and continuance of stereotyped attitudes toward men and women. The subtlety of this influence is emphasized. The facilitator suggests that one way to be able to recognize and cope with it is to seek it out actively and make the covert visible.

II. Participants are assigned to "influence seeking" teams of no more than six members, balanced by sex. Each team is assigned two process observers.

III. Teams are told to create a collage that depicts the common forms of sex-role stereotyping found in the popular media. (Forty minutes.)

IV. Materials are distributed to each team.

V. Process observers are privately instructed to observe the following interactional patterns in the group:[1]

A. *Time Dominance.* Which sex has the most "air time" in the group?

B. *Question Asking and Answer Giving.* Which sex asks the questions; which one gives the answers?

C. *Role Distribution.* Which sex stresses task completion? Which sex takes responsibility for the maintenance function of supporting and encouraging others?

D. *Topical Flow.* Who controls the course of the conversation from one activity to the next?

VI. Near the end of the allotted time period, the facilitator tells each team to select an individual to present its collage to the other groups.

VII. The large group is reassembled and group collages are presented. Similarities and differences are pointed out by the facilitator and discussed by the group.

VIII. A group-on-group design may be used to share the process observers' comments. The facilitator tells the participants what the observers were instructed to note. Then, with process observers in the center of the group, they share their observations on each of the dimensions in step V. The process observers move out of the group to observe the reactions of the teams to what they have said. (This will allow the facilitator an opportunity to observe the teams on the same dimensions.)

IX. The facilitator leads a discussion of the participants' reactions to the activity. (Note: The facilitator may want to discuss personal behavioral change goals at this time.)

---

[1]The process observational dimensions used in this activity have been adapted from Warren Farrell, *The Liberated Man.* New York: Random House, 1974.

Toward a Nonsexist Language: Gaining Insights

Goals

I. To become aware of how language affects sex-linked attitudes.

II. To explore alternatives to sexist language systems.

Group Size

Any number of small groups of four to six members.

Time Required

One to one and one-half hours.

Materials

I. A newsprint pad and felt-tipped marker for each group.

II. Copies of "A Woman Is Not a Girl and Other Lessons in Corporate Speech" for each participant.

Process

I. The facilitator delivers a brief lecturette on the role of language in the shaping of sex-role stereotypes, attitudes, and behaviors. Particular attention is paid to guilt- and shame-provoking phrases such as "that's not ladylike," "that's women's work," "she's a tomboy," and "why does he prefer dolls to baseball?" as definers of what is good and appropriate or normal and natural for individuals in our society. If appropriate, pejorative terms may also be discussed in light of their sex-linked qualities. Note is made of the current difficulty in the usage of he/she, him/her, his/hers because of their sex-linked connotations and how several people—for example, Warren Farrell, who opts for phrases such as "tes" and "ter"—have suggested the need to develop a nonsexist language system.

II. The participants are told that they will identify sex-linked words and phrases that they encounter in their day-to-day lives and look at alternative nonsexist modes of expressing themselves verbally.

III. Participants are assigned to four- or six-member teams, balanced by sex. Each group receives newsprint and a felt-tipped marker. Groups are given fifteen minutes to identify and write down as many sex-linked words and phrases as they can.

IV. Each group then shares its list with the other groups and the facilitator leads a discussion of sex-role stereotyping as illustrated by the samples.

V. The facilitator distributes copies of "A Woman Is Not a Girl and Other Lessons in Corporate Speech" to each participant and allows time for reading, followed by a discussion of the alternatives presented.

VI. The small groups are re-formed and instructed to review their lists of sex-linked terms and look for alternative ways of conveying the same points in nonsexist terms, using the reading for guidelines. (Ample time is allowed to complete the process.)

VII. Participants are reassembled into a large group to share ideas. (Note: In an ongoing group, participants may be instructed to practice alternative forms of self-expression for the remainder of the time spent together.)

Variation

In place of step V, the facilitator may give a lecturette based on the article "A Woman Is Not a Girl and Other Lessons in Corporate Speech."

A Woman Is Not a Girl and Other Lessons in Corporate Speech

Patricia Hogan

If you listen carefully to businessmen's conversations, you can learn much about their attitudes toward women.

SCENE ONE: A planning meeting. Ten men are seated around a large, circular conference table. One of the men leading the meeting has forgotten to bring a crucial document. Discovering this, he says, "I'll have my girl bring it right over." Five minutes later, a woman who appears to be in her early forties knocks at the door, excuses herself for the interruption, and hands the man the document.

SCENE TWO: Mr. Z calls Sally Jones, one of the firm's account executives, into his office to congratulate her on landing an account the company has been pursuing for years.

"Sally, you did a first-rate job on that Mercer account," he says. "You really surprised everyone. Don't get me wrong—it's not that we didn't think you could do the job. It's just . . . well, how did you manage to get old Mercer to sign? Never mind, we won't go into that," he says with a wink.

Later, Mr. Z sees Ms. Jones in the executive dining room, approaches her table, and again congratulates her. "Bet you guys don't know what a terrific little saleswoman we have here," he says to the men lunching with Ms. Jones.

By day's end, Mr. Z has commended Ms. Jones five times on her achievement.

SCENE THREE: Six men and a lone woman attend a luncheon. The table conversation turns to capital gains, product diversification, and a new Management Information System (MIS) that will facilitate financial reporting for the large multinational corporation for which they work.

Halfway through lunch, one of the men leans over and whispers to the woman, "Are we boring you?"

SCENE FOUR: A group of executives meet to discuss a merger. During the course of the discussion, one of the male vice-presidents says, "This is going to be a bitch to pull off." He immediately turns to the two women present and apologizes for the five-letter word.

SCENE FIVE: A male manager has recently transferred to head a new department. On the third day in his new assignment, he emerges from his office and asks a female standing near the Xerox machine to make four copies of a report and to get him a cup of coffee. The woman introduces herself; she is one of the production managers who report to him.

As women advance in the business world, men are often confronted with situations like those above—situations which call for new forms of behavior and a new awareness of and effort to overcome the sexism inherent in daily conversations.

The men in these five situations have violated certain basic communications rules. In the first instance, the man has referred to a mature female as a girl. The term *girl* implies a certain dependency associated with children. The word is as denigrating when applied to a woman as the word *boy* is when applied to a man. Secondly, the businessman identified the woman by her sex and not by her function (in this case, secretary) as would have been appropriate in this situation. Thirdly, the man's use of the word *my* indicates that he thinks of the secretary as personal property rather than as an employee of the company.

In the second example, Mr. Z's repeated and overblown praise belies any conviction that women are competent. His comments demonstrate his astonishment at Ms. Jones's achievement. In addition, he tries to attribute her success to feminine wiles or to sexual favors granted to "old Mercer." Mr. Z also patronizes Ms. Jones by describing her as a "terrific *little* saleswoman."

In the third case, the man's question is based on the assumption that women are not interested in business matters. If he did not accept the stereotype of woman as primarily concerned with domestic and certain other interests, he would not ask the question. The very phrasing of the question ("Are we boring you?") reveals that he views the men as controlling the conversation and the woman as a passive participant. She is seen as a listener and not as an equal partner in the luncheon discussion.

In the fourth instance, the vice-president apologizes not because he thinks he has offended an individual, but because he has been conditioned to believe that certain forms of language are not used in the presence of women. In this particular case, the man apologized despite the fact that one of the women had called the president of the company being acquired a "fucking madman" during the course of the meeting, thus clearly indicating that she took no exception to such language.

The manager in the fifth illustration obviously assigns women to certain roles within the business world. He finds it natural to assume that a woman standing near a Xerox machine is either a secretary or a clerk, and his remarks flow from that assumption.

WORDS OFTEN EXCLUDE WOMEN

Businessmen do no better when it comes to the written word, as an examination of internal memoranda and other documents will show. Indeed, business has created and uses an extensive terminology that excludes women. Some of its more familiar phrases include manpower planning, man-hours, workman's compensation, the right man for the job, etc.

It can, of course, be argued that these terms are meant generically and therefore include women. However, the effect is frequently the opposite. To most executives, *manpower planning* means plotting the future careers of the key men in the organization or matching key men with key positions. Invariably, the generic evokes a masculine image, especially when used in a business environment, which has long been a male preserve.

Most business terminology can be easily changed without resorting to awkward or strained language. For example, manpower planning becomes *staff resources planning*. Workman's compensation becomes *worker's compensation*. Right man for the job becomes *right person for the job*.

Many companies already have issued guidelines to help executives achieve nonsexist writing. (The McGraw-Hill "Guidelines for Equal Treatment of the Sexes" is perhaps the most notable and comprehensive of these. Although aimed at authors of textbooks, the McGraw-Hill guidelines are valuable for everyone.)

De-sexing the spoken and written language, however, requires more than the invention and utilization of nonsexist words and phrases. Behavior modification and attitudinal change are required. And because language is the externalization of our thought processes, it is our thinking about women that must change. Women must no longer be perceived as inherently bound to play limited roles in society. Sexist stereotypes, such as the indecisive female executive, must be discarded.

Businesswomen must be seen as the equals—for better or for worse—of businessmen: competent, aggressive, ambitious, decisive individuals. They must be viewed as people serious about their careers. As effective managers. Only when we think of females in this way will we be able to approach communicating with them in the proper manner.

Compared with the spoken word, de-sexing the written word should prove easy, because people tend to think more carefully about what they commit to print. We take the time to revise and refine our words.

Conversations are more spontaneous, therefore more apt to show people's biases. Also, people sometimes play power games on the conversational field. Conversations can be used either consciously or subconsciously to "put a woman in her place"—to make her submissive. They can be used, as in the Mr. Z-Ms. Jones example, to make a woman doubt her own abilities. They can be used to draw inordinate attention to a woman (causing embarrassment or making an already uncomfortable situation more uncomfortable), as in the case of the apologetic male vice-president who feels compelled to excuse himself for his language. The message he has sent via his apology is that women are a special breed of people who must be protected from vulgar language. (The corollary being, of course, that they must be protected from the harsh realities of the business world and therefore denied the same opportunity for advancement as men have.) He has also called attention to the fact that, as he perceives it, two women are now intruding on the meeting being held by the male executives.

One of the chief mistakes made in everyday conversations is to regard people as the representatives of a group rather than as individuals. The apologetic vice-president in example number four did not consider the people to whom he spoke *as individuals*. If he had, he might have apologized to a man present who found the language being used offensive. If the manager in the fifth example thought in terms of an individual rather than a class of people, he would have taken time to find the woman's position before asking her to make copies of his report and fetch coffee.

Nonsexist speaking habits can be acquired only by redirecting thinking patterns, discarding all the old assumptions and learning to interact on a one-to-one basis.

TIPS ON AVOIDING SEXIST LANGUAGE

Excepts from McGraw-Hill Book Company Guidelines for Equal Treatment of the Sexes

The word sexism was coined, by analogy to racism, to denote discrimination based on gender. In its original sense, sexism referred to prejudice against the female sex. In a broader sense, the term now indicates any arbitrary stereotyping of males and females on the basis of their gender.

Men and women should be treated primarily as people, and not primarily as members of opposite sexes. Their shared humanity and common attributes should be stressed—not their gender difference. Neither sex should be stereotyped or arbitrarily assigned to a leading or secondary role.

Women and men should be treated with the same respect, dignity, and seriousness. Neither should be trivialized or stereotyped. In descriptions of women, a patronizing or girl-watching tone should be avoided, as should sexual innuendoes, jokes, and puns.

No	Yes
the fair sex; the weaker sex	women
the distaff side	the female side or line
the girls or the ladies (when adult females are meant)	the women
girl, as in: I'll have my girl check that.	I'll have my secretary (or my assistant) check that. (Or use the person's name.)
lady used as a modifier, as in lady lawyer	lawyer (A woman may be identified simply through the choice of pronouns, as in: The lawyer made her summation to the jury. Try to avoid gender modifiers altogether. When you *must* modify, use woman or female, as in: a course on women writers, or the airline's first female pilot.)

the little woman; the better half; the ball and chain	wife
female-gender word forms, such as authoress, poetess, Jewess	author, poet, Jew
female-gender or diminutive word forms, such as suffragette, usherette, aviatrix	suffragist, usher, aviator (or pilot)
libber (a put-down)	feminist; liberationist
sweet young thing	young woman; girl
housewife	homemaker for a person who works at home, or rephrase with a more precise or more inclusive term

In references to humanity at large, language should operate to include women and girls. Terms that tend to exclude females should be avoided whenever possible.

(A) The word man has long been used not only to denote a person of male gender, but also generically to denote humanity at large. To many people today, however, the word man has become so closely associated with the first meaning (a male human being) that they consider it no longer broad enough to be applied to any person or to human beings as a whole. In deference to this position, alternative expressions should be used in place of man (or derivative constructions used generically to signify humanity at large) whenever such substitutions can be made without producing an awkward or artificial construction. In cases where man-words must be used, special efforts should be made to ensure that pictures and other devices make explicit that such references include women.

Here are some possible substitutions for man-words:

No	*Yes*
mankind	humanity, human beings, human race, people
primitive man	primitive people or peoples; primitive human beings; primitive men and women
man's achievements	human achievements

If a man drove 50 miles at 60 mph . . .	If a person (or driver) drove 50 miles at 60 mph . . .
the best man for the job	the best person (or candidate) for the job
manmade	artificial; synthetic, manufactured; constructed; of human origin
manpower	human power; human energy; workers; workforce
grow to manhood	grow to adulthood; grow to manhood or womanhood

(B) The English language lacks a generic singular pronoun signifying "he or she," and therefore it has been customary and grammatically sanctioned to use masculine pronouns in expressions such as "one . . . he," "anyone . . . he," and "each child opens his book." Nevertheless, avoid when possible the pronouns he, him, and his in reference to the hypothetical person or humanity in general.

Various alternatives may be considered:

(1) Reword to eliminate unnecessary gender pronouns.

No	*Yes*
The average American drinks his coffee black.	The average American drinks black coffee.

(2) Recast into the plural. (Most Americans drink their coffee black.)

(3) Replace the masculine pronoun with one, you, he or she, her or his, as appropriate. (Use he or she and its variations sparingly to avoid clumsy prose.)

(4) Alternate male and female expressions and examples.

No	*Yes*
I've often heard supervisors say, "He's not the right man for the job," or "He lacks the qualifications for success."	I've often heard supervisors say, "She's not the right person for the job," or "He lacks the qualifications for success."

(5) To avoid severe problems of repetition or inept wording, it may sometimes be best to use the generic he freely, but to add, in the preface and as often as necessary in the text, emphatic statements to the effect that the masculine pronouns are being used for succinctness and are intended to refer to both females and males.

(C) Occupational terms ending in man should be replaced whenever possible by terms that can include members of either sex unless they refer to a particular person.

No	*Yes*
congressman	member of Congress; representative (but Congressman Koch and Congresswoman Holtzman)
businessman	business executive; business manager
fireman	fire fighter
mailman	mail carrier; letter carrier
salesman	sales representative; salesperson; sales clerk
insurance man	insurance agent
statesman	leader; public servant
chairman	the person presiding at (or chairing) a meeting; the presiding officer; the chair; head; leader; coordinator; moderator
cameraman	camera operator
foreman	supervisor

(D) Language that assumes all readers are male should be avoided.

No	*Yes*
you and your wife	you and your spouse
when you shave in the morning	when you brush your teeth (or wash up) in the morning

Insofar as possible, job titles should be non-sexist. Different nomenclature should not be used for the same job depending on whether it is held by a male or by a female. (See also paragraph (C) for additional examples of words ending in man.)

No	*Yes*
steward or purser or stewardess	flight attendant
policeman and policewoman	police officer
maid and houseboy	house or office cleaner; servant

Unnecessary reference to or emphasis on a woman's marital status should be avoided. Whether married or not, a woman may be referred to by the name by which she chooses to be known, whether her name is her original name or her married name.

Males should not always be first in order of mention. Instead, alternate the order, sometimes using: women and men, gentlemen and ladies, she or he, her or his.

Giving Coins-Taking Coins:
Self-Discovery

Goal

To increase awareness of how sex-role attitudes affect actions in a situation of competition and physical give-and-take.

Group Size

Six to twelve participants.

Time Required

Approximately fifteen minutes for each phase, totaling thirty to forty minutes.

Materials

Small change in any denomination participants may have with them.

Process

I. Giving coins.

   A. Participants are told to collect their spare coins and stand in a group in the center of the room.

This activity was adapted from D. I. Malamud & S. Machover, *Toward Self-Understanding: Group Techniques in Self-Confrontation*. Springfield, Ill.: Charles C Thomas, 1965.

B. The facilitator tells participants that their goal is to give away all of their spare change, using any means necessary. They cannot take money from others. To successfully complete the task, participants should not have any change on their persons at the end of five minutes. The facilitator gives no further instructions and tells participants when to begin.

C. The facilitator ends the activity and asks the participants to sit in a circle, either in chairs or on the floor.

D. The facilitator encourages participants to share their reactions to the activity. Some possible probe questions might include:

Was it easy for you to get involved in this exercise?

What kinds of things made getting involved easy?

What kinds of things made it difficult?

Was it easier to give to some members than to others?

If so, what did they do to make it easy for you?

In what ways were your actions affected by the sex of the potential recipient(s)?

E. The facilitator summarizes what has been said and clarifies where necessary. The summary process sets the stage for the next activity. For example, the facilitator might move from one activity to the next by asking the participants how they would act if they had to take coins from each other rather than give them away.

II. Taking coins.

A. After instructing the participants to stand and regroup, the facilitator tells the participants that now their goal will be to *take* all of the coins they can in five minutes, using any means they want. They cannot give coins away. The facilitator tells participants when to begin and gives no further instructions. (Note: If the participants balk at the idea of actively or aggressively taking from each other, the activity can be stopped and the facilitator can lead a discussion about the reasons for the members' hesitation. Much useful information can be generated in this way about how the participants manage anger and assertiveness and the alternatives they choose to making physical demands on others when they want something that is valuable to them.)

B. The facilitator ends the activity and asks the group to re-form into a circle.

C. The facilitator leads a discussion using modifications of the probe questions given in step I-D, focusing on how the participants experienced the differences between giving and taking coins.

D. The facilitator summarizes the learnings from both activities, clarifying when necessary.

SIMILAR STRUCTURED EXPERIENCE:

A structured experience that emphasizes physical power and competitiveness is the Body-Blow Fight, an activity that also requires a high level of trust within the group. (Before selecting this option, however, the facilitator should consider carefully the age and composition of the group members.)

Process

I. Each participant is paired first with a same-sex partner, then with an opposite-sex partner, and allowed two minutes to batter the opponent with pillows, foam rubber blocks, or Bataca Bats. Blows must be limited to the body; facial and genital areas are off-limits. Group members are assigned as referees. (Persons with negative feelings about fighting may be given the roles of spectator, referee, or timekeeper.)

II. Spectators are required to decide who wins each fight by a quick hand vote on such criteria as who inflicted more blows to the body; who fought more aggressively; who stayed on the offensive more; who showed more agility and strength, etc.

III. After each participant has taken part in two fights, the facilitator polls the group members for their reactions, allowing considerable time to process feelings. Some possible probe questions are the following:

Was it easier to be aggressive with the same-sex or other-sex opponent?

How did the women feel fighting men larger or stronger than themselves?

How did the men feel with female partners? Did they tend to hold back?

What feelings surfaced during the fights?

What were the feelings associated with winning or losing or not participating?

How do you usually deal with impulses toward physical aggression?

What were you taught about fighting as a child?

IV. The facilitator leads a discussion of the feelings that surfaced, bringing out the male/female "roles." (Note: The facilitator may want to follow the Body-Blow Fight with an activity that increases cooperation and sharing.)

"Typical" Behavior:
Sex-Role Exploration

Goal

To explore sex-role attitudes toward behavior and roles.

Group Size

Six to twelve members.

Time Required

Thirty minutes to one hour, depending on follow-up activities.

Materials

I. Four large pieces of newsprint and tape to fasten them to the wall.

II. Pencils and a copy of the "Typical" Behavior Personal Information Sheet for each participant.

III. Felt-tipped markers.

Process

I. Prior to the activity, the facilitator posts four sheets of newsprint labeled Typical Male, Atypical Male, Typical Female, and Atypical Female.

II. The facilitator presents the activity as an opportunity to look at how individuals view their own behavior in relation to sex-role stereotypes. He or she distributes the "Typical" Behavior Personal Information Sheets and pencils and allows time for all group members to fill out their sheets.

III. Participants are instructed to write one response from each of the first two questions on their "Typical" Behavior Personal Information Sheets on the appropriate newsprint sheets with felt-tipped markers.

IV. The facilitator might deal with the material in several ways: discuss the lists in the large group, divide the group into male and female groups, small mixed groups, or same- or opposite-sex dyads to discuss reactions to the lists. An informal comfort test can be administered by having participants rate their feelings about each listed behavior as one of the following:

horrified/repelled
slightly uncomfortable
indifferent/so what!
slightly positive
turned on/great!

V. The facilitator emphasizes feelings—how participants feel about their behavior and how it affects them—in a follow-up discussion which could deal with the sources of the attitudes and the avoidance of or ambiguous feelings about certain behaviors or it could center on the learnings about participants' own motivations and attitudes toward others based on stereotypic expectations.

"TYPICAL" BEHAVIOR
PERSONAL INFORMATION SHEET

1. List three activities or things you do that are typical of your sex role. (Women knit, men follow pro football.)

2. List three activities or things you do that are not typical of your sex role. (Men knit, women watch pro football.)

3. Describe something about yourself or your life that you might feel awkward or hesitant about sharing with members of the opposite sex.

4. Describe something about yourself or your life that you might feel awkward or hesitant about sharing with individuals of your own sex.

Seven Questions: A Feedback Activity

Goal

To facilitate feedback about member role behavior and member conformance to sex-role stereotypes.

Group Size

Six to twelve members.

Time Required

One-half to one hour.

Materials

I. Seven sheets of newsprint to post preferences.

II. Blank paper and a pencil for each participant.

III. Masking tape and felt-tipped markers.

IV. A blackboard or newsprint pad.

Process

I. Prior to the activity, the facilitator writes each of the following: Boss, Important Mission, Discuss New Idea, Companion for

---

Adapted by special permission from NTL Institute for Applied Behavioral Science. *Twenty Exercises for Trainers.* Edited by Cyril R. Mill. Copyright 1972 NTL Learning Resources Corporation.

Recreation, Help in Trouble, Marooned on Island, and Escort Spouse at the top of a sheet of newsprint and posts the sheets on the wall.

II. The facilitator introduces the activity with a short lecturette on the need to be more aware of how the group members perceive each other.

III. He or she writes the following questions on newsprint or a blackboard.

Who would be your choice in this group . . .

as a boss?

to send on an important mission?

to discuss a new idea with?

as a companion for recreation?

to ask for help if you were in serious trouble?

to be marooned with on a tropical island?

to escort your spouse across the country?

IV. The facilitator distributes blank paper and pencils and instructs group members to write down their choices. While people are deciding, the facilitator posts the seven sheets, one for each question, around the room.

V. When the choices have been made, each participant is instructed to write his or her own name on each sheet of newsprint, followed by an arrow pointing to the person of his or her choice for that question. Time is allowed for everyone to look at the sheets to see where his or her own name appears and the patterns for others in the group.

VI. The facilitator may wish to concentrate on any or all of the following questions:

What are the bases for certain choices?

Why do some names appear more frequently than others?

Why are some people not chosen at all?

Is there an attraction of opposites? Of the like-minded?

Are any of the choices more influenced by sex-role stereotypes?

Do men's names appear more frequently in some categories than others? Do women's names appear more frequently in some categories than in others?

Ideal Date/Mate and Friend: Information Sharing

Goals

I. To share values and expectations about heterosexual dating relationships and heterosexual friendships.

II. To make explicit any differences in expectations between the two types of relationships.

Group Size

Six to twelve members, an equal number of males and females.

Time Required

Approximately one hour.

Process

I. The facilitator explains that the participants are to look for characteristics that they find appealing for a date or mate in group members of the other sex. Participants are encouraged to move around the room to examine each other. After a few minutes of mixing, the participants are told to choose a partner, based on attributes (physical or otherwise) that they enjoy in other-sex relationships. The dyads are told to choose spots to sit down in privacy to "look each other over" while fantasizing about some kind of heterosexual relationship. The partners are to take turns sharing "If you were my ideal date/mate/betrothed/lover you would . . ." (Ten minutes.)

II. When it appears that the group has reached a stopping point, the facilitator instructs each partner to react to the other's ideals and expectations. (Ten minutes.)

III. The facilitator gathers the entire group together to look for members of the other sex they would enjoy relating to as *friends*. Participants are told to pair off with someone who looks interesting, sit down together, and imagine a friendship with that person. Each partner takes turns sharing "If you were my ideal friend, you . . ." The facilitator explains that it is important for each person to be as spontaneous and detailed as possible. (Ten minutes.)

IV. Partners are told to compare their reactions to each other's statements and to share the differences and similarities between what each expects in a date and in a friend. (Ten minutes.)

V. The facilitator leads a final discussion of the learnings about cross-sexual expectations.

Variations

I. If the group is small enough, each participant may want to share his or her perceptions of this experience.

II. The same activity can be done with same-sex friendship, and the differences can be compared.

Internal Dialogue:
Self-Examination

Goals

I. To explore and integrate conflicting sex-role attitudes.

II. To determine how these attitudes affect behavior.

III. To gain a perspective on how sex-role attitudes affect others.

Group Size

Six to twelve members.

Time Required

Forty-five minutes to one hour.

Materials

A copy of the Internal Dialogue Sheet, blank paper, and a pencil for each participant.

Process

I. The facilitator instructs participants to find their own private spaces within the room.

II. The facilitator notes that every person experiences certain

Adapted by special permission from NTL Institute for Applied Behavioral Science. *Twenty Exercises for Trainers.* Edited by Cyril R. Mill. Copyright 1972 NTL Learning Resources Corporation.

complexities and paradoxes with regard to sex-role attitudes and feelings and suggests that the participants can begin to think in terms of "getting it all together" by conducting an inner dialogue between any of the divergent attitudes within themselves.

III. The facilitator distributes Internal Dialogue Sheets, blank paper, and pencils.

IV. The group members are instructed to conduct an inner dialogue in their private spaces in the group room. (Thirty minutes.)

V. The participants are told to form a circle. Each participant reads the parts of his or her dialogue that he or she would like to share with the group. (This allows the participants to select the areas they want to share without feeling that they must reveal all to the group.)

VI. The facilitator leads a group discussion centered on each individual's dialogue: what it means to him or her in terms of his or her behavior, how others experience it and how they react to the behavior, and what similarities and differences exist within the group by sex.

VII. The facilitator summarizes what has come out of the activity and suggests that the participants continue their dialogues internally, using their new-found awareness. (Note: In an ongoing group, some opportunity for further sharing should be scheduled.)

INTERNAL DIALOGUE SHEET

You may have developed a clearer perspective of the relationship between your attitudes and your behaviors for some aspects of your sex role than for others. If the relationship is not clear, you may experience confusing paradoxes.

We are all a complex blend of a variety of attitudes—of *do* and *don't*, of *yes* and *no*, of *want* and *don't want*. The purpose of this activity is to allow you some time with your complex self to develop a dialogue between your conflicting inner voices. Select an area or issue relating to your sex role that you feel ambivalent about. Try to hear clearly what both parts of you have to say. Write as you listen to what your inner voices are telling each other; let your thoughts be as free and spontaneous as possible. You will be allowed about thirty minutes to complete your dialogue.

Here are some areas that you may wish to deal with:

As a woman, I can (should) . . .; as a woman, I can't (shouldn't) . . .

As a man, I can (should) . . . ; as a man, I can't (shouldn't) . . .

Need for intimacy versus need for privacy.

Emotional dependence versus emotional independence.

To be or not to be committed to a person of the other sex.

Trust versus distrust.

To engage in a particular sexual activity or not.

My responsibility to myself versus my responsibility to her/him.

My masculine self versus my feminine self.

Assertiveness:
Fantasy and Role Play

Goals

I. To learn the components of assertive, nonassertive, and aggressive behavior.

II. To increase awareness of responses to feelings of anger and frustration.

III. To increase understanding of how response patterns are linked to sex-role stereotypes.

Group Size

Six to twelve members, evenly matched for sex.

Time Required

One to one and one-half hours.

Materials

A copy of the Assertiveness Definitions for each participant.

Process

I. Guided Fantasy
A. The facilitator tells participants to get comfortable, relax,

---

Developed by Linda R. Silverman and Sarah Lynne McMahon.

close their eyes, and imagine themselves in the following situation:

> You are waiting at a restaurant for your lunch date—a friend or colleague or acquaintance of the *same sex*—to arrive. You have rushed to be there on time but are the first to arrive. Now you have been waiting for ten minutes. You seat yourself in a central location facing the entrance. You look up each time someone comes in. You check your watch frequently as you have only an hour for lunch. Twenty minutes later your friend arrives. What is your reaction?

B. The participants are encouraged to share their reactions to this situation, including what they fantasized doing when their lunch dates arrived, how they felt during the waiting, and how they felt after their friends arrived.

C. The facilitator repeats the first two steps, substituting a person of the other sex in the fantasy.

D. The facilitator has participants share their reactions to the second situation, using the same questions. The facilitator points out differences in behavior and feelings between the first and second fantasy situation, based on sex-role expectations.

II. Lecturette and Demonstration

A. The facilitator distributes the Assertiveness Definitions to each participant and gives a lecturette describing and defining the three basic behavior responses: aggressive, nonassertive, and assertive, based on "Assertion Theory" or one of the references listed at the end of the reading. The lecturette may also include illustrations drawn from the fantasy experience.

B. The group is instructed to form dyads to role play all three behaviors with samples drawn from the facilitator's experience to make sure that participants understand the differences. (Note: The illustrations and demonstrations should be geared to the general level of the group. As a general rule, situations that invoke anger are among the most difficult for people to deal with assertively, and the more intimate the relationship, the more complex and difficult it is to act assertively.)

III. Role Playing

A. Participants are told to choose other-sex partners for role playing each of the three responses. The facilitator may choose a situation that the group participants can respond to: a situation where personal space is being violated, a friend has let you down, you want to refuse a request from a friend or boyfriend, etc. Each participant is to practice aggressive, nonassertive, and assertive responses to the same situation. (The activity can be repeated in same-sex dyads.)

B. The facilitator brings the group together to share reactions and learnings about sex-role expectations. Facilitators may want to use such questions as:

How did it feel to act out each response?

How did it feel to listen to assertive, aggressive, and nonassertive responses?

Are any of the responses easier to play or receive than others?

Did you respond differently to members of the other sex?

Variations

I. If the group members seem to grasp easily the differences among assertive, nonassertive, and aggressive behavior and enjoy role playing, the facilitator may alter the instructions. Each person can be told to select a situation from his or her own life experience in which he or she finds it difficult to act assertively. This situation can be role played in dyads. Each person in the dyad can be given approximately five minutes to practice each behavior response. The other member of the dyad is told not to respond, but only to listen. When both persons have finished the role play, they are instructed to give each other *only positive* feedback about how each came across in the assertive part of the assignment.

II. In an ongoing group, participants may contract with the group to practice assertive behavior in some situation they have had problems with as a homework assignment.

ASSERTIVENESS DEFINITIONS

Aggressive Behavior. Standing up for oneself without considering the rights of others. Aggressive behavior puts down the other person. The goal is to win.

Nonassertive Behavior. Failing to stand up for one's rights or doing so in an ineffectual way. The nonassertive goal is to appease.

Assertive Behavior. Standing up for one's rights without violating the rights of others. The goal of assertion is to find a mutual solution and to give straight communication.

Assertion Theory

Colleen Kelley

A friend asks to borrow your new, expensive camera . . . Someone cuts in front of you in a line . . . A salesperson is annoyingly persistent . . . Someone criticizes you angrily in front of your colleagues . . .

For many people these examples represent anxious, stressful situations to which there is no satisfying response. One basic response theory being taught more and more frequently in training programs is a theory called Assertiveness or Assertion.

Some important aspects of Assertion theory include (1) the philosophy underlying assertion, (2) the three possible response styles in an assertive situation, (3) some means of outwardly recognizing these response styles, (4) some functional distinctions between the three styles, and (5) the six components of an assertive situation.

THE PHILOSOPHY OF ASSERTION

Assertion theory is based on the premise that every individual possesses certain basic human rights. These rights include such fundamentals as "the right to refuse requests without having to feel guilty or selfish," "the right to have one's own needs be as important as the needs of other people," "the right to make mistakes," and "the right to express ourselves as long as we don't violate the rights of others" (Jakubowski-Spector, in press).

THREE RESPONSE STYLES

People relate to these basic human rights along a continuum of response styles: nonassertion, assertion, and aggression.

Assertion

The act of standing up for one's own basic human rights without violating the basic human rights of others is termed assertion

Reprinted from Colleen Kelley, in J. W. Pfeiffer & J. E. Jones (Eds.), *The 1976 Annual Handbook for Group Facilitators*, La Jolla, Calif.: University Associates, 1976, pp. 115-118.

(Jakubowski-Spector, 1973). It is a response style that recognizes boundaries between one's individual rights and those of others and operates to keep those boundaries stabilized.

When one of her friends asked to borrow Jan's new sports car for a trip, she was able to respond assertively by saying, "I appreciate your need for some transportation, but the car is too valuable to me to loan out." Jan was able to respect both her friend's right to make the request and her own right to refuse it.

Nonassertion

The two alternative response styles represent an inability to maintain adequately the boundaries between one person's rights and those of another. Nonassertion occurs when one allows one's boundaries to be restricted. In Jan's case, a nonassertive response would have been to loan the car, fearing that her friend might perceive her as petty or distrustful, and to spend the rest of the afternoon wishing she had not. Thus, Jan would not have been acting on her right to say no.

Aggression

The third response style, aggression, takes place when one person invades the other's boundaries of individual rights. Aggression, in Jan's case, might sound like this: "Certainly not!" or "You've *got* to be kidding!" Here, Jan would be violating the other person's right to courtesy and respect.

RECOGNIZING RESPONSE STYLES

Some helpful keys to recognizing these nonassertive, assertive, and aggressive response styles in any given situation are (1) the type of emotion experienced, (2) the nonverbal behavior displayed, and (3) the verbal language used.

Emotion

The person responding nonassertively tends to internalize feelings and tensions and to experience such emotions as fear, anxiety, guilt, depression, fatigue, or nervousness. Outwardly, emotional "temperature" is below normal, and feelings are not verbally expressed.

With an aggressive response, the tension is turned outward. Although the aggressor may have experienced fear, guilt, or hurt at one time in the interchange, this feeling has either been masked by a "secondary" emotion such as anger, or it has built up over time to a boiling point. In an aggressive response, the person's emotional temperature is above normal and is typically expressed by inappropriate anger, rage, hate, or misplaced hostility—all loudly and sometimes explosively expressed.

In contrast to the other two response styles, an individual responding assertively is aware of and deals with feelings as they occur, neither denying himself the right to the emotion nor using it to deny another's rights. Tension is kept within a normal, constructive range.

Nonverbal Behavior

Each response style is also characterized by certain nonverbal or body-language cues. A nonassertive response is self-effacing and dependent; it "moves away" from a situation. This response may be accompanied by such mannerisms as downcast eyes, the shifting of weight, a slumped body, the wringing of hands, or a whining, hesitant, or giggly tone of voice.

Aggression represents a nonverbal "moving against" a situation; it is other-effacing and counterdependent. This response may be expressed through glaring eyes, by leaning forward or pointing a finger, or by a raised, snickering, or haughty tone of voice.

Assertion, instead, faces up to a situation and demonstrates an approach by which one can stand up for oneself in an independent or interdependent manner. When being assertive, a person generally establishes good eye contact, stands comfortably but firmly on two feet with his hands loosely at his sides, and talks in a strong, steady tone of voice.

Verbal Language

A third way of differentiating between assertion, nonassertion, and aggression is to pay attention to the type of verbal language being used. Certain words tend to be associated with each style.

Nonassertive words can include qualifiers ("maybe," "I guess," "I wonder if you could," "would you mind very much," "only," "just," "I can't," "don't you think"), fillers ("uh," "well," "you know," "and") and negaters ("it's not really important," "don't bother").

Aggressive words include threats ("you'd better," "if you don't watch out"), put downs ("come *on*," "you must be kidding"), evaluative comments ("should," "bad"), and sexist or racist terms.

Assertive words may include "I" statements ("I think," "I feel," "I want"), cooperative words ("let's," "how can we resolve this"), and empathic statements of interest ("what do you think," "what do you see").

Emotional, nonverbal, and verbal cues are helpful keys in recognizing response styles, but they should be seen as general indicators and not as a means of labelling behavior.

FUNCTIONAL DISTINCTIONS

Outwardly, the three response styles seem to form a linear continuum running from the nonassertive style, which permits a violation of one's own rights; through the assertive style; to the aggressive position, which perpetrates a violation of another's rights.

Functionally, however, nonassertion and aggression look both very much alike and very different from assertion. Nonassertion and aggression are dysfunctional not only because they use indirect methods of expressing wants and feelings and fail to respect the rights of *all* people, but also because they create an imbalance of power in which the two positions may mix or even change positions with each other. In refusing to stand up for his rights, the nonassertive responder creates a power imbalance by according everyone else more rights than himself, while the aggressive responder creates a power imbalance by according himself more than his share of rights.

This power imbalance is unstable; the restricted nonassertive responder can accumulate guilt, resentment, or fear until he becomes the aggressive responder in a burst of rage, or he may mix a nonassertive "front" with a subversive "behind the scenes" attempt to "get back" at the person.

The assertive responder seeks a solution that equalizes the balance of power and permits all concerned to maintain their basic human rights. Thus an imbalance of power, caused by a failure to respect the rights of *all* people and perpetuated by the use of indirect methods, creates a very vulnerable position for both the nonassertive and the aggressive responders, while the more functional assertive responder respects all human rights, uses direct methods, and seeks a balance of power.

COMPONENTS OF AN ASSERTIVE SITUATION

Assertion theory can be helpful in situations in which a person is anxious about standing up for his basic human rights. These situations include saying yes and no with conviction, giving and receiving criticism, initiating conversations, resisting interruptions, receiving compliments, demanding a fair deal as a consumer, dealing with sexist remarks, and handling various other specific situations encountered in one's personal, social, and professional life.

A person may feel capable of being assertive in a situation but make a conscious decision not to be so, because of such things as power issues or the time or effort involved. Before making a decision to be assertive, it is helpful to examine the six components of an assertive situation.

1. The potential asserter's basic human rights and his level of confidence that he has these rights;
2. The specific behavior to which the potential asserter is responding;
3. The potential asserter's feeling reactions to this specific behavior;
4. The specific behavior the potential asserter would prefer;
5. The possible positive and negative consequences for the other person if he behaves as the potential asserter wishes him to behave;
6. The potential consequences of the assertive response for the potential asserter.

Once the situational assertive components have been determined, assertion training techniques provide a means of formulating and enacting an assertive response.

CONCLUSION

Assertion theory offers a model for those who wish to stand up for their own rights without violating the human rights of others. It is a model that can be used in all types of situations—personal, professional, and social—to facilitate honest, direct, functional communication.

REFERENCES

Jakubowski-Spector, P. Facilitating the growth of women through assertive training. *The Counseling Psychologist*, 1973, 4(1), 75-86.

Jakubowski-Spector, P. Self-assertive training procedures for women. In D. Carter & E. Rawlings (Eds.), *Psychotherapy with women*. Springfield, Ill.: Charles C Thomas, in press.

Pfeiffer, J. W., & Jones, J. E. Openness, collusion and feedback. In J. W. Pfeiffer & J. E. Jones (Eds.), *The 1972 annual handbook for group facilitators*. La Jolla, Calif.: University Associates, 1972.

OTHER READINGS

Alberti, R. E., & Emmons, M. L. *Your perfect right: A guide to assertive behavior* (2nd ed.). San Luis Obispo, Calif.: Impact, 1974.

Alberti, R. E., & Emmons, M. L. *Stand up, speak out, talk back!: The key to self-assertive behavior*. New York: Simon & Schuster, 1975.

Bloom, L. L., Coburn, K., & Pearlman, J. *The new assertive woman*. New York: Delacorte, 1975.

Cummings, E., et al. *Assert your self*. Seattle: Seattle-King County N.O.W., 1974.

Fensterheim, H., & Baer, J. *Don't say yes when you want to say no: How assertiveness training can change your life*. New York: McKay, 1975.

Lazarus, A., & Fay, A. *I can if I want to: The direct assertion therapy program to change your life*. New York: William Morrow, 1975.

Osborn, S. M., & Harris, G. G. *Assertive training for women*. Springfield, Ill.: Charles C Thomas, 1975.

Phelps, S., & Austin, N. *The assertive woman*. San Luis Obispo, Calif.: Impact, 1975.

Smith, M. J. *When I say no, I feel guilty*. New York: McKay, 1975.

Here-and-Now Self and Ideal Self: Commitment to Change

Goals

I. To become aware of sex-role stereotypes and their influence.

II. To focus on where participants are and where they would like to be with regard to their sex-role attitudes and behaviors.

III. To provide a transition to changed behaviors in a "real world" setting.

Group Size

Six to twelve members.

Time Required

Approximately one hour.

Materials

I. A newsprint pad and felt-tipped marker.

II. A copy of the Here-and-Now Self and Ideal Self Worksheet and a pencil for each participant.

Process

I. The facilitator summarizes the most significant experiences

---

This activity is intended to be used as a commitment to change after an ongoing group or a day-long workshop.

shared by the participants during previous sessions (or activities, if the activity takes place in a one-day workshop) and lists them on newsprint. He or she then introduces this activity by explaining its goals—transition into the "real world."

II. Each participant is given a Here-and-Now Self and Ideal Self Worksheet and a pencil and is told to answer the two questions as completely as possible. (Thirty minutes.)

III. Participants are regrouped in a circle and are encouraged to share as much of their writing as they feel comfortable sharing with others. The facilitator summarizes, asks for clarification, and points out similarities and differences. (Note: The facilitator may wish to use other structured experiences that are designed to help members determine how to go from where they are now to where they would like to be, such as An Exercise in Change: Commitment, The Interpersonal Contract: Commitment to Change, or Town Meeting: Planning Change in Organizational Settings.)

HERE-AND-NOW SELF AND IDEAL SELF WORKSHEET

You have just spent some time mutually exploring feelings, behaviors, and social influences related to your sex role. You may have received feedback from other participants about how your behaviors and attitudes affect them. We hope these experiences have provided you with more understanding of your feelings and new insights into your interactions with others. At this time, try to summarize and write down as completely as possible how you feel about your sex role—that is, how your sex role influences your values, ambitions, actions, decisions, and interpersonal relationships.

After you have done this, think of how you would like to be ideally—that is, how you would "best" feel and function in your sex role. Write your responses below.

How I Am Now.

How I'd Like To Be.

An Exercise in Change: Commitment

Goals

I. To provide a vehicle for translating general goals into behaviorial change.

II. To teach basic skills in structuring for behavioral change, including the identification of change-related behaviors and personal and external resources.

Group Size

Six to twelve members.

Time Required

One hour or more.

Materials

A pencil and a copy of An Exercise in Change Question Sheet for each participant.

Process

I. The facilitator lists the goals of the activity, presenting it as a

---

This structured experience is designed to follow an activity in which participants have been made aware of their "here-and-now" selves and their "ideal" selves, such as Here-and-Now Self and Ideal Self: Commitment to Change.

means to follow up the Here-and-Now Self and Ideal Self: Commitment to Change or a similar activity.

II. The facilitator identifies and summarizes some of the contrasts expressed by participants when they described their "present" versus their "ideal" selves. The facilitator asks participants to think about how they would *behave* if they were to realize their ideal selves. The facilitator may wish to use questions such as:

How would others *know* that you've changed?

How could others *observe* your change?

What personal and external *resources* would you draw on to make your change?

III. Each participant is given a copy of An Exercise in Change Question Sheet and instructed to complete it as a means of planning and implementing self-directed change in the realization of his or her ideal self. The facilitator circulates around the group assisting individuals in working through the activity. (Thirty minutes.)

IV. After ample time has been given to complete the written exercise, participants are regrouped to share their results, to offer each other feedback, and to clarify further their own feelings about change. (Note: The facilitator may use this sharing process as a basis for forming partnerships in working through the Interpersonal Contract: Commitment to Change.)

Variation

Members can be instructed to form "sharing pairs" to work through the activity. Sharing pairs are useful in making the activity less of a paper-and-pencil task and more of an interpersonal experience.

AN EXERCISE IN CHANGE QUESTION SHEET

The purposes of this activity are to help you define a personal change goal, to identify ways of implementing it, and to identify resources that you may use to facilitate changing. Try to answer each question as fully as possible and keep your focus on specific behaviors that are observable to others in planning your change.

1. If you were to change one aspect of the way you relate to others or of a significant relationship, what would it be? Be specific in describing the behaviors related to this change.

2. What would you accomplish by this change, i.e., if you were to behave differently, what would your behavior do for you?

3. What are the forces in yourself, your relationship(s)—values, fears, expectations—or your environment that may potentially hinder you in making the change?

   (a) Hindering forces in *yourself*:

   How do you intend to work with or around them?

(b) Hindering forces in your *relationship(s)*:

How do you intend to work with or around them?

(c) Hindering forces in your *environment*:

How do you intend to work with or around them?

4. What are the forces in yourself, your relationship(s), or your environment, that may potentially facilitate making the change?

(a) Facilitating forces in *yourself*:

How will you utilize them?

(b) Facilitating forces in your *relationship(s)*:

How will you utilize them?

(c) Facilitating forces in your *environment*:

How will you utilize them?

5. How will you communicate your desire to change to others?

6. How much responsibility will you take for creating the change?

How much responsibility will you share?

7. How strongly committed are you to making this change?
   (Rate yourself on the scale given below.)

   /   /   /   /   /   /   /   /   /   /
   _____
   Not   Very
   committed   committed

   What does your self-rating mean to you?

8. Using the information from questions above, describe the behavioral steps you will have to go through to make this change.

   (a) _____

   (b) _____

   (c) _____

   (d) _____

   (e) _____

   etc.

9. How will you know when you have changed?

10. Who outside of the situation or relationship you are trying to change would you like to assist you in working through the change process?

In what ways do you feel this person would be effective in helping you?

11. When in the future would you like to review your progress in making your change?

Town Meeting: Planning Change in Organizational Settings

Goal

To learn ways to plan change in organizational settings.

Group Size

Any number of groups with four to six members each.

Time Required

One and one-half to two hours.

Materials

One newsprint pad and a felt-tipped marker for each group.

Process

I. Participants are told to pretend that as a group they have received several requests from local organizations to develop programs to change sex-role attitudes among the organizations' staffs. The organizations might include (1) a public school or college; (2) a state or local police force; (3) an industrial firm; (4) a church; (5) a local civic volunteer group; and (6) a mental health agency. (Other organizations may be inserted to fit the unique character of the participant group.)

II. The facilitator assigns participants to small consulting teams of no more than six members, balanced by sex, each group to work with a specific organization.

III. Each team is given a newsprint pad and felt-tipped pen and instructed to develop a flexible strategy with clear and measurable outcomes for affecting change in the organization over a six-month period. (One hour.)

IV. The facilitator tells each group to select a representative to summarize and share its ideas for all the participants.

V. After the groups share their ideas, the facilitator notes common strategies. (Where appropriate, participants may be referred to outside literature in organization development and organizational consultation.)

VI. The facilitator processes the participants' reactions to the activity, focusing on applications "back home."

The Interpersonal Contract: Commitment to Change

Goals

I. To teach basic skills in conflict resolution, identification and usage of personal resources, and structuring for behavioral change.

II. To provide closure and follow-up in an ongoing group.

Group Size

Six to twelve participants or any number of opposite-sex dyads.

Time Required

Three hours or more.

Materials

A pencil, blank paper, and copies of "The Interpersonal Contract" for each participant.

Physical Setting

A room with comfortable seating in which dyads may share experiences without distraction.

Process

I. The facilitator explains that this activity is to be used to teach basic skills and reviews the goals of commitment.

II. The facilitator gives a lecturette covering general concepts such as the contractual nature of all relationships; the benefits of explicit contracts and public commitments; the reasons individuals choose to contract; and the types of contract.

III. Time is allowed for group members to react to the contracting concept and to ask questions.

IV. "The Interpersonal Contract" is distributed to all participants to read and review. The concepts are clarified by the facilitator.

V. Participants are told to think of their personal goals for behavioral change. (In an ongoing group, participants may choose the ones they listed in An Exercise in Change: Commitment.) After goals are chosen, the facilitator instructs participants to find partners, preferably of the other sex, with whom they would like to practice negotiating and writing contracts for behavioral-change goals. (Partnerships can be formed on any basis, providing that they are beneficial to both partners.)

VI. The facilitator asks each participant to share the basis of his or her partnership (reasons for selection) with the group as a whole.

VII. Participants are instructed to reread the Guidelines for Negotiating an Interpersonal Contract, after which the facilitator answers questions and clarifies ambiguities.

VIII. Partners are given paper and pencils and instructed to find private spaces in the room to begin negotiating contracts. The facilitator circulates around the room, assisting individuals in working through the contracting process.

IX. After all contracts have been negotiated, the participants regroup, and the facilitator leads a discussion, with participants sharing their reactions to the contracting process.

The Interpersonal Contract

Clarke Carney   S. Lynne McMahon

The idea of contracting for change in intimate relationships tends to elicit negative reactions from most individuals. In our society, the word *contract* often connotes an impersonal process of tough bargaining in smoke-filled rooms between declared opponents. *Negotiation* evokes a picture of wiley diplomats jostling for power through subterfuge, manipulation, and hints of armed intervention.

Neither of these scenes is readily applicable to personal relationships. Yet all relationships involve negotiated agreements which vary according to explicitness, duration, and restrictiveness. Husbands and wives, for example, develop pacts about household chores, while neighbors contract to form a car pool. Roommates reach agreements about visitors, paying bills, and study times. Teachers and students specify individual learning objectives.

Given its prevalence in our daily lives, the interpersonal contract might be described as the mortar that binds relationships; it lends predictability to our interactions and provides us with a basis for trust.

Implicit and Explicit Agreements

Most of the agreements individuals work out among themselves are implicit and are rarely verbalized. People normally function on the basis of unwritten compacts, seldom recognizing that they have indeed negotiated an agreement.

The most fulfilling means of facilitating change in a relationship, however, occurs when partners make a conscious and consistent effort to negotiate their expectations openly in an atmosphere of mutual trust and respect. In making a public commitment, both partners are more likely to carry out their agreements. Such explicit agreements are easily renegotiated and modified for the mutual benefit of participants.

Reprinted from Clarke Carney & S. Lynne McMahon, in J. W. Pfeiffer & J. E. Jones (Eds.), *The 1974 Annual Handbook for Group Facilitators*, La Jolla, Calif.: University Associates, 1974, pp. 135-138.

Problem-Centered Perspective

People generally approach the process of contracting for change in their relationship from a problem-centered perspective: "We are doing all right, but we have a problem with. . . ." The problem may be one of agreeing on family finances, learning how to express anger, or finding a satisfying means of completing a task. The situation is seen as lacking a necessary element or as an irritant to be remedied.

Though creative growth is seldom given equal attention, it too can serve as a subject for an interpersonal contract. Partners can use their contracts to determine how much energy they will spend on problem-solving and how much on creative development.

Two Approaches

Regardless of the circumstance that prompts them to seek change, partners can use one or both of two approaches in negotiating an interpersonal contract. They can develop a *mini-contract* to deal with situations that have a restricted time limit or scope, or they can seek the more comprehensive goals of a *developmental contract* to maximize the growth possibilities for both individuals and their relationship.

A mini-contract might, for example, specify acceptable means of expressing affection for members of the opposite sex, provide for completing job assignments on time, determine grading procedures, divide household tasks, set up a homework schedule, or designate the children's vacation bedtime.

The developmental contract is more comprehensive, involving decisions about how to implement the ideals of the partnership, how to provide for future changes, and how to work through problems. A couple, for instance, might develop a contract to enhance growth and intimacy in their marriage. Wanting to share in the process of learning together, they could contract to attend marriage-enrichment workshops and free university classes. They might seek to provide a renewed basis for intimacy in their relationships by contracting to spend one weekend a month as a couple—camping, visiting nearby cities, or having a "tryst" at a local hotel.

GUIDELINES FOR NEGOTIATING AN INTERPERSONAL CONTRACT

The Process

Negotiating an interpersonal contract can be a rewarding and illuminating experience, especially when both partners agree to negotiate in an atmosphere that is free of coercion and manipulation. Sitting down and talking things through—sharing your aspirations as individuals and partners—offers you new insights into yourselves, your values, feelings, priorities, and personal viewpoints. It can also help you find and realize rewarding new possibilities for your relationship.

If possible, find a quiet, private, *pleasant place*, free from outside disturbances, to negotiate and write your contract. While you are at it, be good to yourselves. Treat yourselves to a glass of wine, some freshly baked cookies, or any special treat.

Allow yourselves *ample time* to negotiate and write your contract; at least one hour per sitting is most helpful. Guidelines for implementing serious readjustments in a relationship are seldom developed in one sitting—take time over several sessions to let your ideas and feelings percolate and sort themselves out. Each of you could well spend some time alone defining, clarifying, and noting your personal behavioral goals before sharing them with your partner.

When you attempt to define and share your goals, it is important that you consistently *check signals* with each other to make sure you have heard and understood what the other is saying. During the early stages of goal-sharing, you may practice the art of listening and responding by following the succeeding exercise.

Step 1: One person, Person A, takes responsibility for initiating a conversation about a specific topic; in this instance, "What I'd like our contract to do for us." As A talks, B becomes actively involved in the process of listening by nodding his head when he feels he understands, sitting forward in his chair, taking note of things he agrees or disagrees with, and sorting out what he understands from what he doesn't.

Step 2: After A completes his or her statement, B responds, "I heard you say . . ." and repeats what A has said. After B summarizes to A's satisfaction, they continue on to the next step.

Step 3: B attempts to clarify their communication further by expressing his understanding of the feeling aspect of A's message. He completes the sentence, "I think you mean (feel). . . ."

Step 4: After B has completed the process of summarizing and clarifying his feelings, A responds with his thoughts and reflections: "My response is. . . ."

Step 5: The process is reversed and B then engages in a monologue on the same subject.

Tape recording your conversations may help promote effective communication between you and your partner, by giving both of you a more objective view of your interaction.

Most human behavior is guided by "self-fulfilling prophecies." We often get what we expect out of a relationship simply because our expectations guide our behavior in ways that produce complementary responses from others. For example, if a man sees himself as being unattractive to women, he more than likely will approach them in a way that communicates his expectations of himself—"You wouldn't want to go out with me, would you?"

Accordingly, as you enter your contract negotiations, it is important to consider your expectations for yourselves and each other and the influence they may have in determining the success or futility of your efforts. Some assumptions that facilitate or hinder interpersonal communication can be useful as a set of guidelines during your contract negotiations.

These are some assumptions that *facilitate* successful contract negotiations:

The Humility Assumption—I am not perfect, I would like to improve my interpersonal relationships and am willing to learn from you.[1]

The Human Dignity Assumption—I value you and feel you are equal to me.[1]

The Confidentiality Assumption—I will respect confidences which are entrusted to me.[1]

The Responsibility Assumption—I will share equally with you in building and maintaining our partnership.

The Changeability Assumption—I can change and am willing to try. Our relationship can change. We are not set in our ways.

Assumptions that *hinder* contract negotiations:

One (or both) of us "needs help," is mentally disturbed.

Our relationship is poor, hopeless, "on the rocks."[1]

My partner does not know what he's really like. I am going to get him to see the Truth about himself.[1]

All of our problems are my partner's fault. He is the one who needs to change.

My partner had better change, "or else."

My partner has hurt me. Now I am going to get even.

---

[1]This assumption and several of the others in this listing are taken from Kenneth R. Hardy, *The Interpersonal Game*, Provo, Utah: Brigham Young University Press, 1967, p. 4.

We are the way we are. There's no sense in stirring things up.

It seems apparent, then, that an atmosphere of trust, respect, and understanding, in which successful contract negotiations thrive, is most likely to occur when individuals are willing to listen and respond to each other without feeling that they are taking the risk of being manipulated or coerced.

The Product

When writing your contract, strive to avoid either extreme rigidity or excessive generalization in your statement.

Try to *determine your personal priorities* before specifying your goals. Identify your non-negotiables early in the process so you can work with or around them.

Very useful, especially during initial negotiations, is *an outline format*; it reads easily and encourages succinctness and clarity.

In writing each section, go from a *general objective* to the specific steps you will take to realize it. State your *action steps* so that both of you can understand your goal or purpose. Use *specific behavioral examples* to clarify what you mean. For instance, if you are experiencing difficulty in managing conflict, you might state "dealing with conflict" as a general objective. As action steps, you might list the following: "Both partners will define the issue before pursuing the argument"; "John/Margaret calls time out when he/she is no longer able to listen effectively"; "Margaret summarizes what has been said before presenting new information."

It is also helpful to visualize a *sequence of action steps*. In the example given above, "defining the issue" logically preceded the other steps since it is important to agree on the subject for argument before beginning to discuss it.

To avoid confusion, separate each general objective and the action steps connected with it, just as you would a clause in a contract. If you are developing a method for dealing with conflict in one section of your contract, for example, you should not include guidelines for completing chores, unless the chores are directly related to your conflict.

The best way to change is to act differently *now*. People have a tendency to postpone remedial actions, especially when they seem difficult or costly, but the past cannot be relived. Specify your action steps in *the present tense* and in the active voice, such as "summarizes," "clarifies," "asks," "takes," "names."

Have an objective outsider read your contract to make sure your goals and terms are clear. Remember, however, that your purpose should not be to persuade this person to take sides with either partner on an issue.

Finally, specify a time in the future *to review your contract* and negotiate it if necessary. When reviewing your contract, you might ask some of the following questions:

Are the behaviors called for by the contract appropriate to the issue?

Do the action steps adequately represent the behavior associated with the general objective?

Is the contract too rigid or too flexible?

As they are stated, are the objectives attainable?

Do the objectives agree with the philosophy of our relationship and with the aim of shared responsibility?

Contracting explicit, negotiated interpersonal contracts can be a very useful device for change in intimate relationships. The success of the process requires an atmosphere of mutual trust, time, helpful assumptions about each other, clear objectives, and a sequence of specific action steps toward the goal of mutual change.

SUGGESTED ACTIVITY

The facilitator presents the lecturette to a training group. (The participants can be given this material in written form.)

Group participants are then asked to discuss some of their goals for personal behavior change; to select a "partner" with whom they would like to share the process of negotiating and writing a contract; to share the basis of their "partnership" with the group; to read the "Guidelines"; and then to negotiate their contracts privately.

After negotiation, the entire group is re-formed to discuss and respond to the contracting process.

REFERENCE

Sherwood, J. J., & Glidewell, J. C. Planned renegotiation: A norm-setting OD intervention. In J. E. Jones & J. W. Pfeiffer (Eds.), *The 1973 annual handbook for group facilitators*. San Diego: University Associates, 1973, 195-202.

INSTRUMENTS

Bem Sex-Role Inventory (BSRI)

Sandra Lipsitz Bem

For many people, being masculine or feminine is a fairly central aspect of their self-concept. In American society, men are supposed to be masculine, women are supposed to be feminine, and neither sex is supposed to be much like the other. Men are supposed to be tough, dominant, and fearless; women are supposed be tender, sympathetic, and sensitive to the needs of others. The man who gently and lovingly cares for his child or who prefers ballet to football is destined to have his masculinity questioned, just as the woman who aggressively defends her clients in court or who refuses to defer to the wishes of her husband is destined to have her femininity questioned. In American society, masculinity and femininity are seen as opposites, and a person is therefore taking a risk of sorts when he or she ventures into the other sex's territory. Even psychological tests of masculinity and femininity reflect this bias: a person can score as either masculine or feminine, but most tests do not allow a person to say that he or she is both.

In principle, of course, a person can be *both* masculine and feminine. A baby can be dressed in pink on Mondays and blue on Tuesdays; a preschooler can be given both trucks and dolls for Christmas; an adolescent can spend some leisure time playing basketball in the driveway and other leisure time serving as a nurse's aide in the local hospital; and a criminal lawyer can aggressively defend his or her

Previously published in J. E. Jones & J. W. Pfeiffer (Eds.). *The 1977 Annual Handbook for Group Facilitators*. La Jolla, Calif.: University Associates, 1977.

clients in court and then lovingly and gently care for a baby at home. In principle, a person can also blend, in a single act, these complementary ways of dealing with the world. For example, he or she can criticize an employee's job performance straightforwardly but also with sensitivity for the guilt or anger or distress that such criticism inevitably produces. The concept of androgyny (from the Greek *andro*, male, and *gyne*, female) refers specifically to this blending of the behaviors and personality characteristics that have traditionally been thought of as masculine and feminine. By definition, then, the androgynous individual is someone who is *both* independent and tender, *both* aggressive and gentle, *both* assertive and yielding, *both* masculine and feminine, depending on the situational appropriateness of these various behaviors.

The Bem Sex-Role Inventory (BSRI) is an instrument that treats masculinity and femininity as two independent dimensions rather than as opposite ends of a single dimension; in so doing, it allows an individual to say that he or she is *both* masculine and feminine. More specifically, the BSRI consists of twenty adjectives describing masculine personality characteristics (e.g., ambitious, self-reliant, independent, assertive) and twenty adjectives describing feminine personality characteristics (e.g., affectionate, gentle, understanding, sensitive to the needs of others). The particular masculine and feminine characteristics used were chosen because they were all rated by both males and females as being significantly more desirable in American society for one sex than for the other. The BSRI also contains twenty adjectives describing neutral characteristics (e.g., truthful, happy, conceited, unsystematic), which serve as filler items.

On the test itself, the masculine, feminine, and neutral items are intermixed so as to form a single list of characteristics, and a person is asked to indicate on a scale from 1 ("never or almost never true") to 7 ("always or almost always true") how well each characteristic describes himself or herself. The average or mean number of points assigned by each person to the masculine attributes constitutes his or her Masculinity score; the average or mean number of points assigned by each person to the feminine attributes constitutes his or her Femininity score.

Using the median masculinity and femininity scores as the cutoff points, a person is then classified as either masculine (high masculine-low feminine), feminine (high feminine-low masculine), androgynous (high masculine-high feminine), or "undifferentiated" (low masculine-low feminine). According to this definition, over one-third of the males and females in introductory psychology at Stanford University in 1975 described themselves as sex-typed (i.e., as masculine if they were male and as feminine if they were female), approximately one-quarter described themselves as androgynous, approximately one-quarter described themselves as undifferentiated, and fewer than one-fifth described themselves as "sex-reversed."

Scoring

The BSRI is scored in three steps:

1. Calculating masculinity and femininity scores for each individual;
2. Calculating medians for the masculinity and femininity scores based on the total sample, sexes combined. (Or, if preferred, this step may be omitted, and the median masculinity and femininity scores derived at Stanford University may be used instead.)
3. Classifying individuals according to whether their masculinity and femininity scores are above or below each of the two medians identified.

The masculinity and femininity scores are simply the means of the ratings of the masculine and feminine adjectives on the BSRI. That is, a given individual's masculinity score is the mean of that individual's rating on the masculine adjectives, and that same individual's femininity score is the mean of his or her ratings on the feminine adjectives. The placement of adjectives on the BSRI is as follows:

1. The first adjective and every third one thereafter is masculine;
2. The second adjective and every third one thereafter is feminine;
3. The third adjective and every third one thereafter is neutral.

Once each person's masculinity and femininity scores have been calculated in this way, the median masculinity score and the median femininity score for the particular group must then be calculated. The median masculinity score is that score above which 50 percent of the masculinity scores fall; the median femininity score is that score above which 50 percent of the femininity scores fall. Ideally, the scores of both males and females should be considered together when these two medians are calculated, and, if an unequal number of males and females is involved, the numbers should be equalized statistically by weighing the underrepresented sex by an appropriate amount.

Although it would be best to calculate medians as described above, this may not be possible in certain situations. In such a case, it is possible to use the Stanford medians as the basis of sex-role classification. In 1975, the median masculinity and femininity scores for a large sample of Stanford undergraduates were 4.89 and 4.76, respectively. These medians, however, are not necessarily appropriate for a noncollege population. Indeed, it might be equally appropriate to classify individuals as above or below the midpoint (4.5) on the masculinity and femininity scales.

Once the median masculinity and femininity scores have been determined, individuals can be classified as follows:

		Masculinity Score	
		Below Median	*Above Median*
Femininity Score	*Below Median*	Undifferentiated	Masculine
	Above Median	Feminine	Androgynous

As described here, the BSRI can be scored quite easily by hand. Computer scoring may be more efficient in certain situations, however, and a packet of computer programs for scoring the BSRI is available upon request from the author.

REFERENCES

Bem, S. L. The measurement of psychological androgyny. *Journal of Consulting and Clinical Psychology*, 1974, *42*, 155-162.

Bem, S. L. Androgyny vs. the tight little lives of fluffy women and chesty men. *Psychology Today*, 1975, *9*, 58-62. (a)

Bem, S. L. Sex-role adaptability: One consequence of psychological androgyny. *Journal of Personality and Social Psychology*, 1975, *31*, 634-643. (b)

Bem, S. L. Beyond androgyny: Some presumptuous prescriptions for a liberated sexual identity. Keynote address, APA-NIMH Invited Conference on the Research Needs of Women, 1975. In J. Sherman & F. Denmark (Eds.), *Psychology of Women: Future Directions of Research*. New York: Psychological Dimensions, in press. (a)

Bem, S. L. On the utility of alternative procedures for assessing psychological androgyny. *Journal of Consulting and Clinical Psychology*, in press. (b)

Bem, S. L., & Lenney, E. Sex-typing and the avoidance of cross-sex behavior. *Journal of Personality and Social Psychology*, 1976, *33*, 48-54.

Bem, S. L., Martyna, W., & Watson, C. Sex-typing and androgyny: Further explorations of the expressive domain. *Journal of Personality and Psychology*, in press.

Bem, S. L., & Watson, C. *Scoring packet for the Bem sex-role inventory*. Unpublished manuscript, Stanford University, 1976.

Kaplan, A. G., & Bean, J. P. *Beyond sex-role stereotypes: Readings toward a psychology of androgyny*. Boston: Little, Brown, 1976.

Spence, J. T., Helmreich, R., & Stapp, J. The personal attributes questionnaire: A measure of sex role stereotypes and masculinity-femininity. *JSAS Catalog of Selected Documents in Psychology*, 1974, *4*, 43. (Ms. No. 617)

BSRI

Sandra Lipsitz Bem

In this inventory, you will be presented with sixty personality characteristics. You are to use those characteristics in order to describe yourself. That is, you are to indicate, on a scale from 1 to 7, how true of you these various characteristics are. Please do not leave any characteristic unmarked.

Example: _____ Sly

> Mark a *1* if it is *never or almost never true* that you are sly.
> Mark a *2* if it is *usually not true* that you are sly.
> Mark a *3* if it is *sometimes but infrequently true* that you are sly.
> Mark a *4* if it is *occasionally true* that you are sly.
> Mark a *5* if it is *often true* that you are sly.
> Mark a *6* if it is *usually true* that you are sly.
> Mark a *7* if it is *always or almost always true* that you are sly.

Thus, if you feel it is *sometimes but infrequently true* that you are "sly," *never or almost never true* that you are "malicious," *always or almost always true* that you are "irresponsible," and *often true* that you are "carefree," you would rate these characteristics as follows:

___3___ Sly   ___7___ Irresponsible
___1___ Malicious   ___5___ Carefree

Describe yourself according to the following scale:

1	2	3	4	5	6	7
Never or Almost Never True	Usually Not True	Sometimes But Infrequently True	Occasionally True	Often True	Usually True	Always or Almost Always True

_____ 1. Self-reliant   _____ 4. Defends own beliefs
_____ 2. Yielding   _____ 5. Cheerful
_____ 3. Helpful   _____ 6. Moody

_____ 7. Independent
_____ 8. Shy
_____ 9. Conscientious
_____ 10. Athletic
_____ 11. Affectionate
_____ 12. Theatrical
_____ 13. Assertive
_____ 14. Flatterable
_____ 15. Happy
_____ 16. Has strong personality
_____ 17. Loyal
_____ 18. Unpredictable
_____ 19. Forceful
_____ 20. Feminine
_____ 21. Reliable
_____ 22. Analytical
_____ 23. Sympathetic
_____ 24. Jealous
_____ 25. Has leadership abilities
_____ 26. Sensitive to the needs of others
_____ 27. Truthful
_____ 28. Willing to take risks
_____ 29. Understanding
_____ 30. Secretive
_____ 31. Makes decisions easily
_____ 32. Compassionate
_____ 33. Sincere
_____ 34. Self-sufficient

_____ 35. Eager to soothe hurt feelings
_____ 36. Conceited
_____ 37. Dominant
_____ 38. Soft-spoken
_____ 39. Likable
_____ 40. Masculine
_____ 41. Warm
_____ 42. Solemn
_____ 43. Willing to take a stand
_____ 44. Tender
_____ 45. Friendly
_____ 46. Aggressive
_____ 47. Gullible
_____ 48. Inefficient
_____ 49. Acts as a leader
_____ 50. Childlike
_____ 51. Adaptable
_____ 52. Individualistic
_____ 53. Does not use harsh language
_____ 54. Unsystematic
_____ 55. Competitive
_____ 56. Loves children
_____ 57. Tactful
_____ 58. Ambitious
_____ 59. Gentle
_____ 60. Conventional

BSRI SCORING AND INTERPRETATION SHEET

The adjectives on the BSRI are arranged as follows:

1. The first adjective and every third one thereafter is *masculine*.
2. The second adjective and every third one thereafter is *feminine*.
3. The third adjective and every third one thereafter is *neutral*.

Instructions

1. Sum the ratings you assigned to the *masculine* adjectives (1, 4, 7, 10, etc.) and write that total here: _____. Divide by 20 to get an average rating for masculinity: _____.
2. Sum the ratings you assigned to the *feminine* adjectives (2, 5, 8, 11, etc.) and write that total here: _____. Divide by 20 to get an average rating for femininity: _____.

Interpretation

3. Share your scores with others in your group to establish the median scores for each scale. (The median is that score above which 50 percent of the group members scored.)
4. Classify yourself according to the chart below by determining whether you are above or below your group's medians on masculinity and femininity.

Masculinity Median Score _____

		Below the Median	*Above the Median*
Femininity Median Score _____	*Below the Median*	Undifferentiated	Masculine
	Above the Median	Feminine	Androgynous

5. Study the items on the BSRI to explore how you see yourself with regard to your sex-role identity. You may wish to solicit feedback from other group members on whether they would rate you in the same ways.

The Attitudes Toward Women Scale (AWS)

Janet T. Spence

Robert Helmreich

THE ATTITUDES TOWARD WOMEN SCALE
SCORING INSTRUCTIONS

The Attitudes Toward Women Scale contains fifty-five items, each consisting of a declarative statement for which there are four response alternatives: Agree Strongly, Agree Mildly, Disagree Mildly, and Disagree Strongly. Each item is given a score from 0 to 3, with 0 representing choice of the response alternative reflecting the most traditional, conservative attitude and 3 the alternative reflecting the most liberal, profeminist attitude. Because the statement contained in some of the items is conservative in content and the statement in others is liberal, the specific alternative (Agree Strongly or Disagree Strongly) given a 0 score varies from item to item. Each subject's score is obtained by summing the values for the individual items. The range of possible scores goes from 0 to 165. The most conservative possibility is shown. The keyed responses should be covered before copies are made for participants, or items can be read aloud.

Used with permission of the authors. A machine-scorable answer sheet is available from the Department of Psychology, The University of Texas, Austin, Texas 78712.

The statements listed below describe attitudes toward the role of women in society that different people have. There are no right or wrong answers, only opinions. You are asked to express your feelings about each statement by indicating whether you (A) agree strongly, (B) agree mildly, (C) disagree mildly, or (D) disagree strongly. Please indicate your opinion by marking the alternative that best describes your personal attitude. Please respond to every item.

(A) Agree strongly
(B) Agree mildly
(C) Disagree mildly
(D) Disagree strongly

Response keyed 0   (The most conservative alternative, scored 0, is shown)

A   1. Women have an obligation to be faithful to their husbands.

A   ✓ 2. Swearing and obscenity are more repulsive in the speech of a woman than a man.

A   3. The satisfaction of her husband's sexual desires is a fundamental obligation of every wife.

D   4. Divorced men should help support their children but should not be required to pay alimony if their wives are capable of working.

A   5. Under ordinary circumstances, men should be expected to pay all the expenses while they're out on a date.

D   6. Women should take increasing responsibility for leadership in solving the intellectual and social problems of the day.

D   7. It is all right for wives to have an occasional, casual, extramarital affair.

D   8. Special attentions like standing up for a woman who comes into a room or giving her a seat on a crowded bus are outmoded and should be discontinued.

D   9. Vocational and professional schools should admit the best qualified students, independent of sex.

D   10. Both husband and wife should be allowed the same grounds for divorce.

A   11. Telling dirty jokes should be mostly a masculine prerogative.

D   12. Husbands and wives should be equal partners in planning the family budget.

A   13. Men should continue to show courtesies to women such as holding open the door or helping them on with their coats.

D   14. Women should claim alimony not as persons incapable of self-support but only when there are children to provide for or when the burden of starting life anew after the divorce is obviously heavier for the wife.

A   15. Intoxication among women is worse than intoxication among men.

A   16. The initiative in dating should come from the man.

D   17. Under modern economic conditions with women being active outside the home, men should share in household tasks such as washing dishes and doing the laundry.

D   18. It is insulting to women to have the "obey" clause remain in the marriage service.

D   19. There should be a strict merit system in job appointment and promotion without regard to sex.

D   20. A woman should be as free as a man to propose marriage.

D   21. Parental authority and responsibility for discipline of the children should be equally divided between husband and wife.

A   22. Women should worry less about their rights and more about becoming good wives and mothers.

D   23. Women earning as much as their dates should bear equally the expense when they go out together.

D   24. Women should assume their rightful place in business and all the professions along with men.

A   25. A woman should not expect to go to exactly the same places or to have quite the same freedom of action as a man.

A   26. Sons in a family should be given more encouragement to go to college than daughters.

A   27. It is ridiculous for a woman to run a locomotive and for a man to darn socks.

A   28. It is childish for a woman to assert herself by retaining her maiden name after marriage.

D   29. Society should regard the services rendered by the women workers as valuable as those of men.

A   30. It is only fair that male workers should receive more pay than women, even for identical work.

A   31. In general, the father should have greater authority than the mother in the bringing up of children.

A   32. Women should be encouraged not to become sexually intimate with anyone before marriage, even their fiancés.

D   33. Women should demand money for household and personal expenses as a right rather than as a gift.

D   34. The husband should not be favored by law over the wife in the disposal of family property or income.

D   35. Wifely submission is an outworn virtue.

A   36. There are some professions and types of businesses that are more suitable for men than women.

A   37. Women should be concerned with their duties of childrearing and housetending, rather than with desires for professional and business careers.

A   38. The intellectual leadership of a community should be largely in the hands of men.

A   39. A wife should make every effort to minimize irritation and inconvenience to the male head of the family.

D   40. There should be no greater barrier to an unmarried woman having sex with a casual acquaintance than having dinner with him.

D   41. Economic and social freedom is worth far more to women than acceptance of the ideal of femininity which has been set by men.

A   42. Women should take the passive role in courtship.

A   43. On the average, women should be regarded as less capable of contribution to economic production than are men.

D   44. The intellectual equality of woman with man is perfectly obvious.

D   45. Women should have full control of their persons and give or withhold sex intimacy as they choose.

A   46. The husband has in general no obligation to inform his wife of his financial plans.

A   47. There are many jobs in which men should be given preference over women in being hired or promoted.

A   48. Women with children should not work outside the home if
they don't have to financially.

D   49. Women should be given equal opportunity with men for
apprenticeship in the various trades.

D   50. The relative amounts of time and energy to be devoted to
household duties on the one hand and to a career on the
other should be determined by personal desires and interests rather than by sex.

A   51. As head of the household, the husband should have more
responsibility for the family's financial plans than his wife.

D   52. If both husband and wife agree that sexual fidelity isn't
important, there's no reason why both shouldn't have extramarital affairs if they want to.

A   53. The husband should be regarded as the legal representative of the family group in all matters of law.

D   54. The modern girl is entitled to the same freedom from
regulation and control that is given to the modern boy.

A   55. Most women need and want the kind of protection and
support that men have traditionally given them.

Self-Assessment Questionnaire

How would you rate yourself on:

Living effectively in the present

/ / / / /

    Poor   Fair   Average   Above Average   Very Good

Looking to the future rather than the past

/ / / / /

    Poor   Fair   Average   Above Average   Very Good

Setting realistic future goals

/ / / / /

    Poor   Fair   Average   Above Average   Very Good

Expressing yourself in a group

/ / / / /

    Poor   Fair   Average   Above Average   Very Good

Listening to others

/ / / / /

    Poor   Fair   Average   Above Average   Very Good

Open mindedness

/ / / / /

    Poor   Fair   Average   Above Average   Very Good

Decision-making skills

/ / / / /

    Poor   Fair   Average   Above Average   Very Good

The first seven items were written by Lucinda E. Thomas for the *Life Planning Workshop Manual*, University Counseling Center, Colorado State University, Ft. Collins, Colorado 80521. Used with permission.

Awareness of how your attitudes toward male-female relationships influence your behavior

_____/	_____/	_____/	_____/	_____/
Poor	Fair	Average	Above Average	Very Good

Understanding how attitudes toward male-female relationships influence others

_____/	_____/	_____/	_____/	_____/
Poor	Fair	Average	Above Average	Very Good

Relating effectively with opposite-sex friends

_____/	_____/	_____/	_____/	_____/
Poor	Fair	Average	Above Average	Very Good

Relating effectively with same-sex friends

_____/	_____/	_____/	_____/	_____/
Poor	Fair	Average	Above Average	Very Good

Expressing yourself honestly and directly

_____/	_____/	_____/	_____/	_____/
Poor	Fair	Average	Above Average	Very Good

Changing your behavior in desired directions

_____/	_____/	_____/	_____/	_____/
Poor	Fair	Average	Above Average	Very Good

Male-Female Role Questionnaire

* ___ ___ ___ ___ ___
  A   B   C   D   E

1. In your opinion, which sex is better off in this society?
   A. Men are much better off because they have freedom, status, and power.
   B. Men are somewhat better off.
   C. There are complementary advantages to each sex.
   D. Women are somewhat better off.
   E. Women are much better off because they have protection, leisure, and freedom from pressures to achieve.

* ___ ___ ___ ___ ___
  A   B   C   D   E

2. How would you describe your social relationships with the opposite sex now?
   A. Almost always relaxed and at ease.
   B. Moderately comfortable.
   C. Moderately uncomfortable.
   D. Almost always uncomfortable and uneasy.
   E. Rarely have social dealings with opposite sex if I can help it.

---

*Questions with an asterisk were taken from "Woman & Man—A PSYCHOLOGY TODAY Questionnaire" by Carol Tavris in PSYCHOLOGY TODAY Magazine, February, 1971. Copyright ©Communications/Research/Machines, Inc. Used with permission.

* _____ _____ _____ _____ _____
A   B   C   D   E

3. Which of the following would give you the most satisfaction in your life?
   A. Career or occupation.
   B. Family or love relationships.
   C. Friendships.
   D. Leisure-time activities and hobbies.
   E. Running a home.

* _____ _____ _____ _____ _____
A   B   C   D   E

4. Aside from relatives, who have been your closest friends in recent years?
   A. Mostly persons of the same sex.
   B. Mostly persons of the opposite sex.
   C. Persons of both sexes equally.

For each of the following traits, indicate whether you think it is more characteristic of men or women, and, if there are differences, whether they are mostly due to biological (genetic) or cultural (learned) factors.

Male Trait Biological	Male Trait Cultural	No Difference	Female Trait Cultural	Female Trait Biological	
* ___	___	___	___	___	5. Aggressiveness
* ___	___	___	___	___	6. Emotionality
* ___	___	___	___	___	7. Independence
* ___	___	___	___	___	8. Objectivity/rationality
* ___	___	___	___	___	9. Nurturance
* ___	___	___	___	___	10. Intelligence (abstract or math reasoning)
* ___	___	___	___	___	11. Intelligence (verbal ability)
* ___	___	___	___	___	12. Inclined to monogamy
* ___	___	___	___	___	13. Ambitiousness
* ___	___	___	___	___	14. Empathy/Intuition

Agree	Tend to Agree	Don't Know or Care	Tend to Disagree	Disagree	
* ___	___	___	___	___	15. Many qualified women can't get good jobs; men with the same skills have less trouble.
* ___	___	___	___	___	16. Almost all men unconsciously support the notion that females should assume a lesser position in our society.
* ___	___	___	___	___	17. Most women have only themselves to blame for not doing better in life.
* ___	___	___	___	___	18. Men are as likely to take an interest in a woman's mind as in her body.
* ___	___	___	___	___	19. Women are usually less reliable on the job than men because they tend to be absent more and quit more often.
* ___	___	___	___	___	20. Children of working mothers tend to be *less* well-adjusted than children of unemployed women.
* ___	___	___	___	___	21. Women are as capable as men in most things.
___	___	___	___	___	22. Women have the right to compete with men in every sphere of economic activity.
___	___	___	___	___	23. The husband should be regarded as the legal representative of the family in all matters of law.
___	___	___	___	___	24. Women have as much need to "sow wild oats" as do men.
___	___	___	___	___	25. Women should be given equal opportunities with men for vocational and professional training.

Agree

Tend to
Agree

Don't Know
or Care

Tend to
Disagree

Disagree

_____ _____ _____ _____ _____ 26. Women are not intellectually or emotionally capable of holding political offices that involve great responsibility.

_____ _____ _____ _____ _____ 27. Women are more sensitive than men.

_____ _____ _____ _____ _____ 28. There is no particular reason why a girl standing in a crowded subway should expect a man to offer her his seat.

_____ _____ _____ _____ _____ 29. The women's liberation movement will probably improve relations between men and women in the long run.

_____ _____ _____ _____ _____ 30. A husband has the right to expect that his wife be obliging and dutiful at all times.

_____ _____ _____ _____ _____ 31. Complementary sex roles protect the basic institution of our society—the nuclear family.

_____ _____ _____ _____ _____ 32. A woman should not expect to go to the same places or to have quite the same freedom of action as a man.

_____ _____ _____ _____ _____ 33. The working wife who claims economic equality has no more right to alimony from her husband than he has right to alimony from her.

_____ _____ _____ _____ _____ 34. Women should always take the passive role in courtship.

Agree	Tend to Agree	Don't Know or Care	Tend to Disagree	Disagree		
___	___	___	___	___	35.	Despite the American ideal of equality of the sexes, there are certain jobs and certain things a woman just shouldn't do if she wants to be considered feminine.
___	___	___	___	___	36.	Men need ego building; women need to be protected.
___	___	___	___	___	37.	A major fault that women have is their personal vanity, as shown by the exaggerated importance they attach to details of dress and grooming.
___	___	___	___	___	38.	Parental authority and responsibility for discipline of the children should be equally divided between husband and wife.
___	___	___	___	___	39.	The increase of casual dress among both college males and females indicates a decline of romanticism in dating /sexual relationships.
___	___	___	___	___	40.	A female who does not shave her legs or underarms can be as pretty as one who does.

How do you feel about the following:

Approve	Slightly Approve	Don't Care	Slightly Disapprove	Disapprove		
* ___	___	___	___	___	41.	Public day-care facilities.
* ___	___	___	___	___	42.	Abortion on demand by a woman.

Approve
Slightly Approve
Don't Care
Slightly Disapprove
Disapprove

* ___ ___ ___ ___ ___ 43. Equality for men and women in salaries, promotions, and hiring.

* ___ ___ ___ ___ ___ 44. Equal responsibility by man and woman for housekeeping.

* ___ ___ ___ ___ ___ 45. Equal responsibility by man and woman for child rearing and child care.

* ___ ___ ___ ___ ___ 46. An end to sex-differentiated tracking in the educational system, e.g., so that women are no longer counseled into feminine careers.

* ___ ___ ___ ___ ___ 47. A change in or an alternative to the institution of marriage in its present form.

* ___ ___ ___ ___ ___ 48. Child rearing without regard for traditional sex-role stereotypes.

* ___ ___ ___ ___ ___ 49. A U.S. Constitution equal-rights amendment for women.

* ___ ___ ___ ___ ___ 50. What is your general impression
  A   B   C   D   E   of *most* of the women in the women's liberation movement?

A. They are sexually frustrated women who use the movement to work out personal problems.

B. They are aggressive and castrating females who dislike men.

C. They are women who are somewhat neurotic as a result of experiences with discrimination.

D. They are well-adjusted women with justifiable grievances.

E. They are healthy women fighting a sick system.

READINGS

Growing Up Male

Florence L. Denmark

"Growing Up Male,"[1] the title, carries the implications that distinct from growing up female, or just growing up, there is something quite unique about growing up male. Recently, much attention has been paid to the early socialization of females and what it means to grow up female in our society, with special consideration given to the specific contributions of parents, teachers, groups, institutions, and the mass media in the shaping of self-concept, self-image, and future aspirations of girls. Concurrently however, there has been a relative neglect of inquiry into the early socialization of males. Yet from birth onward, sex-differential treatment occurs.

Even *if* certain sex differences in behavior are biologically predisposed, investigators must still recognize and acknowledge the effects of the difference in eliciting differential interaction with the neonate, and the resultant on-going treatment of infants and young children. This differential treatment then serves to maintain, magnify, and distort the male-female dichotomy. As in other areas of investigation, the nature-nurture issue serves to divert attention from the more important questions relating to process. Therefore, the focus here will be on socialization practices.

Sex-prescribed treatment begins at birth with the assignment of sex-related color to the clothing worn by infants: blue clothing announcing the presence of a male infant and pink for female, although

---

[1]Susan McCandless provided invaluable assistance in obtaining some of the included data.

this practice has changed somewhat during recent years. Style of clothing is similarly affected, with the assumption that even the infant male requires clothing that is sturdier and less confining than the feminine and frilly dress. In fact, stereotyped behavior expectations for sons begin even prenatally, to the extent that the sex of an active fetus will often be inferred as male, and a more quiescent fetus as female (Lewis, 1972a). Based on such expectations and related societal values, parents may frequently have a preference for a child of one sex or the other. One study (Jaccoma & Denmark, 1974) indicated that parents would like to select the sex of their unborn child. Boys were preferred over girls with an increase in this preference for a son as the firstborn child. The preference for a male firstborn was apparently based on the feeling that a girl should have an older brother who would be stronger and wiser, thus equipped to guide and protect her.

Labelling, another phenomenon beginning at birth, can be as insidious as it is relentless. Money & Ehrhardt (1973) report that the behavior of parents toward their young baby changes radically if it is discovered that the child, born with ambiguous genitals and having been assigned one sex at birth, could more feasibly develop the gender identity of the opposite sex and is reassigned accordingly. Such parents have the unique opportunity to be aware of and to report that the same child will elicit different responses from them when the sex has been changed. In one case reported by Money and Ehrhardt even a three year old brother radically changed his behavior toward his sibling.

Lewis (1972a) analyzed the behavior of mothers and infants and found additional evidence that parents do change their behavior measurably as a function of the sex of the child. For six months or so, infant boys have more physical contact with their mothers than infant girls, but by the time boys are six months old, this relationship reverses and girls receive more physical as well as non-tactile contact. It has also been noted by Moss (1967) that boys were held more between the age of three weeks and three months. However, from the earliest age, girl infants are looked at and talked to more than are boys (Goldberg & Lewis, 1972). In addition, physical contact with their mothers is diminished at a later age (Lewis, 1972a). It is not clear why mothers touch boys more frequently during the first six months of life. Perhaps it is because they are more valued, or perhaps it is because they are more irritable and have longer periods of wakefulness than do girls. After six months, the motive for less contact also can be cultural, in that mothers may believe that boys should be more independent and that they thus require assistance towards exploration and orientation towards the mastery of their environment (Aberle & Naegele, 1952; Lewis, 1972a).

There seems to be a relationship between these early sex differences in touching and physical contact, and with the touching practices of adult life. In American society, men and women are allowed considerably different "degrees of freedom" for touching (Lewis, 1972a). Men do not ordinarily make physical contact with other men, except in explicitly sanctioned situations. The fear of homosexuality is reported to be much stronger in boys than in girls (Douvan & Adelson, 1966). Although there has been some recent movement in the direction of greater freedom here, men still feel uncomfortable about close physical contact with others. Circumstances of crowding, with the possibility of unwelcome or unacceptable physical contact seem to make men more hostile and aggressive, whereas, women, in contrast, tend to become more friendly (Lewis, 1972b).

By the age of thirteen months, boys spend longer periods of time away from their mothers, venture further distances and spend less time looking at and talking to their mothers than do girls of the same age (Lewis, 1972a). The fact that nursery schools receive far more applications for boys than for girls (Sherman, 1971) may suggest that mothers are more willing to separate from sons than from daughters. Possibly this willingness might indicate a greater need for relief of the mother as caretaker of a nursery-aged boy because of his supposed greater activity and more vigorous exploratory behavior. The daily routine of a young mother may often become compatible with the sex-role prescribed activities of a little girl (i.e., baby or dolls and dishes or both), and it is possible that this same sex identification with a daughter, juxtaposed against the ambivalent feelings which each sex feels for the other, is strong enough to affect even the mother-child relationship.

It should be mentioned at this point that not all of the sex differences cited here will appear in the early years, and that the difference between the sexes is always one of degree. To say that a boy is one thing does not imply that a girl is not, but merely is a statement that one sex demonstrates a particular behavioral trait with relatively more force and/or frequency than does the other. Within group differences are invariably greater than between group differences.

One stereotype about early sex differences in behavior appears to be supported by experimental evidence, namely that males are considerably more aggressive than females under almost all conditions studied (Oetzel, 1966; Mischel, 1970; Maccoby & Jacklin, 1974). Sex differences in aggressive behavior are even observed at early ages, a finding which suggests that boys are more aggressive even before they are taught that aggressiveness is an attribute of masculinity. However, while males seem to have this greater predisposition of aggress, insofar as they are physically rougher in play activities from early childhood onward, it should be also kept in mind that aggressiveness is an attribute of masculinity. Thus, we would expect that sex-typed socialization practices would serve to amplify existing sex differences. Males and females may also merely express their aggressive feelings in different ways, since females have been found to exhibit more verbal aggression and prosocial aggression than do males (Feshbach, 1970).

The male is physically stronger, but more vulnerable to stress, major diseases and adverse environmental factors (Garai & Scheinfeld, 1968). He is reported to have a higher touch and pain threshold (Lipsett & Levy, 1959; Rosenblith & Le Lucia, 1963), although a recent review of all existing studies by Maccoby & Jacklin (1974) suggests that this is a premature generalization. Such a difference, if true, may facilitate more fearless and assertive environmental exploration in the male during early infancy, although here also, there is no clear-cut evidence for a sex difference in motor activity in neonates (Garai & Scheinfeld, 1968; Maccoby & Jacklin, 1971).

Although Maccoby & Jacklin (1974) state that the evidence does not indicate a difference, many other investigators have stated that there is a sex difference in responsiveness and/or preference for sense modalities such that males are visual and females auditory (e.g. Garai & Scheinfeld, 1968; Watson, 1969). If so, this would imply that males and females are likely to respond differently to both the same and different stimuli (Kagan, 1969), with possible facilitation of the development of one skill for males (spatial), and another for females (language).

The female's recognized early superior verbal skills, and greater nurturance and affiliation tendencies serve to facilitate communication and shape her perceptions along interpersonal/aesthetic dimensions. In comparison, the male's greater mathematical skills, and greater independence and achievement aspirations focus his interests more on objects and ideas (Hutt, 1972; Carlson, 1971). In play, he is interested in constructing and playing games of power and dominance (Rosenberg & Sutton-Smith, 1960, 1964).

In addition to the possibility of early differences which may predispose infants to different learning experiences in the two sexes, young children begin to learn the existence of gender concepts. Kohlberg (1966) points out that by the age of two a boy has learned that certain objects are called boys and men; others, girls and women. These definitions are learned by the observation of the behavior, appearance and attire of these individuals. This categorization is one of the earliest conceptualizations made by a child. Initially, it is not based on anatomical distinctions, nor do young children consider it to be a permanent, unchangeable human quality (Kohlberg, 1966). At a somewhat later age, children broaden their conceptions of gender to include psychological traits. Young children agree that males are more dangerous and punishing than females. Six year old boys classify their fathers and themselves as darker, larger, more dangerous, and more angular than their mothers and other females (Kagan & Lemkin, 1960). Osgood found these perceptions to occur also in other cultures (Osgood, 1960 and 1964). The perception of the boy role, and the perception of the adult expectations for the behavior of boys eight and eleven years old were found by Hartley (1959) to include, other than the usual physical and game prowess, behaviors and attributes stressing superiority over girls, and the avoidance of girl-appropriate activities. The boys' perception of the adult male role included occupational abilities, physical skills, dominance, and importance.

The learning process is often made difficult for a young boy by the frequent unavailability of a male model in his immediate life. The safest and simplest solution for such a boy is to define 'maleness' as 'that which is not female.' An avoidance of perceived female attributes thus results. Indeed, young boys growing up without any male model may develop an extreme stereotyped masculinity—sometimes to the point of exhibiting juvenile-delinquent behavior. Lacking a complex example of human masculinity, they draw their knowledge from other sources, such as peers and the media. The media tends to present men in occupational roles, concerned with self, and prone to varying degrees of violence, power and status concerns. It also portrays boys and men with far greater frequency than girls and women, which constitutes a more frequent presentation of this stereotypical behavior with resultant facilitation of "skewed" learning (Task Force, 1972; Kay, 1973; Sternglanz & Serbin, 1974).

The greater frequency of portrayal of males can also lead to the internalized understanding that males, as a group, are more important and salient in life. This understanding is further reinforced by the fact that females, when they appear at all, are portrayed as relatively passive and ineffectual.

At about five or six years of age, the young boy increases his imitation of the father and usually has the opportunity to enjoy various activities with him (Mischel, 1970). The child's attitudes and orientations are shaped and molded by strong parental influences

(Fagot, 1974). The boy's imitation of the father is enhanced if the father is perceived as warm and powerful, power being the more important dimension. Thus, a young boy will imitate or identify with a powerful mother even if the father is perceived as warm. Conversely, for girls, warmth seems to be the significant dimension. A young girl will imitate a warm mother, regardless of which parent is seen as the more powerful (Hetherington, 1965).

Beginning at the age of five or so, the father attains a status of increasing salience in a young boy's life. He exerts more power (reward and punishment) toward the son than toward the daughter (Emmerich, 1962), and is more likely to use corporal punishment methods with him (Tasch, 1952). Findings show that boys tend to receive both more deprivation of privileges and more attention from the father (Devereaux et al., 1963), as well as more physical control, hostility, neglect, and less love and nurturance (Droppleman & Schaefer, 1963). Adolescent boys receive more pressure and discipline than girls, in particular from the father (Bronfenbrenner, 1960). From middle childhood through adolescence the theme of conflict, power, and concern about independence become prominent in the life of a male (Douvan & Adelson, 1966).

The importance of the father in his son's development is underscored by findings which suggest that a father is characteristically more prone to the sex-typing of activities than is a mother, and is particularly concerned that a son be 'appropriately' masculine (Tasch, 1952; Goodenough, 1957; Lansky, 1967). The father's interest in the development of his son's motor ability increases with the age of the boy, and he becomes an active participant in motor activities with him (Tasch, 1952). When questioned on areas of major concern regarding a son's behavior, a typical father will cite lack of responsibility and initiative, poor school work, insufficient aggressiveness, athletic inadequacy, over-conformity, excitability, excessive tearfulness, and 'childish behavior' (Aberle & Naegele, 1952).

Fathers appear to be less tolerant of dependency in sons than in daughters (Rothbart & Maccoby, 1966). This may lead the father to draw the son into more independent behavior. In contrast, "being a good girl" may reap rewards for a girl, and thus assume more importance for her. This would promote conformity, dependent behavior, tractability and passiveness.

If a boy were to continue to behave in a dependent manner, he would encounter increasing disapproval from his parents, especially his father. In grade school, he would experience censure from his peers, both males and females. In fifth or sixth grade, boys with a high need for approval are among the least popular, whereas the converse is true for fifth and sixth grade girls (Tulkin, Muller, & Conn, 1969). Thus, a boy who doesn't exhibit 'naturally' independent behavior will meet varied and powerful environmental pressures. They are pressured to turn to their peers for acceptance, and to develop internal criteria and objective achievements.

Same-sex peer group relationships seem to serve a different purpose for boys than for girls. Young boys appear to engage in group activities and sports not so much for the opportunity to be with each other, but primarily for the activity itself. Girls are less likely to play in large groups, but rather to pair off with one or two close companions (Maccoby & Jacklin, 1974). Perhaps this is because the activity is secondary to the relationship for girls. This difference continues into early adolescence, during which boys still tend to be less involved in close friendships. The tendency is to form 'gangs' which serve to provide peer group support in the male quest for autonomy. The authority and solidarity of the group qua group is much valued (Douvan & Adelson, 1966).

The on-going attempt to match the male's attributes to his sex-role ideal allows him to display a more intense involvement in difficult intellectual and mastery problems than does the female. Males are expected to be more competent in science and mathematics. Girls, believing that they should not be overly competitive, must frequently inhibit intense intellectual striving. The male grows up anticipating a career, with intellectual concerns linked to that end. National surveys of adolescents have found that a boy's identity is directly fused with his vocational aspirations and plans. Boys stress education and work, and dream of outstanding achievement in an area of personal interest (Douvan & Adelson, 1966). Girls frequently do not perceive any incentive or need for concern over intellectual mastery.

Yet in the early school years girls outperform boys (Lynn, 1972). The ratio of boys to girls with speech, reading, and other language problems ranges as high as 10 to 1 (Bentzen, 1963). One explanation for this disparity may be that young boys perceive school as a feminine place under the jurisdiction of female teachers who value obedience and the suppression of aggression and motor activity—precisely the behaviors regarded by boys as more appropriate for girls (Kagan, 1964).

In an investigation into the reactions of first and second grade teachers to fictitious boys and girls portrayed to manifest achieving, aggressive or dependent characteristics, the teachers did not indicate greater approval or liking for sex-stereotyped children. Achieving children met with equal approval. While the dependent girl was liked more than the aggressive girl, the aggressive boy was not liked more than the dependent boy (Levitin & Chananie, 1972).

However, the gap in scholastic performance between boys and girls during the elementary years is soon obliterated and eventually reversed. At puberty, perhaps as a function of new awareness and perceived adult role requirements, boys begin to improve their scholastic competencies, and girls decline (Lynn, 1972). A great deal of time and effort is spent by teachers and volunteers in training boys in verbal skills, and with good results. Such remedial reading programs, designed and promoted by educators, are commonplace features in the early grades. Can you imagine what a comparable benefit would result to girls if intensive training in spatial skills and problem solving were offered!

In junior high and high school, the school experience continues to favor the male. In a recent study, junior high teachers of both sexes were found to initiate more positive contacts with boys, facilitate more interactions of all types with boys, provide boys with more opportunities to respond, and give more affect (both positive and negative) to boys. Male teachers were more likely to praise boys for correct responses, and merely to affirm the correct responses of girls. Other significant interactions have implications for promoting sex differences in the direction of higher achievement motivation and more analytical skills for the male students (Good, Sikes, & Brophy, 1973). Thus, boys are provided with skilled cross-sex models in their early years—both their mothers and their teachers. The same is not true for girls.

To counterbalance this discrepancy, it would seem advisable that the care of young children be shared by both parents (Biller, 1972). The role of the father should have equal importance to that of the mother, and enhancement of the ability to establish contact with young children should be encouraged in the male. In this way, children of both sexes would have the opportunity to see fathers, as well as mothers, in a nurturant role. Exposure to a male model who spends more time with his children and exhibits a wide range of diverse behaviors would help promote a more complex, human conception of masculinity in both sexes. Attributes of stereotypes would not be as crucial to the young child.

Toys and play activity are of equal importance to children of both sexes and at all ages. Through the opportunities provided by play—exploration, manipulation, and role-playing—intellectual functioning and creativity are stimulated. The child's physical development is also, to a large extent, dependent on play. The needs of young boys and girls are similar, and if given the opportunity, both will develop strong bodies and increase their skills through physical activities. In fact, if given similar practice, no sex differences should appear in motor ability in the childhood years.

Sex differences in play are also culturally conditioned and socially reinforced. Girls generally have been restricted by the kinds of activities and toys chosen for them by parents, or through the advertisements which stress products in sex-typed promotions. Boys are given room and leeway to be active, to achieve skill, and to engage in more imaginative play in preparation for life, whereas girls have been oriented toward passivity. Exciting activities have always been the special province of boys, while a girl's place has always been with dolls and other sedentary domestic activities. Along with the supposition that boys are usually better endowed in mechanical and analytical skills, it must be acknowledged that they have been encouraged to manipulate mechanical toys such as cars, trains, and construction sets. These differences in play activities have resulted in different methods of learning in school for boys and girls, as well as in differences in the expectations of parents and teachers.

Masculine or boyish activities have been associated with greater freedom, privileges, and status. Through play, boys derive a sense of themselves as powerful, effectual, instrumental, and "in control." Boys tend to rely on themselves for direction in their activities. They have greater opportunity to manipulate toys and not just accept them as they are. The possibilities of a set of blocks are infinite compared with a doll's house. A doll's house will still be a doll's house, despite redecorations and revamping of the furniture layout. Blocks can be constructed to form anything, bounded only by the imagination and creativity of the child. The manipulation of blocks provides an additional opportunity to become familiar with spatial attributes and abilities.

It is very likely that the independence and activity which has been encouraged in boys may contribute to a rise in their achievement as they grow older. By encouraging girls as well to experiment more freely with toys which invite imagination and manipulation, their intellectual potential may also be enhanced. A greater variety of role possibilities will be opened to both sexes if their early play activity were not so restricted to stereotypically prescribed future occupations, either out in the world or in the kitchen. Parents should become less preoccupied with stressing sex-limited behavior at every turn and more dedicated to providing both sexes with opportunities and materials for exploration and experimentation.

The games and physical activities of boys also serve as preparation for what they will do when they grow up. In competitive sports they experience victory and defeat. Effort and experience become salient; they learn to try harder, to reach a bit higher each time, and gradually and steadily improve the development of achievement skills and competitive behavior skills. They also learn that failures are commonplace and do not necessarily indicate that an individual is inadequate.

Both competition and winning are fairly unfamiliar experiences to women. They are taught that such activities will lead to negative consequences (Task Force, 1972; Boslooper & Hayes, 1973). Particularly in mixed sex situations a victorious female is likely to encounter negative reactions from others. As a consequence, girls learn early that losing is a more tolerable outcome (Horner, 1970). When the sexes do compete, they often do so for different reasons. Men compete for awards signifying excellence and women compete for men or approval from others (Boslooper & Hayes, 1973).

Games and play activities of young children are not inconsequential activities, activities which have no importance once one leaves the realm of childhood. They foster skills and personality attributes which are transferred readily to more grownup pursuits. They can be likened to models: smaller scaled-down versions of the "real-thing." For instance, competitive team sports involve power, cooperative effort, and physical skill. The training in strategy, especially if accompanied by parental encouragement towards achievement and social responsibility, should facilitate preparation for a responsible role in life (Roberts & Sutton-Smith, 1969; Roberts, Sutton-Smith, & Kozelka, 1969).

In the above sense then, perhaps the game can be won at least partially on the "playing fields." Boys are given active training for later success and power roles through involvement in competitive games and sports. Games of chance and interpersonal affairs mirror feminine skills. Fairy tales and other stories are like literary games. Boys identify with the male hero models whereas girls succumb to the same hero models; a girl is *Cinderella*—it is the boy who imperially selects her and carries her off on a white charger. Games can have disadvantages for men if they feel that they *should* only "play" a particular role, or constellation of roles, in life. Some men feel threatened unless the activities of the sexes are rigidly dichotomized into mutually exclusive roles. For some, a sense of independence requires that another be dependent. For others, self-esteem and a perception of importance may hinge on seeing oneself as superior, particularly to one's wife (Komarovsky, 1973). Unfortunately, some returning Viet Nam prisoners of war are very unhappy about their wives' newly found autonomy and competency.

Unhappily, competition in games has gone haywire. Too often, sport is no longer play, but a very serious business. It has become a test for and proof of masculinity, and a facilitator of further aggressiveness. Instead of being used and enjoyed as a vehicle to develop skills and evaluate their improvement, the focus has narrowed to that of the end result: winning or losing. A game is no longer a game in the sense of a child's approach to it. The symbolic meanings embedded in sports have robbed such activities of their playfulness. Men can't afford to participate in sports because the possibility of failure is too devastating. The result is a nation of spectators: observers of the gladiators. Yet creators know that discovery will not occur if one is terrified of the prospect of failure. Scientists and artists must withstand repeated failures before ultimately they obtain the result they are seeking. And competition, in the best sense of the word— including through sports—should provide such a valuable set of experiences for both sexes. It should help make men and women readier to accept the challenge of natural obstacles and the unknown—to teach them how to win and to lose, and to keep on trying.

Although there is much to be said against the rigid and confining nature of the masculine role, it does provide for unity in terms of an individual's physical and psychological development. At puberty, boys are encouraged to continue strengthening their physical competitiveness and aggression but girls are asked to give up their physical competency which has contributed to their identity for the first decade. When boys are asked to add intellectual concerns to their athletic interests, girls are asked to reduce their intellectual competency. In adolescence, boys increase their skills in both areas, whereas girls are left with neither (Rosenberg, 1972).

Just as women can learn from the positive features of growing up male, and discard the negative features, so men can learn from the so-called "feminine ideal."

The freedom of emotional expression permissible to women represents a great advantage. Similarly the reach for independence and competence in males is also important. Our society should be neither masculinized nor feminized, but should blend the best of both. A society may make women and men temperamentally different or it may create instead a "human" personality. Men, like women, can be anything society makes them.

REFERENCES

Aberle, D. F., & Naegele, K. D. Middle-class father's occupational role and attitudes towards children. *American Journal of Orthopsychiatry*, 1952, 22, 366-378.

Bentzen, F. Sex ratios in learning and behavior disorder. *American Journal of Orthopsychiatry*, 1963, 33, 92-98.

Biller, H. B. Sex role learning: Some comments and complexities from a multidimensional perspective. Paper presented at the meeting of the American Association for the Advancement of Science, Washington, D.C., December, 1972.

Boslooper, T., & Hayes, M. *The femininity game*. New York: Stein & Day, 1973.

Bronfenbrenner, U. Some familial antecedents of responsibility and leadership in adolescents. In L. Petrullo and B. M. Bass, eds., *Studies in leadership*. New York: Holt, 1960.

Carolson, R. Sex differences in ego functioning: Exploratory studies in agency and communion. *Journal of Consulting and Clinical Psychology*, 1971, 37, 267-277.

Devereux, E. C., Bronfenbrenner, U., & Suci, G. J. Patterns of parent behavior in the United States of America and the Federal Republic of Germany: A cross-national comparison. *International Social Science Journal*, 1963, 14, 2-20.

Douvan, E., & Adelson, J. *The adolescent experience*. New York: Wiley, 1966.

Droppleman, L. F., & Schaefer, E. S. Boys' and girls' report of maternal and paternal behavior. *Journal of Abnormal and Social Psychology*, 1963, 67, 648-654.

Emmerich, W. Variations in the parent role as a function of the parent's sex and the child's sex and age. *Merrill-Palmer Quarterly*, 1962, 8, 3-11.

Fagot, B. I. Sex differences in toddlers' behavior and parental reaction. *Developmental Psychology*, 1974, 10, 554-558.

Feshbach, S. Aggression. In P. H. Mussen, ed., *Carmichael's manual of child psychology*. New York: Wiley, 1970.

Garai, J. E., & Scheinfeld, A. Sex differences in mental and behavioral traits. *Genetic Psychology Monographs*, 1968, 77, 169-299.

Goldberg, S., & Lewis, M. Play behavior in the year old infant: Early sex differences. *Child Development*, 1969, 40, 21-31.

Good, T. L., Sikes, J. N., & Brophy, J. E. Effects of teacher sex and student sex on classroom interaction. *Journal of Educational Psychology*, 1973, 65, 74-87.

Goodenough, E. W. Interest in persons as an aspect of sex difference in the early years. *Genetic Psychology Monographs*, 1957, 55, 287-323.

Hartley, R. E. Sex role pressures and socialization of the male child. *Psychological Reports*, 1959, 5, 458.

Hetherington, E. M. A developmental study of the effects of sex of the dominant parent on sex-role preference, identification, and imitation in children. *Journal of Personality and Social Psychology*, 1965, 2, 188-193.

Horner, M. S. Femininity and successful achievement: Basic inconsistency. In Bardwich, J. M., Douvan, E., Horner, M. S., & Gutman, D. *Feminine personality and conflict*. Belmont, California: Brooks Cole Publishing, 1970, 45-74.

Hutt, C. *Males and females*. Middlesex, England: Penguin Books, Ltd., 1972.

Jaccoma, G., & Denmark, F. L. Boys or girls: The hows and whys. Unpublished master's thesis. Hunter College, 1974.

Kagan, J. The emergence of sex differences. *School Review*, 1972, *80*, 217-228.

_____ Continuity in cognitive development during the first year. *Merrill-Palmer Quarterly*, 1969, *15*, 101-119.

_____ The child's sex role classification of school objects. *Child Development*, 1964, *35*, 1051.

Kagan, J., & Lemkin, J. The child's differential perception of parental attributes. *Journal of Abnormal and Social Psychology*, 1960, *61*, 446.

Key, M. R. Male and female in children's books—dispelling all doubts. In F. Denmark and R. Unger (eds.), *Women: Dependent or independent variable?* New York: Psychological Dimensions, Inc., 1975.

Kohlberg, L. A cognitive-developmental analysis of children's sex role concepts and attitudes. In E. E. Maccoby (ed.), *The development of sex differences*. Stanford, California: Stanford University Press, 1966.

Lansky, L. M. The family structure also affects the model: Sex-role attitudes in parents and preschool children. *Merrill-Palmer Quarterly*, 1967, *13*, 139-150.

Levitin, T. E., & Chananie, J. D. Responses of female primary school teachers to sex typed behaviors in male and female children. *Child Development*, 1972, *43*, 1309-1316.

Lewis, M. Parents and children: Sex-role development. *School Review*, 1972, *80*, 229-240. (a)

_____ Culture and gender roles: There's no unisex in the nursery. *Psychology Today*, May 1972, *5*, 54-57. (b)

Lipsitt, L. P., & Levy, N. Electrotactual threshold in the human neonate. *Child Development*, 1959, *30*, 547-554.

Lynn, D. B. Determinants of intellectual growth in women. *School Review*, 1972, *80*, 241-260.

Maccoby, E. E., & Jacklin, C. N. *The psychology of sex differences*. Stanford, California: Stanford University Press, 1974.

_____ Sex differences and their implications for sex roles. Paper presented at the American Psychological Association, Washington, D.C., 1971.

Mischel, W. Sex typing and socialization. In P. H. Mussen (ed.), *Carmichael's manual of child psychology*, Volume II, 3rd edition. New York: Wiley, 1970.

Money, J., & Ehrhardt, A. A. *Man and woman: Boy and girl.* Baltimore: Johns Hopkins Press, 1972.

Moss, H. A. Sex, age, and state as determinants of mother-infant interaction. *Merrill-Palmer Quarterly,* 1967, *13,* 19-36.

Oetzel, R. B. Annotated bibliography. *The development of sex differences.* Stanford, California: Stanford University Press, 1966, 224-321.

Osgood, C. E. Semantic differential technique in the comparative study of cultures. *American Anthropologist,* 1964, *66,* 171-200.

———— The cross-cultural generality of visual-verbal synthesthetic tendencies. *Behavioral Science,* 1960, *5,* 146-169.

Osgood, G. L., & Tannenbaum, P. *The measurement of meaning.* Urbana, Illinois: University of Illinois Press, 1957.

Roberts, J. M., & Sutton-Smith, B. Child training and game involvement. In Loy, J. W., & Kenyon, G. S. (eds.), *Sport, culture and society.* New York: Macmillan, 1969.

Rosenberg, B. G. Sex, sex role, and sex role identity: The built-in paradoxes. Paper presented at the annual meeting of the American Association for the Advancement of Science: Washington, D.C., December, 1972.

Rosenberg, B. G., & Sutton-Smith, B. The measure of masculinity and femininity in children: An extension and revalidation. *Journal of Genetic Psychology,* 1964, *104,* 259-264.

———— A revised conception of masculine feminine differences in play activities. *Journal of Genetic Psychology,* 1960, *96,* 165-170.

Rosenblith, J. F., & De Lucia, L. A. Tactile sensitivity and muscular strength in the neonate. *Biologia Neonatarum,* 1963, *5,* 266-282.

Rothbart, M. K., & Maccoby, E. E. Parent's differential reactions to sons and daughters. *Journal of Personality and Social Psychology,* 1964, *4,* 237-243.

Sternglanz, S. H., & Serbin, L. A. Sex role stereotyping in children's television programs. *Developmental Psychology,* 1974, *10,* 710-715.

Sutton-Smith, B., Roberts, J. J., & Kozelka, R. Game involvement in adults. In Loys, J. W., & Kenyon, G. S. (eds.), *Sport, culture and society.* New York: Macmillan, 1969.

Tasch, R. J. The role of the father in the family. *Journal of Experimental Education,* 1952, *20,* 319-361.

Task Force of Central New Jersey N.O.W. *Dick and Jane as victims: Sex stereotyping in children's readers.* Princeton, New Jersey: Women on Words and Images, P.O. Box 2163, 1972.

Tulkin, S. R., Muller, J. P., & Conn, L. L. Need for approval and popularity: Sex differences in elementary school students. *Journal of Consulting and Clinical Psychology,* 1969, *33,* 35-39.

Watson, J. S. Operant conditioning of visual fixation in infants under visual and auditory reinforcement. *Developmental Psychology,* 1969, *1,* 408-416.

Men's Responses
to the
Changing Consciousness of Women

Joseph H. Pleck

I will first describe some different theoretical approaches to under-standing men's attitudes toward women in non-traditional or chang-ing roles, and the research that these different theoretical approaches has generated. I will then describe the particular issues that arise in men's responses to women's changing roles in two special contexts: work environments, where men are increasingly having to respond to female co-workers as equals or superiors, and in intimate relation-ships, especially marriage, where men are increasingly having to re-spond to women whose work is becoming as important to them as their own work is to themselves. Finally, going beyond the level of individual male response, I will briefly examine the larger social-political responses that men are making to women's changing con-sciousness, especially the response of men's liberation.

Formal psychological research on men's attitudes toward women has been underway for a long time. There has been a range of studies, for example, relating traditional or restrictive attitudes to-ward women to the psychological trait called authoritarianism, find-ing that men with restrictive attitudes toward women have more rigid, conventional, and negative social attitudes generally (Nadler & Morrow, 1959; Centers, 1963; Pincus, 1971; Brannon & Dull, 1971; Worell & Worell, 1971; Goldberg, 1972). There is also a group of studies relating traditional attitudes toward women to low self-esteem, finding that men who believe that women should stay in their traditional roles see themselves negatively (Miller, 1972; Vav-rik & Jurich, 1971). These two theoretical approaches to traditional

Reprinted from *Women and Men: Roles, Attitudes, and Power Relationships*, E. L. Zuckerman (Ed.). Used with permission of the publisher, The Radcliffe Club of New York, Inc. Copyright 1975.

sex role attitudes, though compatible with each other, suggest somewhat different attitudes toward men with traditional attitudes. The former portrays traditional males rather negatively, as bearers of undesirable and conservative social views generally, while the latter portrays them, perhaps more sympathetically, as rather unhappy people who don't like themselves very much, and whose views toward women are best seen as a symptom of this more general personality issue. Now, neither type of research really "explains" traditional sex role attitudes in men (or in women, either), but these two different approaches illustrate a fundamental value dimension which is extremely important to make explicit in research on traditional male attitudes.

Sometimes in these studies of sex role attitudes, it is found that there are substantial differences between the attitude that men express toward freedom for women in the abstract and the attitude they express toward specific changes or implications of change for women in their more immediate lives. Sometimes it is noted that men's attitudes are contradictory, at the same time espousing freedom for women and no change in their own lives. These discrepancies or contradictions have often been interpreted as showing that men will try to appear "liberal" to others, or even actually believe they are liberal, while actually being quite conservative at a deeper, or real level (Steinmann & Fox, 1966; Komarovsky, 1973). More recently, though, some researchers are suggesting that men hold truly contradictory values and wishes about women, valuing both equality and superiority, both change and the status quo, without the implication that the expressed liberal values are merely superficial while the conservative ones are men's "real" values. In fact, most of us hold contradictory or conflicting values about a wide variety of issues. These two approaches—the "superficial vs. real values" approach and the "conflict in values" approach—have, of course, quite different implications for how one views men who hold any traditional attitudes. If one believes that men have genuine value conflicts about women, then one has some basis for working toward change, which one does not have if one believes that men's underlying values are inevitably traditional. At a broader level, there have been two dominant theoretical approaches to understanding male sex role traditionalism. The first approach derives from psychoanalytic theory, and postulates that the early relationship of the child to the mother leaves a residue of lifelong concern in males to avoid and fear being in relationships with females in which one is subordinate (Horney, 1932; Lederer, 1968). According to various formulations of this theory, this lifelong concern about being dominated by women leads men to want to restrict women and their potential power or competence, to exclude them from competition with men, and so on. Following this theory, it was argued in one study, for example, that younger men in business firms had more negative attitudes toward female co-workers than did older men (and, incidentally, age is typically positively related to prejudice against other groups, not negatively related as in this study) because younger men are still trying to free themselves from actual or potential domination by women (Bowman, Worthy, and Greyser, 1965). Though some observed phenomena are consistent with this theory, there has not been any definitive research in its support. There have not been studies, for example, in which men's sex role traditionalism has been correlated with the extent to which they were dominated by their mothers. In fact, the few available (though not definitive) studies of the association between men's relationships with their parents and their attitudes toward women's roles find either that the closer the relationship with the mother, the more positive are males' sex role attitudes (Rapoport & Rapoport, 1972; Meier, 1972), or that sex role attitudes are not associated with males' relationships to their mothers, but rather with their relationships with their fathers (Worell & Worell, 1971). So, though the psychoanalytic approach to male sex role attitudes seems plausible, we should be cautious about accepting it too uncritically.

The second dominant theoretical approach to male sex role attitudes comes from social-psychological research on intergroup relations and attitudes, particularly on the effect of intergroup contact on change in attitudes toward other groups. This research approach, sometimes going under the name of "contact theory," finds that the terms on which groups interact is a major determinant of whether intergroup contact reduces false stereotyped and negative attitudes. If the less valued group interacts on an equal basis with the more valued group, then attitudes toward the less valued groups improve; but if the less valued group interacts in inferior roles relative to the more valued group, then negative stereotypes and attitudes remain. Consistent with this theory, one study found that business managers who worked with women of equal status had more positive attitudes toward women workers than did managers who worked with women only as subordinates (Bass, Krusell, & Alexander, 1971). This approach to understanding male attitudes toward women, emphasizing the powerful effect of just what terms men and women interact on, clearly has different implications than the psychoanalytic approach which argues that men's liberal or restrictive attitudes toward women depend on the early relationship they had with their mothers.

The point I want to draw from examining these different pairs of theoretical perspectives I have described—authoritarianism vs. self-esteem; the "superficial vs. real values" approach vs. the "conflict in values" approach; and the psychoanalytic approach vs. the inter-group relations perspective from social psychology—is that there are some ways of viewing traditional attitudes of men toward women that describe men negatively or conservatively, or see men's attitudes as inevitable and determined at a very early age, while there are other approaches that view men more sympathetically and allow for change. Seeing traditional men as authoritarian, and pretending to be liberal while really being chauvinistic, and all because of their early relationships with their mothers, has quite different implications than seeing traditional men as not liking themselves, and being in genuine conflict about their values about women, and open to real attitude change depending on the circumstances in which they relate to women. What concerns me is not so much that the one view takes a less favorable view toward men than the other, but that it makes change-seem practically impossible, and makes men seem uniformly negative. How we define the problem determines how we work for the solution. All true revolutionaries must believe in the possibility and the reality of change, most of all in ourselves. We need a view of men that does justice to men's variety, and men's potential for change.

Let us turn now to two specific contexts or environments in which men are increasingly having to respond to changing con-sciousness in women: work environments, and intimate relation-ships.

Up to the present, there has not been a large volume of research on male attitudes toward women in work settings (but see Thorsell, 1967, for a compendium of Scandinavian research). No doubt, the advent of affirmative action will generate much new research in this area. Several themes emerge in the studies that are available. First, there is a special concern about attitudes to working women who are in higher positions relative to men, especially supervisory ones. Male attitudes in this situation are sometimes found to be particularly negative, and have been interpreted in the light of psychoanalytic hypotheses about male needs to get away from domination by women (Bowman, Worthy, & Greyser, 1965). Other studies, however, indicate that the most negative attitudes are held toward women in low positions relative to men, in light of the intergroup relations hypothesis mentioned earlier (Bass, Krusell, & Alexander, 1971). There has also been some speculation that the most threatened re-sponses by males might occur toward women who are in positions equal to those of male respondents, because these women are the ones that individual males experience themselves in competition with (again, Bass, Krusell, & Alexander, 1971). One variation of this speculation is that males find it uncomfortable to be in equal, and therefore competitive, relationships with women in work settings because competition inevitably involves aggressive feelings, and aggression by males toward females is especially severely punished and prohibited in male socialization (Caplow, 1954, p. 221). So, in effect, there is a different theory accounting for why each of the three possible types of status relationships between women and men in work—superior, inferior, and equal—should be the most threatening or generate the most negative attitudes in men! Perhaps we will ultimately need to draw on all three approaches in understanding and promoting desegregation in work settings.

My current research gives some attention to male attitudes to women in work environments, and the self-esteem approach has been particularly useful here. In a preliminary analysis of survey data (Pleck, Staines, & Jayaratne, unpublished), it was found that men who believe that women do not work as hard as men do—a specific negative attitude toward women in work settings—rate themselves as less competent at the work they themselves do—a specific component of male self-esteem, in the work context. It makes sense, in fact, that men who evaluate themselves positively as workers—who are sure of where they stand—are less likely to be threatened by women as equals, or as subordinates or superiors either.

Turning to men's responses to change in women in intimate relationships, especially in the family, we find a substantial backlog of formal research in two areas: first, attitudes on whether wives should work outside the home, and second, attitudes toward intelligence or competence in women whom one is in an intimate relationship with. In the first area, until very recently, studies have universally found that males generally do not approve of their spouses working outside the home (Payne, 1956; Christensen, 1961; Dunn, 1960; Axelson, 1963; Nelson & Goldman, 1969; Entwisle & Greenberger, 1972; Brown, 1972). It is especially striking that one of Ruth Hartley's studies showed that even very young boys of 5 or 6 already had formed negative attitudes about whether their hypothetical future wives should work (Hartley, 1959-60)! More recent studies, however, show a marked change in this attitude. In two samples of college males, one studied by Mirra Komarovsky (1973) and the other a sample of mine (Pleck, 1973), over 50% of the males studied expected that their future wives would have full-time careers. Of course, there were only expectations or intentions at this point in these men's lives, and a lot may happen before these men actually have career spouses, but nonetheless it is striking that so many men now have an attitude that was so rare only a few years ago. Recent writing on dual-career marriage is increasingly focusing attention on the role of husbands in the dual-career situation, emphasizing how these husbands work out patterns of giving support and taking real satisfaction from their wives' careers (Rapoport & Rapoport, 1972, 1973).

A second area of formal research concerns men's responses to generalized intelligence or competence in women they are in intimate relationships with. Some earlier studies indicated that a substantial proportion of men can relate only to women whom they perceive as less intelligent than themselves, and suggested that these men tend to have low self-esteem and to be insecure in their own sex role generally (Beigel, 1957). My own major research (Pleck, 1973) has been in this area, and indicated that using a projective measure, men could be classified according to the extent to which they experience competence in female intimates as threatening. I found that threatened men, in a sample of college men in dating relationships, tended to perform much better than usual, or "super-perform," when competing with their dating partners on an intellectual task, and at the same time, reported that they wanted to leave the competitive situation. Equally important, these threatened men showed relatively little involvement when working with their partners on an intellectual task in a cooperatively structured situation. That is, these men got "psyched up" when working against their dating partners, but found it hard to become involved when working with them. The most important distinguishing characteristic of the threatened group was their low self-esteem, as well as their tendency to relate to women whom they perceived as lacking in self-confidence (though their partners did not see themselves this way), which perhaps made their partners seem less threatening to them.

Taking a broader perspective on the impact of the changing consciousness of women on men in intimate relationships with them, there seem to be at least two critical issues in the new types of relationships which women and men are working out today: the first having to do with sexuality, and the second having to do with the problems of accommodating two careers in one relationship. To consider sexuality first, there has been considerable concern in the media about the potential negative effects of women's equality on male sexuality, or to put it succinctly, that women's liberation will make men impotent (Nobile, 1972). To respond to this media concern, there is actually no clear data indicating that there has been an increase in male impotence or other sexual dysfunctions in recent years. One gets the sense that this is one of those phenomena which, in Voltaire's phrase, if it didn't exist, it would need to be invented. If adequate data were examined, my own expectation would be that change in women is leading some men to experience more sexual difficulties, while at the same time causing other men's sexuality to be enhanced—so that on balance, there is no overall trend in either direction. The issues of men whose sexuality is impaired, for one reason or another, by change in women are important, and need to be considered most sensitively and seriously. But there is an even greater need for due emphasis on the positive effect that women's changing consciousness is having on other men's sexuality. It is important that we present positive models of adaptation to change, instead of the negative ones our media are so full of.

While some men report that these specifically sexual issues are central to their response to change in women (e.g., Julty, 1972), other men report that for them sexual equality is easiest to achieve in bed, and hardest to achieve in much more mundane matters of whose work or career gives way first to the demands of household work or childcare, and whose career takes precedence (e.g., Miller, 1971). That is, males' investment in their careers may set an upper limit on how much childcare or household responsibility they can accept, which in turn set a limit on how much their partners are free to invest in their own careers. It is hard for women to have "two roles"—work and family—unless men opt for two roles as well. Perhaps the clearest direct data on this issue, presented by Lotte Bailyn (1973), confirms this effect. In a sample of couples with highly educated wives, Bailyn showed that the men with the highest career motivation had wives with traditional roles, in spite of their education. Bailyn also found that the wives of men with the lowest career motivation also had careers outside the home relatively infrequently. It would make sense that men who rejected careerism for themselves would have difficulty accepting it in their spouses. Bailyn concludes, then, that emotionally supporting one's wife in a career and making the necessary accommodating changes in one's own life is associated with moderate career motivation, as well as other traits suggesting some rejection of traditional male goals and interests. It is becoming increasingly clear that men's attitudes toward careers for women in their lives relates in many complex ways to their experience of themselves in their own careers.

The relationship between men's responses to changing roles for women in work environments and in marriage can be understood in different ways. Rhona and Robert Rapoport (1972) argue, for example, that change for women in work is stimulating change for women in the family. In their view there is, however, a "psychosocial lag" between the extent to which men accept new roles for women in work and the extent to which they accept new roles for women in the family. That is, while women are increasingly accepted by men in the work world, their husbands generally continue to make traditional demands on them, and do not adjust their own participation in the family to accommodate the changes made necessary by their wives' employment. The Rapoports believe that this psychosocial lag represents a transitional problem of adjustment which will diminish over time as the family catches up with what they see as the primary change taking place for women in work. It may be that we are also seeing the causality beginning to work in the other direction as well. Increasingly, young couples are adopting primary values about sex role equality in marriage which then sets limits on the types of careers that they consider possible. That is, many couples are realizing that if you want sex role equality in your marriage, then you may want to reconsider certain highly demanding careers which make it much more difficult. (Here, too, we should not overestimate the difficulties of dual-career marriages involving highly demanding careers, viewing them as beyond the capacities of devoted and serious individuals to adapt to. Rather than be discouraged by its problems, those of us in this situation must learn how to give and receive support from each other.)

To summarize, there have been several different approaches to understanding traditional male attitudes about women, some of which are harsh and make change seem next to impossible, and others which are more sympathetic to men and view change as a real possibility. We can separately analyze the psychological issues in men's accommodation to the changing status of women in the world of work and in the world of intimate environment of the family, and describe how changes in the two areas are related. After this review of research on male responses to change in women, focusing at the individual level, I will close by looking at the larger social-political response men are showing to the women's movement and the social forces it represents and expresses.

There has certainly been no absence of negative social-political responses, as in the recent writings of Norman Mailer, Stephen Goldberg, and George Guilder—on the part of men whom Barbara Seaman calls the "male sexual gatekeepers" of our society. But there has been another response as well, one which I believe will be ultimately much more significant, the response of men's liberation (see Pleck & Sawyer, 1974; Farrell, 1974; Fasteau, forthcoming). In this symposium of "Masculinity and the Changing Woman," it would indeed be a strange omission not to discuss men's liberation.

At present, men's liberation is not so much a "movement" as it is an idea and a vision of how men can be. Many men have been stimulated by the feminist movement to examine how their own sex role has limited them, how male sex role demands to "get ahead" and to "stay cool" have limited us in relationships with women, relationships with other men, our involvements with children, and our experience of work. This self-examining response of men's liberation directly helps men, but has a long-term roundabout effect on women as well. Of the many varied themes in the literature I reviewed earlier, the one that seems to come up in the most different contexts and which seems most far-reaching in its implications is the notion that male self-esteem determines male responses to equality in women. But to fully understand the significance of self-esteem in men's responses to women, and to connect both to men's own liberation, we need to understand that the primary component of self-esteem in men is men's sense of how well they are doing *relative to other men*. As men begin, as part of men's liberation, to examine the stress on competition and relative evaluation with other men inherent in the male sex role, men's sense of themselves will begin to change in ways that will benefit women as a side effect of their liberating effect on men. Ultimately, men cannot go any further in responding to equality in women than they have been able to go in dealing with the uneasy equality they have had with other men for so long. Men's equality with other men, which has proved so really troubling for so many men, has left a backlog of unresolved issues which, in fact, traditional relationships with women have often served primarily as a refuge from. It is precisely these unresolved issues which men's liberation is at last beginning to take up.

REFERENCES

Axelson, L. J. The marital adjustment and marital role definitions of husbands of working and non-working wives. *Marriage and Family Living*, 1963, *25*, 189-195.

Bailyn, L. Family constraints on women's work. *Annals of the New York Academy of Sciences*, 1973, *208*, 82-90.

Bass, B. M., Krusell, J., & Alexander, R. Male managers' attitudes toward working women. *American Behavioral Scientist*, 1971, *15*, 221-236.

Beigel, H. The evaluation of intelligence in the heterosexual relationship. *Journal of Social Psychology*, 1957, *46*, 65-80.

Bowman, G. W., Worthy, N. B., & Greyser, S. A. Are women executives people? *Harvard Business Review*, 1965, *43*(4), 14ff.

Brannon, R., & Dull, C. Racism, sexism, and fascism of white males: empirical interrelationships. Paper presented at the meeting of the American Psychological Association, Washington, D.C., August, 1971.

Brown, S. E. *Husband's attitude and consequences of wife-mother employment*. Ann Arbor, Mich.: University Microfilms, 1970, No. 71-6973.

Caplow, T. *The sociology of work*. Minneapolis: University of Minnesota, 1954.

Centers, R. Authoritarianism and misogyny. *Journal of Social Psychology*, 1963, *61*, 81-85.

Christensen, H. T. Life, family, and occupational role projections of high school students. *Marriage and Family Living*, 1961, *23*, 181-183.

Conyer, J. E. Exploratory study of employers' attitudes toward working mothers. *Sociology and Social Research*, 1961, *45*, 145-156.

Dunn, M. Marriage role expectations of adolescents. *Marriage and Family Living*, 1960, *22*, 99-105.

Entwisle, D. R., & Greenberger, E. Adolescents' views of women's work role. *American Journal of Orthopsychiatry*, 1972, *42*, 648-656.

Farrell, W. *Beyond masculinity*. New York: Macmillan, 1974.

Fasteau, M. *The male machine*. New York: McGraw-Hill, forthcoming.

Goldberg, P. Prejudice toward women: some personality correlates. Paper presented at the meeting of American Psychological Association, Honolulu, August, 1972.

Horney, K. The dread of women. *International Journal of Psychoanalysis*, 1932, *13*, 348-360.

Julty, S. A case of "sexual dysfunction." *Ms.*, November, 1972, 18ff.

Komarovsky, M. Cultural contradictions and sex roles: the masculine case. *American Journal of Sociology*, 1973, *78*, 873-884.

Lederer, W. *The fear of women*. New York: Grune & Stratton, 1968.

Meier, H. C. Mother-centeredness and college youths' attitude toward social equality for women: some empirical findings. *Journal of Marriage and the Family*, 1972, *34*, 115-121.

Miller, S. M. The making of a confused, middle-aged husband. *Social Policy*, 1971, *2*(2), 33-39.

Miller, T. W. Male attitudes toward women's rights as a function of their self-esteem. Paper presented at the meeting of the American Psychological Association, Honolulu, August, 1972.

Nadler, E. B., & Morrow, W. R. Authoritarian attitudes toward women and their correlates. *Journal of Social Psychology*, 1959, *40*, 113-123.

Nobile, P. What is the new impotence, and who's got it? *Esquire*, October, 1972, 95ff.

Patrick, C. Attitudes about women executives in government positions. *Journal of Social Psychology*, 1944, *19*, 3-34.

Payne, R. Adolescents' attitude toward the working wife. *Marriage and Family Living*, 1956, *18*, 345-348.

Pleck, J. *Male threat from female competence: an experimental study in college dating couples.* Ann Arbor, Mich.: University Microfilms, 1973, No. 74-11, 721.

Pleck, J., Staines, G., & Jayaratne, T. Survey data on male attitudes toward women and women's liberation. Institute for Social Research, unpublished.

Pleck, J., & Sawyer, J., eds. *Men and masculinity.* Englewood Cliffs, N.J.: Prentice-Hall Spectrum Books, 1974.

Pincus, F. L. Relationships between racism, sexism, powerlessness, and antihomosexuality. Paper presented at the meeting of the American Psychological Association, Washington, D.C., August, 1971.

Rapaport, R., & Rapaport, R. *The dual career family.* London: Penguin Books, 1971.

Rapaport, R., & Rapaport, R. Working women and the enabling role of the husband. Paper presented at the Twelfth Family Research Seminar, International Sociological Association, Moscow, 1972. To be published in the *Proceedings of the International Sociological Association.*

Rapaport, R., & Rapaport, R. Family enabling functions: the facilitative husband in the dual career family. In R. Gosling, ed., *Support, innovation, and autonomy.* London: Tavistock, 1973.

Smith, J. H. Managers and married women workers. *British Journal of Sociology*, 1961, *12*, 12-21.

Spence, J. T., & Helmreich, R. The attitude toward women scale: an objective instrument to measure attitudes toward the rights and roles of women in contemporary society. *JSAS Catalog of Selected Documents in Psychology*, 1972, *2*, 66. (a)

Spence, J. T., & Helmreich, R. Who likes competent women? Competence, sex-role congruence of interests, and subjects' attitudes toward women as determinants of interpersonal attraction. *Journal of Applied Social Psychology*, 1972, *2*, 197-213. (b)

Steinmann, A., & Fox, D. J. Male-female perceptions of the female role in the United States. *Journal of Psychology*, 1966, *64*, 265-276.

Thorsell, S. Employer attitudes toward female employees. In E. Dahlstrom, ed., *The changing roles of men and women.* London: Duckworth, 1967.

Vavrik, J., & Jurich, A. P. Self-concept and attitude toward females: a note. *Family Coordinator*, 1971, *20*, 151-152.

Worell, J., & Worell, L. Supporters and opponents of women's liberation: some personality characteristics. Paper presented at the meeting of the American Psychological Association, Washington, D.C., August, 1971.

The Great American Male Stereotype

Patrick Canavan

John Haskell

The Great American Male Stereotype exists in every aspect of American life—politics, religion, the arts, education, business, health, government, etc. It defines for many men the type of life to lead, the things to do, the places to go, and the people to be with. A white, middle-class stereotype, due to the influence of the media (particularly television), our educational system, and other people in our lives, it has had impact on all Americans, regardless of economic status, ethnic origin, or job function.

STATING THE CASE

In American society, men must deal with the conflict that is generated between the realities of their lives and the stereotype of the Great American Male—the male who is:

1. Successful in business—has a high corporate position with a great deal of responsibility, power, etc.
2. Financially productive—owns a house, has a car for himself and wife, has good clothes.
3. Sexually attractive—physically in good condition and attractive so that women other than his wife find him physically desirable.
4. Physically productive—can build things, repair cars, etc., as well as be capable of producing physically attractive offspring.
5. Knowledgeable—about the business world, the state of the economy, the political situation, and his own personal and professional goals and directions.

Few American males can say that they fit the Great American Male Stereotype (GAMS). Some say they have no interest in achieving such a goal and that to try to do so is a waste of time and energy and a denial of the constraints of reality. However, so much time, concern, and energy (consciously or unconsciously) goes into achieving GAMS that the different aspects of it and the resulting messages delivered to American males of all ages need to be analyzed and discussed.

American men need to consciously decide which elements of the GAMS they desire and why; American children need to be exposed to both the *costs* and *benefits* of pursuing GAMS. To date the cost has not been thoroughly exposed and discussed in the same way the benefits have.

The cost of pursuing GAMS can be physical disability or early death, heart disease, fatigue, heart failure, overweight, ulcers, high blood pressure, frustration, anger, hostility, alcoholism, drug dependency, cigarette smoking, few intimate relationships, failure, and few collaborative relationships.

The benefits of achieving GAMS are clearly pointed out by the advertising media: popularity, happiness, satisfaction, access to quality goods, attractive surroundings (including people), feeling of security, power, and sexual pleasure.

Behind the stereotype are achievement; competition; power; success; and conflict—each with its own relevance and role to males.

Achievement. The need for achievement is high in American males because achievement means status and acceptability. Achievement is defined by society as successful performance in the work world. Status is awarded to men who are professionally and/or financially successful. Academic achievement is considered important because it is perceived as the major path to professional and financial success.

Competition. Beating someone else is considered to be the way to obtain success. Beginning in early childhood play with neighborhood children through the work years into retirement, score cards are kept—first by the parents and, once learned, by the men themselves. The question is always "How am I doing compared with others?" The score card gets carried into school (grades), sports (best athlete), sex (how many, how often, performance), work (advancement, salary, title), home (house, cars, family), and retirement (travel, time demands). As a consequence of this competition, a sharp sense of analysis is developed. Others' strength, vulnerability, and potential is quickly assessed. The defensive nature of this process makes it extremely difficult to develop collaboration and intimate relationships.

Power and Success. The stereotype overemphasizes power and success. If a man has influence over others and decision-making powers within an organization, then he is considered to be successful. The emphasis on power and success means that a male is usually striving toward a goal somewhere in the future. Consequently, his energies are put into achieving that goal and rarely if ever into the reality of the present. The unhappiness of not being something or not achieving anything takes precedence over the reality of now. Today seems unimportant, the experience of today is denied, and the relationships and tasks of today are forgotten.

Conflict. Because of the competitive element to the male stereotype, the combative technique of problem solving is much easier for men to use than the collaborative technique. The male world is filled with conflict, but males generally do not distinguish between productive and dysfunctional conflict but use conflict as a vehicle for advancing themselves by eliminating or badly damaging the competition. The dependence on conflict as a prime method of problem solving often limits the long-term growth and development of the individual male.

The elements of GAMS—conflict, success and power, competition, and achievement—result in male behavior that values work as the number one priority in life. Only through work can the male achieve GAMS, and consequently the other elements of life (family relationship, friends, recreation, growth, and development) take second or, more frequently, lower priority.

To the male, *task orientation* is essential if he is to be successful at work, where tasks need to be defined, delegated, pursued, and accomplished in an orderly, rational manner. Additionally, task orientation is so strong that many males must deal with immediate, concrete problems and have difficulty or no ability when dealing with the intangible, more amorphous processes of such items as long-range planning, either for an organization or for their own personal and professional development.

Task orientation also requires a perceived ability to make fast, concrete, perfect, and irrevocable decisions. Any male who can do this is perceived as being extremely capable, talented, and having the potential for achieving GAMS. Because of the competitive position accepted by men, the need to be defensive of one's position and abilities is paramount, and therefore the brittleness of these processes and the individual is well hidden and rarely, if ever, is perceived by others. The "capable male" never shows how afraid or fragile he is while operating in this mode.

Task orientation of males means that men are not very conscious of or skilled at the maintenance functions of life. From childhood into the work world, men have had the maintenance functions delegated to women (mother, lover, wife, secretary). Because women have performed the maintenance functions, men have been allowed (or forced) to concentrate primarily on the task at hand. Mother helped to develop dialogue between two quarreling children or between a child and the father. The lover/wife takes on the cooking, recreation planning, or household chores, and the secretary makes coffee, sharpens pencils, or soothes feelings to make her boss's job easier.

Men are comfortable in dealing with women on a sexual level or in a maintenance role. Today's resistance to women (much of it covert) in middle and top level management positions is due to women no longer being in an easily identifiable role (sexual object or maintenance) and demanding to compete on an equal level. This demand is not easily accepted by the male in pursuit of GAMS because it moves a woman from being primarily maintenance oriented into the predominately male category of task orientation and asks that a woman be treated like a male.

The denial of past roles by women challenges men to assess their own behavior and their attitudes toward their own roles at work and at home. However, the optimal resolution of this problem is not to have women adopt male attitudes and behavior. Much is wrong with the male stereotype and little has been done to effectively explore other alternatives or to encourage experimentation. The choices seem to be as follows:

1. To adopt GAMS and become task oriented;
2. To adopt the traditional female role and become maintenance oriented;
3. To take the desirable characteristics of each role and let each person select that which suits him/her best (the androgynous option).

The latter refers to a changing definition of what is appropriate behavior for men and women at home, at work, or in their social lives. To become androgynous is to have a wide behavioral spectrum—behaviors that have been traditionally labeled as "male" as well as behaviors that have been traditionally labeled as "female."

For most men, becoming androgynous means acquiring maintenance behavior in addition to the more familiar task-oriented behavior. Thus, a man who is androgynous is able to support other men and women when support is needed, collaborate or take a secondary role when the situation warrants it, listen to and counsel subordinates and peers about personal problems—i.e., to let emotions show, to do things that support, help, and develop themselves and others. For most women, becoming androgynous means developing the task-oriented, problem-solving, and rational thinking aspects of their behavior.

Of course, these examples are based on stereotypes. To become androgynous, each of us must assess the characteristics, skills, and behaviors that he/she currently uses and ascertain where development is necessary. Androgyny as a goal requires that each of us has available those characteristics, skills, and behaviors that have been traditionally seen as male as well as those characteristics, skills, and behaviors that have been traditionally seen as female. For some men and women, this means concentrating on the development of the task-oriented side; for other men and women this means concentrating on the development of the maintenance-oriented skills.

Historically, behavioral choices have been narrowed by our sex. It is now time to increase the choices and educate everyone in the processes of choice and selection, not in the behavior and attitudes of a specific sex role. The Women's Movement has begun this process and many men have quietly made their own decisions and choices. New individual decisions still need to be made.

FINDING A WAY OUT

Alternative Behaviors

A simple model of being human is that each individual has five *centers*, each of which provides the person's major focus in a certain way at any given time. Each has a *place* which, if recognized and utilized as a source of important data, allows an individual to "check in" and read himself or herself.

Intellect. The mind and its consequent focus on rational thought, problem solving, and task analysis—deliberate, logical, and controlled. The intellectual center operates through the *mind* and communicates through a person's thoughts. The other centers can and do interface with the flow of this "computer" (e.g., strong feelings), but the intent of the mind is to process information, subjective as well as objective, without distortion.

Emotions. Feelings and the emphasis on comfort or discomfort with ourselves, others, and our situations—spontaneous, irrational, autonomous, and uncontrollable. A person's emotional center operates through the central nervous system, the "gut," and the heart. The direct emotional flow of person with environment is influenced by past learnings and norms (typified by children who respond directly and overtly to fear, concern, excitement, and joy).

Physical. Body energies and the focus on pleasurable and painful sensations. Our physical center "speaks" to us through the flow of blood, breathing, and the muscular system and skeleton. Illness and good health are the sensed opposites in this center.

Sexual. Our genital responses and the awareness of tension and release—powerful, private, and highly socialized. Our sexual center "speaks" to us through our genitals and erogenous areas. Sexual fantasy, a product of the intellectual center, is an example of how this center can be influenced.

Spiritual. Growing and transcending, with its emphasis on aliveness and stasis, ephemeral, transpersonal, and holy. The spiritual center is experienced through an awareness that we are no longer simply "I" and separate, bounded by time and the immediate. The spiritual center, when primary in our lives, takes us beyond ourselves, closer to more ultimate concerns, calls purposes into question, and exposes us to the cosmic.

Life is a flowing through situations wherein these centers "share the spotlight." At times we choose where to be centered (e.g., when we choose to learn computer programming [intellectual center] and apply ourselves until we have the thought processes necessary for developing this skill). At other times our center of operation is determined by an event in our environment (e.g., a loved one questions his or her commitment to a primary relationship, and strong feelings of vulnerability and rejection become the focus of our lives [emotional center]). The ebb and flow of these centers within each of us is occurring in a social milieu where others are also ebbing, flowing, changing, and operating with varying degrees of awareness of which center is "onstage." The more attuned a person is to the tones, shifts, and cues of the varying centers, the more conscious that person can be of "life." Conversely, the more out of touch, blocked, or denied the person is in relation to his or her own centers, the less able to transact effectively with the environment the person will be in having needs met and in growing as a person.

Interpersonal transactions occur through these centers. Growthful, life-enhancing relationships result from *resonance,* the accurate "picking up on" where the other is centered. This requires a developed sensitivity (innate and/or learned) to the self and a willingness to allow the other to pass into the self. This difficult skill is the basis of interpersonal relationships.

Centers and Androgyny

If movement toward androgyny is valued intellectually, speaks to emotional comfort, holds out pleasure to the senses, is sexually releasing, and/or enlivens the humanness of the person, *then* facilitating changes in all of the centers is called for. The following is a discussion of actions for all centers which, in concert, can help a *male* experience various aspects of androgyny and the potential it has for developing him as a human being.

Intellect. The concept of androgyny has some immediate appeal—a broader range of behaviors, liberation from unrewarding patterns, a hope for healthier relationships. There are, however, years of entrenched patterns and programs that speak to being male—those GAMS outlooks and behaviors that account to a great extent for how we see ourselves today. Letting go of the GAMS personality, values, thoughts, plans, and predicted rewards is no easy matter. The mind tapes cannot be "erased." They can, however, be altered by application and practice. Information can be introduced that counterbalances existing thought structures, accentuates the GAMS-androgyny dilemmas, and adds a vocabulary to our "inner conversation" that can result in new learnings.

Some suggestions for working with the intellectual center are as follows:

- Join a men's group.
- Read articles and books on men's liberation, androgyny, women's liberation.
- Read reactionary male literature, anti-liberation literature, radical, and anti-male feminist literature (to get to know the extremes).
- Do a cost-benefit analysis for yourself of GAMS and androgyny.
- Change one relationship consciously toward a more androgynous definition and study the consequences.
- Write a one-page statement on androgyny and you.
- Fantasize your answer to the question "If I were more androgynous in a world that supported this, I would find myself . . ."
- Fantasize your answer to "By becoming more androgynous I would give up . . . and I would gain . . ."

Emotions. As males, we live under the shadow of a stereotype that labels us as cold, distant, critical, and *emotionally unexpressive.*

Note: the stereotype does not label us as unemotional, but as inhibited in expression of feeling. Also, the stereotype pins on us the inability or reluctance to take in, allow, accept, and encourage the expression of feelings by others.

In men who accept GAMS, emotionality is "managed" through the mind. Childhood experiences, peer group pressure, and the norms of the working world have conspired to limit the male to a range of acceptable feelings running from "I'm fine" to "I'm feeling lousy." The rich vocabulary of emotions, the experiential depth of feelings, and the much feared sense of being "out of control" (i.e., out of one's mind and genuinely into the emotional center) are suppressed, avoided, denied, and, when too powerful to be kept down, allowed to explode onto the surface in unmanageable, violent, and destructive ways or to implode with those same consequences incurred by the person himself.

Some suggestions for working on the emotional center to bring it beyond the atrophied GAMS state are as follows:

- T-groups and encounter groups set up with this goal in mind.
- Reading.
- Taking risks with allowing glimmers of feelings. (Typical cues are sweaty palms, preoccupation, lump in the throat.)
- *Not* changing any current behavior, but allowing the feelings about it (e.g., work, primary relationship, etc.) to occur and giving these feelings time and space to be, to work themselves out, and to evolve as they do when accepted.

Physical. Health, pleasure, tone, agility, and grace are the values of most cultures, primitive or civilized. Neglecting the body or over-purchasing services to avoid doing physical activity is debilitating, speeds the aging process, lessens the availability of energy, and destroys the "mood" and projection of the self.

Sadly, too many males abandon their bodies through devotion to the job. Sitting, driving, drinking, and overeating, as well as lack of exercise, nervousness, tension, cigarettes, and other contributors to ill health are too often combated with drugs rather than intelligent cultivating of the body. If no effort is made to stop the entropic processes, the body is prone to illness.

Some ways to counter cellular death and to create a healthy physical center are as follows:

- Meditation.
- Fast days.
- Isometrics.

- Acceptance of the body (using a mirror and some caring).
- Adequate sleep.
- Massage.
- Stretching, exercising, jogging.
- Dancing.
- Sensory awareness exercises.

Sexual. The sexual center is problematic to manage because it involves the ego and has its own cycles and rhythms. Sex is as basic as breathing and other biological needs. As a symbol and an act of intimacy, openness, and connectivity, it can be a fragmented portion of the self, a life and measure of its own that acts as a barometer of our attractiveness and "loveworthiness."

When inappropriately managed, the sexual center invades the process of living through doubt, guilt, compulsion, and, most sadly, as a filter through which personal relationships are seen. Male-female relationships in our culture are "polluted" by the silent, covert, desperate underworld of disowned but strongly felt sexual intentions. Going beyond this is a necessary step in dechauvinizing the culture.

Some activities that contribute to better management of the sexual center are as follows:

- Reading (especially Reich, Horney, and May).
- Honest dialogue with primary partners.
- Human sexuality programs.
- Systematic self-analysis of intentions in relationships.
- Observation of responses to new people—awareness.
- Owning needs for intimacy and closeness and distinguishing them from the need for sex.
- Experimentation with sexual rhythms.
- Awareness of fantasies and critique of content and frequency.

Spiritual. The spirit is experienced via *transcendence* in the secular sense of the word. The awareness of larger order purposes, the "high" experiences of nature—childbirth, discovery, orgasm, accomplishment—are the indicators of our higher order human nature, the tastes and glimpses of our own evolution. We are rarely involved in our own transcendence and growth; too frequently we are rooted in the humdrum and routine. We feel that our spiritual center, the level of our purpose and meaning manifested in experience, is outside of ourselves, a product of "twists of fate." But within each of us is a *readiness* for new experience that we can impact, and it is toward this that we can focus our energies.

Some methods of developing the spiritual center are as follows:

- Prayer.
- Focus and clarity during religious services.
- Regular meditation.
- Chanting.
- Rhythmic dancing.
- Reading.
- Study with a spiritual leader.
- Great endeavor in search of the miraculous.
- Fasting extensively.
- Being "high."

With some effort, each of the named centers can receive our attention, energy, and care so that we can grow beyond the male stereotype and into our whole selves—into our androgynous conditions.

GAMS AND THE WORLD OF WORK

Labor Versus Work

A premise of ours is that if one's centers are not in tone, available, and engaged while one is focusing on a task, then one is *laboring*. Only when one is fully present while engaged in a task can one say that one is *working*.

Most people with whom we have come in contact are in the "world of labor," operating below potential, half there, and creating problems by being problems to themselves. The personal growth aspect of management and organization development is to us the legitimization of the whole person.

The Career

For most of us, a profession, a job, or the job we are preparing for represents a significant portion of our time allocation. With an average of fifty-six of 168 hours in the week spent in sleep, there are only 112 hours left to allocate. The time spent commuting, being on the job, and thinking, feeling, or dealing with it at other times easily takes fifty hours per week, so our careers take up to 45 percent of our waking time. This time investment reaps a return unique to each of us. How do GAMS attitudes and behaviors influence the quality of that return on investment?

Work, Self, Family

Again, most of us put our energy and attention into four major spheres of life: a job; our own upkeep (talking to ourselves, tending to our hygiene, planning); our families; and activities, commitments, clubs, worship, civic service, friendships, and social functions—the collection of roles that makes up a person's life space. The spheres are interconnected and in or out of balance with one another depending on our skills in managing ourselves and prevailing conditions in our contingent environment. Schematically, we can be seen as:

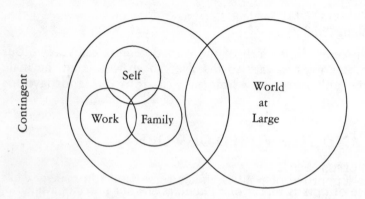

Because 45 percent of our time is spent in the work sphere, it behooves us to look at the quality of work life to see how it contributes to intellectual, emotional, physical, sexual, and spiritual well-being.

Organizational Excellence

Organizational excellence refers to (1) the clarity of *purpose* on the part of the organization and its members and the attainment of goals set by the organization in all its spheres of operation; (2) the congruency of the *process* for goal attainment, problem solving, and resource development with the needs of the people in the organization and the unique demands of the organization's tasks; and (3) the quality of life generated through the interaction of the members with their tasks, or *performance*.

When GAMS is highly revered in an organization, certain outcomes can be predicted:

- Male managers will define their success in terms of individual accomplishment.

- Conflict will be avoided and/or treated in win-lose fashion.
- Task centeredness will reign.
- Committees, groups, and task forces will tend to be ineffective and criticized.
- Information management will be secretive. Information will be treated as a currency, with rumors flying like brushfire through the building when the slightest deviance in behavior or standard operating procedure occurs.

As the delivery of services and manufacture of goods grows more complex, rapid, turbulent, uncertain, and problematic, management becomes a more challenging task. The environment calls for organizational responses that are timely, thoughtful, active, and graceful, utilize varying resources, effectively use group time, and are creative, self-critical, and well monitored.

Now, if we take a step back and try to match GAMS and androgynous behavior with simple and complex organizational situations, an interesting set of relationships should emerge. GAMS is individualistic, competitive, political, defensive, noncollaborative, and pursuant of individual power and control. These behaviors fit well when an organization addresses itself to fixed resource situations, is supportive of politics and intrigue (and top management engages in same), and the environment is viewed as something to master and control. Under these conditions, GAMS behavior can lead to organizational success.

When the organization addresses itself to expandable resources, is supportive of authenticity and collaboration, views its developmental and growth prospects as complex opportunities for multi-talented problem solving, and sees the environment as a mix of hostile and benign forces to be understood and adapted to, then androgynous behaviors contribute to organizational excellence. The question for each manager is: What kind of organization is this? If the answer is "a complex and evolving" organization, then strictly GAMS behavior will obstruct organizational excellence. In fact, just a few key managers playing out their careers in GAMS fashion can limit a complex organization's effectiveness by:

- Making all conflict win-lose so collaborative behavior is loser behavior.
- Making information scarce and costly.
- Using information as a tool for attack.
- Undermining joint effort with attitudes and behaviors that discount the contributions of others.

- Climbing to the top via pursuit of goals that further the individual at the expense of overall organizational effectiveness.
- Creating a climate of closed, mistrusting, defensive norms.
- Eroding organizational health by treating people as mechanical parts of an impersonal system.

In conclusion, let us simply state that complex problem-solving and growth situations demand a complex repertoire of organizational behavior—the androgynous option. Certain situations demand simple, rigid behavior—GAMS.

Issues and Problems

An organization provides the resources and opportunities to do more than any individual can do alone, but an organization constrains its members from being as they might otherwise be via norms, communication networks, hierarchies, and emphasis on command and control. Both personal and interpersonal issues result.

Personal

1. *Being real*—allowing feelings, thoughts, and behaviors to be expressed in an uncensored and spontaneous way. The nature of most organizations and the behavior of people in organizations require communications of feelings and/or thoughts to be evaluated politically before they are expressed. Consequently, what is communicated is very often not what someone is feeling or thinking. The result is that the real thoughts and feelings never are clearly stated and/or emerge in subtle or not so subtle ways.

2. *Owning "self"*—accepting strengths/weaknesses and the implications for one's career. Demands on performance and upward mobility are linked to system rewards. If these demands fit with one's interests and skills, then there will be comfort, and the only issue is developing an appropriate work pace. Most often, the fit is imperfect and stress results from wanting to gain a particular level in the organization and/or acquire a specific set of skills and not having the correct skills, personality, or time to do so. A male characteristic is to perceive this stress as a sign of failure and/or inadequacy. Consequently, the signal is denied, ignored, or avoided at all costs and a "work harder and longer" philosophy is adopted. An objective assessment of the causes of the signal and a cost-benefit analysis of the various reactions to the signal rarely take place.

3. *GAMS lifestyle.* The GAMS lifestyle is most appropriate when it has been *chosen.* Most men do not explore the cost or benefits of GAMS until a crisis occurs in their lives. A colleague's heart attack, a divorce, the loss of a job, or children on drugs and/or alcohol or in trouble with the police are often causes for evaluation and assessment of one's life style. Additionally, a discussion of life styles and professional and personal goals does not occur with the women and/or children in one's life. Consequently, many of the decisions to pursue GAMS are unilateral, although the costs and the benefits are shared by all.

Interpersonal (Male to Male)

1. *Insufficient support.* When a male is (a) successful, he competes with other males; (b) a failure, he is avoided by other males; (c) in trouble, he is talked about by others; (d) planning or performing, communication stays task centered; (e) in a crisis, support *can* be given. Consequently, support from other men is, at best, spotty and difficult to count on. This results in a distance between men, isolates each man and his problem, and makes it difficult for men to collaborate with men easily. Collaboration usually results from a long-term relationship in which parties have had sufficient experience to develop mutual trust.

2. *Intimacy.* The possibility of intimate male-male relationships at work is short-circuited by conscious and subconscious unverbalized sexual fears and discomfort with closeness, although male co-workers can share intimately if "high" together (as in late-night drinking sessions on business trips). It is not uncommon, however, for men to feel vulnerable after sharing major issues, concerns, or problems with another man. The statement "I wish I hadn't said that" or concern about the impact of an intimate discussion on a career often follows such a conversation.

3. *Destructive and wasteful connecting.* Male-male conversations stabilize at the "storytelling" stage (news, politics, the score of last night's hockey, basketball, or football game, there-and-then vignettes). The practice of beginning a meeting with this type of conversation when burning issues need to be resolved results in frustration and wasted time for most participants. Men also relate to men at the expense of women. The sharing of sexist jokes and sexist comments come about as men try to relate to men. Those who utilize this style of relating are blind to the costs to women. Women are depersonalized, made into sex objects, and used as objects of ridicule.

Interpersonal (Male to Female)

1. *Unspoken, covert intentions.* The primary model for male-female relationships is social-sexual. Because this is ruled out in the work place, these intentions are acted out in hidden, secretive, "unstraight" ways. Humans are attracted to other humans, and the attraction occurs in the work environment as often as it occurs elsewhere. The assumption that a man and woman who travel together professionally or have lunch together or a drink together are having an affair is dysfunctional to the organization, as well as to the people involved. Considerable time is wasted in organizations because employees are not exposed to men and women working together as peers and colleagues. Consequently, when cross-sexual interaction does occur it is a cause for rumors, subtle questions, innuendo, and gossip.

2. *Low value.* The male style of providing input in the work environment is task and goal oriented. Men talk in a knowledgeable, convincing way and compete to see who can create the best solution to a problem. Women who do not act like men are ignored or discounted. In mixed-sex meetings, men are often given credit for ideas proposed by women; women are ignored until coffee is needed or minutes have to be taken; and women have to be aggressive in order to get a word in.

The acceptable style for success in an organization is usually defined in narrow male terms. Thus, if a woman is to be successful she must be manlike (tell jokes, work long hours, be goal oriented, be competitive, etc.). If she is, men perceive her as being unfeminine, not very interesting, and a threat—a castrating woman out to break as many men as possible. Such behavior is usually attributed to a woman being frigid, not interested in men and children, and/or being incapable of landing a man.

The woman who is feminine in the work environment is perceived by men as soft-headed, not capable of making tough decisions, not interested in and/or capable of a career, and not worth investing in (developing skills, grooming for a higher position, etc.). Most men do perceive this kind of woman, however, as easy to talk with about both personal and professional issues.

Women are perceived by many men as low-value peers and colleagues. If they become male-like, then they are something to stay away from; and if they are feminine, they are not really serious about working. This perception limits the relationships of men and women and seriously underutilizes a valuable organizational resource.

3. *Sexism.* Men create sexual fantasies about their women co-workers, which puts up a barrier to the development of colleague-ship. As women become more liberated in any organization, the difficulty of sexist relationships *increases*, because men have even more difficulty taking risks in dealing with their thoughts, words, and actions. The fear of being punished by women for sexual fantasies increases as women become more assertive in dealing with men in the work environment.

CONCLUSION

It would be very satisfying to write a short list of prescriptions and proscriptions to help each of us reduce his sexism, be more fulfilled as a person, and contribute more effectively to the success of the organizations to which he belongs. But the daily sex-role stereotyping dilemmas that confront us are so varied and so numerous that this is not possible and will not be possible for years to come. Within reach are increased awareness, actions to change the stimuli in our immediate environments, and realistic steps toward lessening behaviors that our informed awareness tells us are self-defeating and unrewarding to ourselves and to others.

We have attempted to paint a picture of American maleness as we have experienced it in ourselves, learned about it through the research and writings of others, and heard about it through the disclosures of clients, colleagues, and friends. We have explored the costs and benefits of the current stereotypic value system and criticized the nonchoice aspect of GAMS—the condition of living without the awareness that some different values and behaviors, which we call "androgynous," might also be legitimate and appropriate.

A model of the person was presented using a construct of five centers. Using this view of *what* and *how* and *why* a person is, we made connections between a GAMS person and an organization and an androgynous person and an organization. Our purpose was to show that the present-day concern with sexism and sex-role stereotyping is not a faddish "social issue," but an important aspect of the presence or absence of quality and effectiveness in organizational performance. We showed that GAMS behaviors are appropriate to certain organizational situations and androgynous behaviors to others. The critical difference is *awareness* of the existing situation so that *choices* concerning process and behaviors can be made.

Finally, we mentioned some issues that our consulting has shown us are experienced by males in their organizations and which create difficulties for men as they try to deal with their sexism.

In closing, we feel confident in pointing up the following actions we have taken in our own lives to begin our movement from GAMS toward androgyny:

- Lessen total task-oriented view of life.
- Increase supporting others.
- Increase self-disclosure.
- Increase openness to own and others' emotions.
- Ask for help.
- Develop the five centers.

These actions, although different in detail for each of us and needing a lot of energy, time, and effort, have yielded very rewarding results. Our relationships with our colleagues are more fun and productive; our capacities to have varied and satisfying relationships with our friends have expanded; our love and respect for our loved ones have intensified; and our professional activities have been more effective and satisfying. As a result, the *quality* of our lives has improved.

Reflections of a Male Housewife:
On Being a Feminist Fellow-Traveler

Kingsley Widmer

For quite a time I've been an enthusiastic advocate of Women's Liberation. Yes, I know, there's something a bit suspicious about aging and burly husbands who "me, too" the pronouncements of what sometimes are undoubtedly castration-minded females. That's almost as inappropriate as fat-assed matrons burbling over their husband's skills at sports or dead-faced businessmen praising charity. I, too, rather dislike—perhaps with a touch of jealousy—other men who come on heavy about chauvinism and sexism, even muttering to myself, a few whiskies to windward, "That over-compensating sonofabitch has probably been kicking the shit out of women all his life." More soberly, I agree that women have to speak for women, as blacks for blacks. For social change, the new consciousness of the oppressed, not the moral voyeur's logic and sentiments, provides the radical force.

Still, I have some qualifications as a fellow-traveler for Women's Lib. They have nothing to do with being *simpatico* with the usual feminine, which I'm not—no sympathetic menstrual cramps. Nor am I desperately latching on to an ideological substitute for all the other Movement causes—Peace, Civil Rights, etc.—that have partly failed in recent years. No, I go back further than that, almost a "birthright" feminist. I've argued for woman's equality for nearly forty years, which means I started as a toddler. No overstatement there. My mother died when I was two. That unforgiveable insult on her part should, and does, make me rather hostile to women. But I've long

Revised version of an essay that appeared in the *Village Voice* (June 10, 1971). Original Copyright *Village Voice*. This version reprinted with the permission of the author and the second publisher KNOW, INC. (P.O. Box 10197, Pittsburgh, Pa. 15232). ©Kingsley Widmer (San Diego State Univ.).

known that, and leaned back over. Moral allegiances often reveal such perverse histories: the peasant-identifying aristocrat, the intellectual joining the proletarians, the white Negro—and we Male Feminists.

Perhaps most crucial in my developing such consciousness was that one of the first of the various women who served me as maternal surrogate was a vociferous "feminist" grandmother. Literally, some of my earliest memories are of my sweet old grandmother chain-smoking and, with whiskey glass beside her, a bit mawkishly expounding on the "rights of women." In place of the usual sentimental strings to maternal pieties of the stock sort, I'm attached to female equality, as well as to bourbon and tobacco.

As an adolescent I used to take a self-congratulatory pleasure in talking about my feminist grandmother. She appeared to me all the more heroically "emancipated" a woman because most of my other relatives so vehemently disapproved. Now I have mixed feelings about my grandmother's feminist heroics because I realize that they were sometimes self-serving. A rhetoric of "advanced ideas" was a necessity for her, not only as the first woman newspaper reporter in her midwestern area but more personally. Her doting publisher-father had raised his first-born girl as a substitute son and she had taken up what were then, before the first World War, considered purely masculine "vices." She chain-smoked to her death at almost eighty. She drank and swore. She bobbed her hair early. She read notorious books. She was divorced from her adventurer husband, for no practical reason, and stored her only child with relatives. She even, one of my great-aunts anguishedly whispered to me before her death, had once had a "nigger paramour."

No doubt my heroically emancipated grandmother was also a tiresome leech as well as what they used to call "a loose woman." She didn't really make it as a professional journalist—"solely because of male envy" was probably at best a part-truth—but moved herself and various perhaps hysterical illnesses in on reluctant relatives. While waiting for another temporary job or man to show up, she would expound her pop-feminism, wheedle money, and insist also on the prerogatives of more traditional feminine roles though she didn't do well as mother and homemaker. She disliked children, except as a captive audience, and used to beat me for interrupting her reading. She despised housework, was a poor cook, and righteously went out of her way to affront smalltown Protestant neighbors. When her attention was drawn once too often to dirty clothes, unmade beds, and barely edible meals, she would dramatically rage about "female slavery," and then huff off to the next relative. She was right enough but at the same time a self-pitying poseur. So, too, with some of her feminist descendants. But that should serve no condemnation of the women's movement, then or now, since all ideologies will service some people's personal weaknesses. The conservatively smug anti-ideologies, such as snide anti-feminism, are usually the nastiest that way.

And what was a woman without much in the way of resources or usable talents or stoic character to do in a society that demanded submissive females? So the equality of woman seemed heroic principle to me when I started on my own, and I imposed it on most of the young women I bedded and boarded for the best part of a decade. Feminism usually came out as number three in my domestic sermons, right after radical politics and a romantic view of the uniqueness of the artist (which just happened to be exemplified by me). I was a bit of a fundamentalist about my feminism, eager to use it to excuse any awkwardness in seduction. I also rarely made love to a girl more than twice before setting up a household based on "rational" principles of fairly divying up financial and housekeeping "duties." Looking back, I detect considerable misogyny in my claims for "women's rights." Indeed, the hasty householding of what used to be called "love affairs" is itself rather suspect; I wanted those women domesticated—only after that submission could they claim equality.

Obviously, too, I revealed considerable contempt, in a reversed style; I scorned each woman's lack of "emancipation," and was eager to direct her on how to overcome the terrible limitations of her anti-feminist background and servile "girlishness." She damn well would have to be equal, by which I often ended up meaning "man-like." She certainly had to contribute share and share alike to household expenses (and sometimes to *my* expenses), regardless of frequently making less money. My fair-square arrangements in fact meant that the woman usually worked more than I. Parallel lines were not to be bent by mere arithmetic and larger social realities. After all, wasn't I scrupulous in doing a full half of the housework—dishes, laundry, shopping, cleaning, even mending—as well as money-making? Be equal, you bitch!

Thus, at least at my worst, I managed to fuse misogyny and feminism. It was sometimes a bit impractical. Gradually I discovered, or at least admitted, that there might be natural division of talents, not necessarily just sexual. Some things I did well (cleaning) and some badly (cooking), and they didn't really have much to do with male and female natures, with anatomical destiny. My obtuseness here was encouraged by convention; my cooking, for instance, came out patently inferior to that of most of the women I knew—perhaps a legacy from my grandmother, plus a learned indifference (as soldier, migrant worker, etc.) to artful meals. No matter what, I fall back on my days as a short-order cook—something quick fried, a tomato expertly sliced on the oblique, a slap, dash and done. My meals have all the patient subtlety of the hamburger joint (my children of course unfairly rate me lower than that). Is my non-cooking really a covert way of emphasizing a masculine role?

With some men it surely would be. But I do rather well on other housewifery. If there's much chauvinism in my domestic performance, it more likely comes out in inverse ways, as in my too great willingness to announce that I don't know any woman who can clean a house as well as I. My wife only proved her prerogative to sometimes iron my shirts when she clearly demonstrated not only that she was faster than I but that she, too, could iron ancient male style, on any handy surface instead of on an ironing board. (You must, of course, lay down a couple of folded sheets, but ironing boards, like anything more than a bent fork for scrambling and whipping things, tends to corrupt the craft.) I always keep a mocking eye out for any feminine ritualization of housework, for the pathetically self-sanctifying elaborateness of domestic method which has become the consumerized society's cover-up for degrading work and the great mythology for product exploitation.

When I settled into an enduring relationship, it was clearly agreed that we would share domestic chores as well as economic roles. Nothing big about that. Both professional, if often marginal, intellectuals, the kind of job holding we did, or later going to graduate schools together, or taking academic positions, easily encouraged certain kinds of equality. When educated couples end in chattel-like relations, it's a willed effort on someone's part. When I didn't have a job and my wife was working as a researcher, obviously I should be the housewife. She did the larger part of the domestic labors when I was finishing my Ph.D. thesis, as I did when she was finishing hers. Whichever one of us is completing a book or an article is not for the moment the one to wash and wax the kitchen floor or bake bread. If either one of us regularly feels so beat-out from his or her job that they can't do a share of housework, then screw the job which is obviously screwing us.

If I hardly ever make dinner, that less comes from male unfairness than from my wife's good taste—*her* grandmother was a good European professional cook. And I have my own domestic masteries.

Usually we find reasonable tradeoffs, with the divisions of labor rather more by talents and needs than by sexual roles. Still, it is, as they say, a chauvinist culture, and male-female roles even at best remain ambivalent, and these problems never altogether resolved. In this society, authentic personhood, of whatever sexual cast, tends to dissolve into function. Unjustified social patterns covertly envelop one. Jobs, for example. Though my wife has a doctorate and publications and is both a better, a more student-responsive, teacher and less of a bureaucracy-baiting trouble-maker than I am, she has always gotten less salary, and never gotten tenure. Women's Lib is mostly right on the bigoted economics, and any decent man knows he has to work against the grain of our institutional wood in very specific ways for things to come out anywhere near fair.

Some of the other perplexities of a woman's role, however, didn't really get to me until recently, until, due to various family illnesses, I ended up with a year's leave of absence from my college job while my wife, energies drastically limited by recovery from surgery, was teaching at a university. Then I had to take over most of the domesticities, and discovered in myself some new resentments and rages. I had become a male housewife.

Much of that, I believe, must be blamed on suburban lifestyle. Affluence, energetic sons and animals, and obstreperous landlords had driven us into a suburban house-machine. I was more bemused than angry at the consequent "male" demands—repairs, yard-work, the contractor who would only discuss remodeling with "the Mister." But a suburban house also metaphysically demands a housewife. Its spaces and equipment—and considerable mis-equipment—its aesthetic order and social functions, will allow no other management: housewifeism. (Out of decency, of course, I ignore here the partial suburban alternative—the vicious practices euphemistically lumped under "having help in.") Be you man or woman, a bouncy Home Ec. specialist or a disgruntled literary scholar, if you are going to keep a nuclear family going in an affluent American suburban home, then somebody is going to have to be a traditional housewife. And that is a naturally resentment-breeding job. Currently, I'm it. Much of present feminism not only speaks to me but for me.

Don't misunderstand; I'm truly pleased that my wife is teaching again, even though still too frail to do much else. And I readily grant the justice of my doing the housewifery, of the turnabout in previous stock roles which we never consciously chose anyway. About time. That I'm now on leave to write a book certainly should not, under the circumstances, exempt me from the chores and errands. Still, I hadn't realized some of the psychic prices of reversed roles until several recent episodes. Male and female images of ourselves may be partly fun and games but the pains that go with them are real.

Take the little episode of my going into a store recently to replace the cover of a casserole (a gift) that I broke doing dishes. A bit guilty about breaking it, I gave the salesgirl a hard time in making sure that I got an exact match in the replacement. Consequently, I suspect, she gave me a hard time about taking my check, until suddenly she broke into a smile of recognition: "But you must be the husband of Professor Eleanor Widmer? I had her course on the political novel. It was groovy!" I forced a smile, acknowledged the relationship, and thanked her for the compliment to my wife. She cashed my check without further ado. I also suppressed a desire, quite unreasonable, to say more, such as that I was sometime-professor, too, who could give groovy courses, and indeed, probably knew a bit more about the political novel than that *other* Professor Widmer. Naturally I was pleased that the young woman liked my wife's course. And of course I didn't really resent being identified as my wife's husband. Of course not!

But in emotional fact, I did a bit resent it, as many women do the parallel situations, and not just because I'm a beastly male egotist. It's a lonely and indifferent mass social order without much sense of community. As with most people, I'm bound in this society to often feel inadequate identification as me, as a locus of meaningful things in my own right. Right now I can't fall back on the usual self-preoccupation with a "man's work," with my job. Currently, what I actually and mostly do is keep house for my working wife and two boys in school. But, surprisingly often, I remind myself that such is not really me; only temporarily a housewife, I'm a scholar writing another book—that's what I really do. For who could settle for being a suburban housewife, regardless of sex, for all that petty and repetitious routine? And that my book isn't going well, that must be the fault of all the shitty little housework!

I discover other resentments. At *her* departmental cocktail party, I know who I am—everybody announces it—I'm *her* husband, and somehow the conversations eddy past me, as if I were some minor obstruction in the knowledgeable flow of things. Since my wife is out in the world more than I am, she gets more of the invitations. Of course she kindly takes me along—it gets me out of the house and my sweatshirt. At the last two large social gatherings, I found myself over in the corner swapping domestic anecdotes with a non-academic scientist whose government-funded research project folded, leaving him, wife employed, a somewhat irritable house-keeping man. He understands me.

We male housewives rise to other, and quite traditional, rages as well. "Which of you goddam kids tracked up my clean kitchen floor?" "And who spilt juice in the refrigerator and didn't wipe it up, after I just finished cleaning it?" "And that phony new detergent doesn't get the stains out." "And if that phone comes up with a wrong number once more when I'm swabbing out the toilets, I'll rip it out!" "I'm out of paper towels—and what else was it I have to get in the next shopping?" "Look at everybody sitting around on their asses listening to records while I'm slaving away! How about a little consideration for a change?"

There's something about the over and over and over of housework that encourages righteousness, male as well as female. But my real complaint is that the persistent fracturing drag of domesticities doesn't let me get my own intellectual work done. Admittedly, I can't quite explain why that should be. How much of each day does cleaning and laundry and shopping and errands, and the rest, take? A bit hard to figure since there's no neat piece of work to be polished off, which is psychologically part of the problem. Still, I am faster than I am fastidious, and it must come out to, say, four hours or so a day—a half-time job, as I've more than once told my wife in the past. Unfairly, of course, I've the "manly things"—the yard, the car, etc.—to also take care of. Even so, there should be plenty of time for research and writing.

But there doesn't seem to be. Something perhaps about work rhythms. For years I've done my writing at the deep hours of the night, when things are quiet and I can be abstracted from the family and the rest of the world. Thinking requires the feeling of the free-play of time. And a sense of autonomy. (It must be that which explains why slaves and servants rarely write books, though they are frequently more intelligent than their masters. And why wives, even when more intelligent than their husbands, write less!) These days I must get up early, help the kids off, drive my wife to the university, then do a few chores—the breakfast clean-up, a washer load of laundry—before I go to my desk, where the phone or doorbell are sure to interrupt me. By then it's already getting on to noon. Might just as well get a few other chores out of the way and then eat lunch. Lunch always leaves me a bit soggy; I didn't eat it in the past, but then I didn't have to get up and run around so early either. One thing leads to another, which then leads nowhere—the housewife's lament.

After lunch, I glance through a magazine, sort of prepping my-self to go to my desk. That's a new habit. When I'm finally ready to go to work, I realize my youngest boy will soon be home from grade school. I wasn't going to pick up his room, superfluous order, but, what the hell, he's been upset lately about that lousy teacher so I guess I should give him a little sense of comforting—get out some-thing special for a snack, too. And I suppose I could strip all the beds while I'm at it and do another laundry. Kids come home and on top, errands, dinner, dishes. Forgot to put away the laundry. And I'll do a bit of picking up so I'll be ahead for tomorrow and a good clear day. No use working now; I'm a bit tired; watch TV for a change. But isn't that what I said last night? Another new good American suburban habit—the usual routine is making *me* into a suburban habit. Might just as well get to bed early, cleared away for some "real work" tomorrow. Tomorrow? I'll have to do a big shopping, replace the broken plug on the iron, wash the kitchen floor. . . . And what about my own work? Housewifery is a father-fucking machine!

I think I know what's wrong, and it isn't just, or even primarily, the sexist roles of man wired up as bureaucratic functionary and woman short-circuited as a suburban housewife machine. The major-ity of routines in present America show this intellectually and emo-tionally demoralizing order. We can't help but know that so much of it is arbitrary, that fatuous repetition, those fraudulent rewards (or the cheating lack of them), these imposed inequalities, and that lack of real human autonomy—all apply in the larger world as well as in the home. It takes a considerable willed, even eccentric, effort to break beyond them. Discouraged by the ambiguities of male housewifery, I have faltered.

Middle-class lifestyle, and its epitomization in the nuclear sub-urban family, comfortingly rewards the faltering and the muddled, pays off arbitrary sexual roles. What earlier had some anatomical—strength and child-rearing—justifications, no longer persuades. Our false divisions of labor for the male as well as female worlds, house-keeping and working patterns which dully atomize and privateeringly punish-reward with our machines and luxuries, leave us with a terri-bly precarious sense of self. A quite different communal sense and social order will be required to really change, for most, the arbitrary housewife machine and the rest of our false division of identities and labors.

So I listen sympathetically to Women's Lib, though I don't take some of it literally. It may have over-focused on sex—partly yet again for male titillation?—when much of the problem is social, the divisions and the gratifications of our activities. The sexual emphasis tends to end up in a clit-happy solipsism. (Sure, get your pleasures as you can and must, but a narrowly masturbatory sexual ethos, single or multiple, is not very enriching—and we still need each other.) I understand current feminists as speaking for a larger social liberation and equality, a more radical transformation of our divisions and identities and actions than some of them face up to. And, as my personal examples hope to illustrate, this applies to the educated middle class, not just to the more gross underclass brutalization of women.

Of course I have objections to some Liberationist arguments, not confined to my roles as a male and a housewife. (For instance, I see Kate Millet's *Sexual Politics* as badly confusing the issues, sadly evident in her ignorant and callow chapters on literature; in my books on Henry Miller and D. H. Lawrence I, too, criticized their misogyny but at least tried to be both accurate and understanding.) As a long-time feminist, I react against the reformist-trap now getting a big lib-ladies play (proper language there). In sum, I think they accept the male workaday world on its own terms, only demanding a sexual correction as to who gets the ball-cutting power. In illustration, liberationists in the academic make much of the fact that the upper ranks of the professorate—especially in my wife's and my field of English—include disproportionately few women. Quite correct, but instead of drawing the just, and radical, conclusion that the academic order is mostly fraudulent—a crypto-military structure of domination that is anti-intellectual and generally anti-egalitarian as well as anti-feminist—they just want to get more women into it. That will reinforce rather than remove a phony and unjust hierarchy. That kind of *mere* sexual politics, which also applies to many other of our institutions, comes out essentially reactionary.

How one can really be a feminist without being radical, I don't see, since women's functionary oppressions come not only as part but as the packaging of many others. Sure there must be specific grievances and changes as well as consciousness of the larger needs for equality and liberation. I think I feel some of them. Next year my wife and I will have to partly reverse roles again. With cutbacks in the universities, and the nasty controlling pedants' hostility not only to women but to teachers who are intellectuals and sympathetic to students, one Professor Widmer will be teaching less. Guess which sex! So I'll go back to work full-time. (The one just arrangement, both of us working part-time, both academically and domestically, is systematically disallowed in this society for reasons of subordination and control. Men and women must display themselves as functionaries, not as varied and full human beings.) My wife may stay home for awhile, with mixed feelings since she well knows that what is speciously treated as the "man's world" is little more justly humanized than what is speciously treated as the "woman's world." There won't be much justice and fulfillment in the one without justice and fulfillment in the other.

Domestically, we will no doubt make some further adjustments in sharing and equality. For as a male housewife, I've learned some things on my nerves that I should have known but somehow didn't—good intentions never being sufficient for existential understanding. But after again working awhile in the educational bureaucracies—also a dubious and hypocritical trade, even though better recognized and rewarded than domestic labors—I may even yearn to get back to being a male housewife. But let me not forget those non-male housewives who lack some of my freedom of choice and my double consciousness. The very least I can do is continue as a feminist fellow-traveler.

Working in "A Man's World":
The Woman Executive

Roslyn S. Willett

In most countries of the modern world the character of life is established by men's decisions. Thinking women have come to believe that a major reason for the social, economic, and political muddle in the world is precisely men's one-sided assumption of decision-making and responsibility. It is becoming clear that complementary decision-making that makes real use of the differences in temperament and talent of the two sexes is absolutely necessary.

It is generally accepted that males of most species tend to be more aggressive than females. Most women and men agree that men tend to fantasize more than women. The combination of the two, aggressiveness and fantasy, may be useful for developing ambitious plans and elaborating abstract systems and structures. But ambitious plans and abstract systems and structures are ineffectual without the counterbalance of a sensitive perception of what is really happening in the real world and a sustained interest in getting a real job done.

When they are solely responsible for making policy and decisions, men tend to overemphasize the aggressive and fantastic components of possible solutions to a problem. It seems clear, however, that if women take on their proper responsibility as half of the human race, and contribute their organic awareness of what has to be done, all kinds of human needs will be met with less waste of energy. The male aggressiveness that has been overdeveloped for lack of feedback will be better proportioned to real-world requirements. The perceptions of women will be fully utilized, along with such

Chapter 22, "Working in a 'A Man's World'": The Woman Executive, by Roslyn S. Willett, from *WOMAN IN SEXIST SOCIETY: Studies in Power and Powerlessness*, ©1971 Basic Books, Inc., Publishers, New York. Used with permission.

male biological aggressiveness as must remain, to create a fine balance between the two complementary sides of the human temperament. With a righting of that balance, the probability of a saner, more wholesome society for *both men and women* is enormous, irrespective of the particular structures of the society.

This essay is an attempt to explore working relationships between men and women, the complementary distribution of working talent between the two sexes, and their possible relationships to biological differences. Its intention, finally, is to suggest fruitful ways of working together.

WORKING NOW

This is a time of transition in the working relationships between women and men, characterized by certain themes. One of them is women's poor image of themselves. Believing themselves to be lesser, smaller, more passive, weaker, more trivial, incapable of coping with men and other women as equals, incapable of taking hold of a *big* job, they behave as if they *are* this way and then get confirmation from others of their own beliefs.

Another theme is men's belief that women cannot really do big jobs, that women are not creative, and that women in offices, government, and industry should hold the jobs closest to housekeeping and a wife's duties. That is, that women should take care of the routine activities, the maintenance chores, the lubricating trivia while men do the big thinking and contact work. Men feel that in helping a man "do his thing," most women derive their satisfactions and feeling of being needed. And finally, they feel that any woman who does big jobs, is creative, and is successful must be a hard, nasty bitch, or sleeping with a guy who put her where she is.

These are myths. But they have been the operating myths of the working world, and they help to explain why it is that women are offered and accept low pay; that capable, educated women accept dead-end office-wife types of jobs; that women who work full-time also do virtually all the housework and child care without complaint in a family where a husband is also present. They also explain the "volunteer" syndrome in suburbs—the middle-class housewife who does not think she is worth much as a worker, but wants to work, and fritters her time away in volunteer chores where she feels "needed," but not *valued*.

Statistics from the Women's Bureau of the Department of Labor tell only part of the story. Incomes of women working full-time

average about three-fifths of those of men working full-time; the gap
has been widening rather than narrowing. Women clerical workers
earn less than three-fifths of what men clerical workers earn; women
sales workers earn about two-fifths of what men in similar positions
earn; women managers, officials, and proprietors earn slightly more
than half of what men in equivalent situations earn. The narrowest
gap between the two is on the professional and technical level:
women earn about two-thirds of what men earn. Some of the gap is
attributable to the fact that women tend to drop out of work during
the time that their children are young, so that their accumulated
experience may be somewhat less. In addition, a higher proportion of
black women than white ones are dependent on jobs; since black
women's jobs tend to be low-paying and unskilled, their higher rep-
resentation skews the averages.

However, even among women and men of equal educational
attainment, the median annual salary of women scientists in 1966 was
about $3,000 a year lower than the median annual salary of all scien-
tists of both sexes. Starting salaries offered for women whose qualifications were equal to those of men were usually lower. (Engineering
shows the smallest gap—a difference of only a few hundred dollars a
year.) One-third of all working women were in seven occupations in
the late 1960's. One-fourth of them were in four: they were secretaries, retail saleswomen, household workers, or teachers in elementary schools; the next three occupations were bookkeeper, wait-
ress, and nurse.

Myths about the working possibilities of men and women have
been the foundation on which these atrocious figures rest. It would
be easy to say that prejudice against women by men is the primary
cause. It would be easy, but it would be only half the story. The
trouble with working women lies also in themselves, in their definition of themselves and of each other.

Experiments reported in *Trans-Action* magazine several years
ago showed that when an identical lecture was delivered by a female
instructor and by a male instructor, women college students rated the
male "better."

Most working girls and women, even young ones, have permitted their roles to be defined by others, even in contradiction of
their own perceptions. Most working women perceive very clearly
that their (male) bosses are not particularly bright. Over a period of
time, they also become aware that they are themselves as capable as
men, and in some areas—for example, responsiveness to situations,
insights, and ability to carry a job through to completion—
particularly good. They simply do not reach for the rewards of their

capacity or even for ordinary equality. If they expected equitable evaluation on their merits and behaved as if they expected it, they would get it more often.

Considerable thought about the difference between the women who have "made it" and those who have not makes it clear that the women who *have* behave as if they expected to be treated as equal. They know the myths about women, but they do not believe them. They rely on their own perceptions of reality and respond directly to that reality. It is no wonder that over a period of time they act on those perceptions with increasing confidence and become notable in a world of mythmakers for bluntness, directness, and effectiveness. These women have the fewest working "discrimination" stories to tell. They talk sense, and they are listened to. The problem for these women is that men *who do not know them* may not interview, hire, or promote them. They may not get as far, therefore, as men with similar capacities.

On the other hand, women who have been brainwashed early about the inferiority of women do not admit their own perceptions. The idea of equality has no meaning to them. For example, twenty-six years ago, a large company in midtown New York that was advanced enough to have hired an ordinary (not gorgeous) black woman as a receptionist, still required that women smoke cigarettes in the ladies' room, while men were permitted to smoke at their desks. My mere challenge to the personnel department sufficed to undo the ban on women's smoking. Why had the other women waited so long in such a ridiculous situation? It was obviously their feeling that despite the masters degrees in chemistry that a number of them had, they were only women.

Another example of women's bad self-image was in the questionnaire sent to successful women by two women authors of a book on careers for women. The questionnaire asked who had "helped" these women at a number of different stages. Would a man's career be defined by the "help" he had received along the way, making of him a passive recipient of favors? Should it not be as plain for women as for men that a career is not "helped"—that its advancement comes from others' recognizing capacity and making sensible economic use of it?

Demeaning images of women are even disseminated by educated women who are "experts." During the 1950's, a woman Ph.D., working for the then-largest advertising agency in the country as a market researcher, made a career for herself by defining women for the benefit of male marketers as emotional, trivial, and distractable—a great soap opera audience. These qualities could more readily be attributed to temporary isolation from meaning and responsibility than to feminine nature. But there was no differentiation in this analysis. Furthermore, it was extremely satisfying to her male audience, who developed marketing plans and advertising based on it. And handsome young, married, gray-flannel-suit account men confessed with pleasure they could not "understand" women.

Home economists are among the few professional women employed in considerable numbers in industry. They have been charged by manufacturing and communications firms with interpreting women to their male bosses. Unfortunately, these women's training is more in specific technical areas—food, clothing, household maintenance—than in the liberal arts, psychology, or communication. In addition, home economics as a field of study has not attracted many high-powered women. The result, again, has until recently been a concentration on technical detail and further dissemination of clichés and conventional wisdom about women and their interests. Fortunately, these women have begun to see themselves differently, and a mutter of discontent may be heard at their professional meetings with male speakers whose lack of respect for these women's professional and business attainments expresses itself in silly sexual flattery.

Plainly women can and are beginning to think bigger about themselves and the work they can and should be doing. But, as I indicated at the beginning of this section, the trouble is more with men. Not all of them. Only enough to create difficulty. It is a matter of fact that in the scientific and engineering fields, into which few women have ventured, there is less discrimination than in fields that deal more with symbols. It may be that the habit of dealing with *things* realistically—a simple requirement in successful engineering—permits engineers to evaluate women's talents realistically, and let them work accordingly.

In areas where symbols and fantasy dominate work, women are more troubled by male misunderstanding and more subject to unexamined male prejudice, even if they hold good jobs. This is particularly true where what is being "sold" is image more than product, as it is in magazine publishing, advertising, and public relations. In 1950 when I was one of 140 applicants for a job as editor of a trade magazine and the only female applicant, I was hired because I had taken the trouble to look at the magazine before the interview and outline plans for changing it. The publisher disliked having a woman editor and was nervous about reader acceptance. I was introduced to the readership as "R. L. Willett, our new editor, who takes a tough shirtsleeves approach . . ."

One woman who is now president of her own manufacturing company tells a story of the difference between realism and fantasy in another area. In 1960 she had left a company where she had been in charge of systems design and development on a new computer for the American Stock Exchange. She was one of the few people in the country who had designed and built real-time systems and had the only experience in the country with the requirements of a stock exchange. She was interviewed by an official of the New York Stock Exchange for the job of administrator of their data-processing study group, and after extensive checking of her experience, hired. She accepted very happily; as she puts it, "enchanted with the prospect of another big system." However, because the job was a management job at a very high level, she had to be approved by the Executive Board of the New York Stock Exchange. This was generally a formality. In this case, it was not. The men on the board said no, to the considerable embarrassment of the man who had been delegated to find the best-qualified person in the country. His moralistic explanation of their rejection was, "They said you might hear dirty words on the Exchange floor." As she tells it, they hired one man after another—including one who had been her junior in a previous work situation. None of them did the job adequately, and the New York Stock Exchange muddle continued for years.

Inability to believe that women are worth considering outside women's traditional jobs formerly characterized many employment agencies. In the mid-1950's, when I was running the major industrial accounts at a public relations agency, I registered with an employment agency that specialized in public relations executives. I put down my then salary, about $10,000, and the accounts I was working on (mostly in the institutional and packaging fields). The agency principal interviewed me briefly, deciding *a priori* that I was what was known in the trade as a "recipe peddler." (A woman who devises new consumer recipes for use with clients' food products and places them in newspaper and magazine food pages. This happens to be the most usual job for women in public relations, also the lowest paid.) I said I had *never* done that—my experience was entirely industrial, much broader, on a much higher level, and I was paid accordingly. The only job the agency ever offered me was one for a recipe peddler—at almost $3,000 less than I was earning.

Troubles like this continue. A short time ago I received a letter from a professor in the graduate school of business administration of the University of Colorado that said in part:

As you well know, it is a formidable obstacle to a woman graduating senior to get through the door into the business world. In twenty-nine years of doing what I can to help men and women find promising positions, I realize that women must have extra help. Most of our women graduates who have gotten into business have proven their ability to carry executive responsibilities, just as have our men graduates. I can point to many around the country.

More and more men and women executives recognize this and acknowledge that their acceptance is gradually improving, but it is still quite difficult for women to get through that first door. Legislation has not solved the problem.

Can you help? Will you make yourself available to these proven graduates who wish to start their careers in business? I am not soliciting lip-service, or clerk-type openings for these women, but am requesting your whole-hearted, active effort to help a woman graduate when she, or we contact you for your energetic help.

We want your name in our active file. The higher you stand in executive position, the more valuable is your personal availability and participation, just as theirs will be when they reach a level where they can help women graduates that follow. *You* will be greatly appreciated by all concerned, you may be very sure!

Also, we want names and addresses of those persons who you know will cooperate with this program. Please supply us with their names, and the details necessary for making contact with them.

The Wall Street Journal was impressed enough with this kind of effort (directed to only 200 women in the country!) to give it front-page mention a few weeks later.

Working women have had other kinds of problems in being treated as "equal." In the late 1940's I was promoted to a "man's job" in charge of technical service and development on food products in a company that sold celloidal materials to a number of different industries. I was promoted in the first place (from the job of technical and patents librarian) because I had the background, and because the technical director judged that I had the "guts" that the depression-wounded, MIT-educated chemical engineer I was replacing did not have. But, he said, very seriously, "Ros, one of the—things the job requires is that you drink with the boys. Can you do that?" As the single female member of the technical planning committee there, I had other problems. We met at the Chemists Club, and women were not admitted to the bar. I was literally collared on my way out of the meeting room after a long morning by the company president demanding to know where I thought I was going. He had assumed I was heading to the bar. Far from it: I was heading for the ladies' room—which was almost equally inaccessible.

Other public accommodations problems present themselves: the Advertising Club, a professional, not social, organization, segregates members. Women members are only permitted to entertain in certain rooms, far from the nicest. Until recently United Air Lines ran an all-male executive flight to Chicago at 5 p.m. from Newark Airport. I make frequent trips to Chicago, and Newark is an hour closer to where I live than Kennedy, which was for years the only alternative. My secretary pointed out that I was an executive and so listed in several Who's Who's. No admission. I wrote to the Civil Aeronautics Board complaining about discrimination against women on this convenient plane. They said the all-male executive flight was merely promotional, and that if women wanted an all-female executive flight that they would put one on. I pointed out the explosive black-white analogy, suggesting that they tell black people that they were not discriminated against on most flights, but on one flight a day, which was purely promotional, only whites were to be admitted; and if blacks wanted an all-black flight, all they had to do was create effective demand. United also said they scarcely ever had any complaints from women. This went on all through the 1960s until early 1970. I did not use United Airlines for any flight during that period and only use them now when they are the only airline into a city.

Inside organizations and even among male colleagues whom one likes, other kinds of experience indicate how hard it is for men to let women rise to their own level. Some years ago, I was a department head in a public relations agency, running several large industrial accounts. I was in a small office with a window, equipped with a standard office desk. The agency head learned of the availability, from a travel agency that was moving, of two tiny desks with drawers the size of those in a sewing machine cabinet—big enough to hold spools of thread. He bought the desks for five dollars each and then came into my office to tell me I was about to be the recipient of a "lady's desk," so that he could give my desk to a newly hired male writer. I pointed out that the folders and papers I used would not fit in the drawers of the "lady's desk," that my efficiency would be diminished by this inappropriate little table, that he would be wasting part of the pretty good salary I was being paid, that the work I did had nothing to do with being "female," and finally that I would not accept the little desk. He stomped out of my office virtually apoplectic with rage about "women." (He had another idea sometime later that my office, with a window, would be more appropriate for a man, who was my junior in age, experience, and responsibility. Again, my answer was no, with an explanation of why I felt it was wrong. The explanation was unheard. The response was that I was an irrational woman, exceptionally difficult to deal with.)

On other occasions where as an "expert" I have organized technical programs and delivered long, well-received talks to large audiences, the only comment from a "friendly" male colleague was that I said "hell" once and "damn" twice, during one speech. The implications were that he had a right to censure my unladylike behavior, and that the audience would be seriously disaffected by it. On another speech-making occasion, I was introduced to an audience of fellow consultants as "our cute, little, bright, girl consultant." When I said I was far from a little girl, being in my mid-forties, and that gender had nothing to do with this kind of work, I was labeled, again, "difficult."

Another example of unthinking put-down is the story of a professional woman who had been employed as a regional dietitian, supervising the entire Midwestern area school lunch programs and exercising her own initiative successfully for a number of years. She was hired to do similar work by the public relations agency at which I worked. She made her own schedules and handled her own correspondence and contacts with immense success for the years I was there. My successor was a man, a nice man. The head of the agency told him idly one day that he was to "boss" the school lunch representative, taking over her correspondence and contacts and making her travel schedule for her.

(It should be said, incidentally, to clarify what follows, that I was told while I was there that I was "boss" of a couple of very competent men, and expected to "boss" them. Since they were aware of their assignments and produced their work reliably, and since they knew I would be glad to help if they ran into any trouble with which I could help (technical or writing), I did not exercise my boss prerogatives in any noticeable way. Just saw to it that we got the work out.)

Nothing loath—my successor told the school lunch lady the news and asked that she turn her files and contact list over to him, thereby in one swoop making an independent and capable woman into his flunky. She refused. He called to tell me this story with the comment that she was as irrational as most women, very difficult to deal with. I pointed out to him that he had no real function to serve in this case that she was not already performing better, and that he could have said so to the agency head. Also that her response was direct and to the point. If a man had suffered this indignity, he might not have been so direct. A man might have said, "Yes, but we'll have to wait a few days till I get things in order," or devised some other scheme for evading the problem, and finally when it could not be avoided, disappeared into a bar or come down with a psychosomatic disorder that necessitated his absence until, hopefully, it was forgotten.

Men who can stand competent women as long as their biological differences can be ignored become terribly solicitous when biology comes to the fore. Every single woman who has looked for a job has been asked what she would do if she got married. (The responsibility for her departure always seems imminent to men who can ignore their own job turnover very comfortably.) If she is married, the probability of an instant baby overwhelms the interviewer. It required very blunt talks several times to lay that suspicion to rest in my own career. I had been married for ten years before I decided to have a child. When I changed jobs during that period, it was necessary to point out that I had a diaphragm and a fair amount of successful experience in using it.

Finally, when I did decide to have a child, most people, male and female, were "worried" about my continuing to work. I did work until the night before the baby was born, putting on a very successful client party less than two weeks before, at which I did not sit down at all. Two weeks after, I spent a day touring a client factory. My feeling about work was clued by my observation of pregnant alley cats. Belly or no, they continue to jump over fences and grub around in garbage cans. So can most women. When I was asked how I could continue to work with such a massive handicap, the answer was easy: a big belly only interferes with tying your shoelaces; it does not impair your intelligence. Ask any man with one.

Blunt, straightforward talk and action, and ad hoc responsiveness to real-world situations are very characteristic of women. But it is precisely because men do not want or expect directness—and often do not get it from each other, particularly in the white-collar world—that they find it incomprehensible. They prefer fantasies about what women are like and about what their work and organization are about.

A publishing affiliate of one of the best-known "thinking" corporations in the country asked me some time ago to write a book about dealing with women in industry and business for the benefit of male executives and middle management. I wrote to the editor and said they would not want the kind of book that I would write: describing many problems as men's problems with their own myths about women. I outlined a few. The answer was that I was right. It would comfort no executive to hear this kind of thing; he would not buy such a book.

But the situation is changing. The most serious business magazine in one field in which my firm works as consultants has for years been run mostly by women. But the title "editor" or "editorial director"—the magazine's public image maker—has always been awarded to a man of variable competence, who did not last long.

Until lately; a year or two ago the farce ended. The woman "managing editor" became "editor." Other publications in the field have since followed suit as have at least some consumer publications, but the few latter only in the fields defined as "women's."

There are few women in contact positions in advertising and public relations agencies because the men who run them are worried about whether business*men* may not be disturbed at the idea of dealing with a woman. All other things being equal, agency heads have not wanted to disturb possible client prejudices, even in the interest of getting a good job done. Yet, when the question is treated on its merits—and a matter-of-fact evaluation of the requirement for getting a good job done is made—businessmen in heavy industry, high technology, and other fields can and do deal with women without comment. Agency fears have not been justified in my experience, and they are beginning to give way.

The question of competence and ability rarely comes up these days. Most men do not, in the face of evidence to the contrary, say that women *cannot* by their nature do a job; plainly they can and are doing many jobs exceedingly well.

Mary Wells Lawrence runs a dynamic and highly profitable advertising agency and is herself a very creative advertising person. Katherine Flack, administrator of institutional services for the New York State Mental Hygiene Department, has done the pioneering work on creation of a supplies system meeting the requirements of forty-six institutions which house and feed tens of thousands of people. Esther Conwell Rothberg, a physicist, did most of the theoretical work on the behavior of semiconductors. Vera Jenkins, a manufacturers' representative in the Southeast, has turned in the best sales record in the country for Amco Wire Products. General Electric has appointed a woman sales manager in New York for its commercial equipment. Marianne Moore is widely considered one of the country's foremost poets. Margaret Mead and Ruth Benedict have done as much creative thinking in anthropology as any man (and the results do not distort life so much as structural anthropology in the style of Lévi-Strauss). Louise Nevelson's and Marisol's works are as serious and consequential as any male's sculpture; Mary Bauermeister and Helen Frankenthaler, Bridget Riley, and Georgia O'Keeffe, are as creative as any male painter. Mme. Alexandra David-Neel is a fair mystic. Susanne Langer's contributions to philosophy are more important in my opinion than those of any other currently working philosopher. Karen Horney's contribution to self-analysis and human typology are wearing better than much work done by male psychiatrists in the same period.

Geraldine Stutz, Dorothy Shaver, and Mildred Custin among others have been extraordinarily successful retailers. Katherine Meyer, Dorothy Schiff, and Alicia Patterson have been exceptionally creative publishers of very profitable newspapers. Margaret Chase Smith has a record of courage and good sense in the Senate equaled by few men. Female writers from Sappho to authors of virtually all the masterpieces of the Heian period of Japan, from Mary Wollstonecraft Shelley to George Eliot to Iris Murdoch, Sigrid Undset, Virginia Woolf, Doris Lessing, and Marguerite Duras, have produced creative work on a par with that of men. Martha Graham's dance compositions surpass those of any other choreographer now working.

Although the number of women physicians in the United States is not high (about 7 percent of the total), in Russia women are 75 percent of the total and they do not treat only women and children (see Solzhenitsyn's *The Cancer Ward*). The number of women lawyers in the United States is small, about 2½ percent; the number of woman lawyers in official positions is even smaller. But in 1959, a UN study quoted by Doris Sassower in *Trial* magazine showed that women were 14 percent of all lawyers in France, 9 percent of the public prosecutors in Hungary, 25 percent of the judges in Poland, and 50 percent of the law students in Denmark.

The trouble with advancement of women in business and industry no longer lies with the idea that they are incapable of doing the job. Plainly women can do well virtually anything there is to do. It lies instead in the male expectation or belief that women tend to be irrational and difficult to deal with. This is a self-serving myth perpetrated by those men who cannot cope with reality, but must impose fantasy on it. They define responsible women variously and pejoratively as, "a little nutty," domineering, masculine, aggressive, feminine, hard to get along with, and impossible to understand. So defined, few women can get past a middle level in any organization or be considered for public "image making" in non-sex-related jobs by the organization.

ARE THERE BIOLOGICAL AND BEHAVIORAL DIFFERENCES?

There are no absolute biological differences other than the clear-cut differences between primary and secondary sex organs (and even these seem to be blurred in a few unfortunate individuals). Human characteristics appear in distribution patterns like those of any other measurable factors—on a scale from "most" to "least," with a sizable group in the middle, and a trailing off of individuals to either side. This would be true of height, weight, muscularity, strength, and various specific abilities in verbal ability, math, games and strategies, peak-type energy output versus sustained energy output.

Since this is so for both men and women, it would be idiotic to say without qualification, "*All* men are good at math, strategy, peak-type pushes, have more mechanical aptitude, are better at manipulating spatial relationships; *all* women have better vocabularies, speak earlier and better, are higher in sensitivity and suggestibility, and can better sustain long energy outputs." Men and women vary; there are women who are stronger, more aggressive, and more capable of high-level mathematical abstraction than most men. There are men who are more aware and sensitive, have better vocabularies, and are more nurturing in their responses than most women. (This distribution of characteristics should not be regarded as making a man less male or a woman less female.) The distributions may be affected by social expectations as much as by biology. The precise etiology of human characteristics in inborn temperament or training is far from defined. But where measurements have been made, it would appear that the above differences are more likely to be true. Most of these differences are suggested by *Human Behavior: An Inventory of Scientific Findings* (Berelson and Steiner), by M. F. Ashley-Montagu, and others.[1]

Unquestionably, most people perceive that there *are* differences between men and women, although one should not demand them of any *individual* man or woman; if one examines the statistical distribution of characteristics, the median for men will be in a different place on the curve from the median for women. These differences manifest themselves early.

One of the easiest to see is musculature. Boys and men have, on the whole, larger, stronger muscles and considerably more muscle tension. This is clear, for example, in classical and folk dancing—where with equivalent or less training, men jump higher—and in athletics, where even the best women do not compete with men in track events.

There is an interplay between body structure and temperament. The tension in muscles requires release in activity. In our society boys are often called "immature" (in nursery and elementary school), "hyperactive," and other pejorative terms. The basic fact is that they are likely to require more activity to release perfectly normal muscle tensions that build up as a result of their normal structure and hormone supplies. Instead of seeing that the "trouble" lies in muscle tension that can be utilized physically and creatively, educators tend to equate maturity and the capacity for learning with the ability to sit still and look attentive. This may explain why girls get better marks in school until adolescence—when they discover that they are not supposed to be smart.

Any kind of tension, including normal muscle tension, is released by strenuous physical activity. It may be *expressed* by aggressive behavior. Our society tends to deplore acts it labels aggressive as if they were bad. But seizing a problem, attacking it with energy, and worrying it through to some kind of solution are all aggressive, human, and necessary. If, as is generally the case, men have more muscle tension and tend to be more aggressive as a result of biological structure, recognizing the biological base for such characteristics and planning to enjoy and use the results seem no more than common sense.

The paucity of research on any of these differences is pointed up by the few reports we do have. For example, J. J. Gallagher makes the point that differences between boys and girls on written tests were undetectable.[2] They score about the same, except that the girls were *better* at giving solutions to hypothetical problems and the boys were more expressive (should we say aggressive?) in the classroom.

Another possibly biological difference between men and women that has not yet been adequately investigated, but seems to express itself in behavior, has to do with rhythmic cycling and peaking of activity. Possibly because of differences in muscle and hormone tensions, men seem to require a peak-type push and all-out activity at fairly short intervals, with all-out relaxation between. Observation indicates that most women prefer sustained activity without high peaks or deep drops of energy output. Women's activity preferences are much less on an "either-or" basis.

Many primitive societies take advantage of the probable difference in biological rhythms to divide the work between men and women accordingly. The intermittent, maximum-energy-output, then-relaxation jobs are usually men's jobs. In primitive society, hunting is the man's job. The men organize for a hunt, mobilize maximum energy and strategic capability in doing it; encounter very real danger and hardship, and come home with prizes. They then relax, tell stories, fantasize about hardships and danger, reconstruct heroic acts, eat, sleep, and gossip. Women in such societies handle the day-to-day activity, all the businesses, farming, and maintenance.

Aside from possible quantitative differences, there are qualitative differences, some of them perhaps because of training, but many at least partly inborn. One is the nature of perceived reality and how it is dealt with. For reasons that are not entirely clear, men seem to fantasize more than women. This may be one component of their biologically determined aggressiveness. And, perhaps in consequence of an innate difference in ability to perceive spatial relationships and of an interest in strategy and games, men tend to impose abstract structures on reality, and then to perceive reality in terms of their abstractions.

This could be, and often is, extremely fruitful. Abstractions are needed for thinking, for predicting, for developing new ideas. But if the map (the abstraction) does not match the territory (reality), it misleads and confuses. A great many masculine generalizations, abstractions, and "theories" are fake maps aggressively imposed on the real world. Their presence hampers perception of the real world and flexibility in response to it.

With a generally lesser component of aggressiveness and a generally smaller need for fantasy, women are often quite free to perceive the world as it is. The directness and organic wholeness characteristic of feminine perception is called "intuition," "earthiness," "common sense" in everyday affairs. It is also often strikingly new and insightful, creating great "maps" of previously uncharted "territory" like Susanne Langer's *Mind: An Essay on Human Feeling*.

Greater responsiveness to human situations—unvoiced and abstracted—may be somewhat more characteristic of woman *only* in consequence of the *absence* of the hormone and muscle tension that makes males aggressive. On the other hand, some investigators think there are real nervous system differences between men and women. Most women, however, are more likely to believe that sensitiveness and responsiveness are not necessarily positive, *feminine*, built-in characteristics, but qualities that are present in both sexes as part of the *human* endowment, but are covered up by tensions and aggressiveness in the male. The latter are reinforced socially and later become habitual. Possible innate female sensitivity is enhanced by women's experience of nurturing new life and of other *roles*—working and family—in which it is reinforced and deepened.

Apropos of biological differences, it is sometimes said that women are more emotional than men. It is more accurate to note that in our society it is not permitted to men to be as *expressive* of emotion. Women are permitted to be expressive in situations where men are not considered manly if they are expressive. Easy expression of feeling should not be assumed to correlate with intensity of feeling. Women are not necessarily more emotional than men; these things are individual. It may be that the habits of *repression* of feeling (which is masculine) and of imposing abstractions and fantasies on reality actually make men more "emotional." (Evidence exists in their fantasies, in their responsiveness to abstract stimuli for sex, in their preponderance in the crime and violence statistics.)

"Emotional behavior" by women may be related to frustration of their intelligence and capacities, to being put automatically in second place when they are capable of better. Women who work their way out of the second-place role tend not to have to be "emotional."

Granting the really minor differences between men and women, a question arises in the minds of both men and women as to why men have been permitted to dominate affairs for so long. There are several factors involved. First, most women know that the relationships are skewed, but they also know that men have been taught to relate their ego needs to their mythical superiority. Destroying the myths would be destructive of many men. Few women are willing to undertake a *destructive program* even for their own advantage. They know they themselves can readily make adjustment to reality. With their emotional affiliations to particular men, they cannot lightly countenance the possibility of damage to them. (This is not to say that in women's frustration and ambivalence toward the situation in which they find themselves they do not sometimes engage in destructive behavior. They do. But not with that avowed intent.)

Second, although most women perceive the masculine-imposed abstractions on the real world to be faulty, good new structures are not instantly available. In the meantime, it is extremely difficult to substitute for a dazzlingly simple structure (no matter how poorly it matches reality), a nonstructure, a set of ad hoc behaviors that cannot easily be taught or learned, but must be felt. Even discussion or argument about some male-made abstractions is difficult. As the semanticists would say, the formulations may be ultimately meaningless—not discussable.

The problems with the masculine imposition of not-necessarily-matching structure on the working world are all too evident. Economic theory is elaborated but quite often fails to be predictive, although that is its ostensible purpose. "Games" and "strategies" are pursued in business and politics, with immense waste of energy and loss of real purpose. Abstract structures are mistaken for reality, metastructures are imposed on the original abstractions. The whole male-dominated world shows symptoms of a progressive removal from the *real* world with its stubborn ad-hoc-ness and variability. The faulty abstractions aggressively imposed by men on the real world condition decision-making. The new nonverbal, reality-oriented "human potential" and "sensitivity training" movements suggest how urgently a counterbalance is needed.

WHERE DO WE GO FROM HERE?

The division of responsibility between men and women is beginning to right itself. Perhaps the recent progressive trivialization of women, in which a woman who could do effective work or even think was regarded as a freak, has run its course. The mere fact that a Gallup poll could question women recently as to whether they or men have a more "pleasant" life is a sign of change. The majority of women said that women have a more pleasant life. No one asked what has happened to their self-respect in accepting it.

It would be interesting to examine the death rates of men and women in societies in which work and responsibility are shared, comparing them with those in the United States, where women outlive men by seven or eight years. It seems probable that if the hazards of childbirth (which increase the death rate of young women in primitive societies) are not present, and work and responsibility are shared equally, the death rates should be more nearly equivalent.

Men die much earlier in industrial societies mainly because of undue stress. There are a number of factors involved in creating stress. One may be the unnecessary and excessive organization and routinization of work in modern society. This requires that men supplant their possibly more "natural" high-energy-output/relaxation cycle with sustained day-to-day routines that do not suit them as well. The other factor is the overload of responsibility they take on in most families.

Most married men take on the responsibility of earning most, if not all, of the family income. Where necessary, that may mean carrying *two* wage-earning jobs. Since most families are really economic arrangements, to which the money coming in is basic, this is an enormous responsibility. In addition, most men take on the responsibility for making major decisions about where to live, the kind of domicile, the kind of education for the children, the exterior and large-scale maintenance of housing and furnishings, as well as the care and repair of autos, dealings with government, and care of tax, legal, and financial matters. Women in such families do the shopping, take care of cleaning, cooking, laundry, children's errands, some bill-paying, and the social and cultural activities. They are generally under no time pressure. There is no demand that they politic in a hierarchical structure, waste time commuting, or live by the external pressures of the clock. They have reserved much of the very pleasant family business for themselves: the children, entertaining and cultural activity.

In families where married women work full-time (fewer than half), they usually carry a double burden of household activity and work, and the responsibility may be more nearly shared. But often these women are doing too much of the routine work which should *also* be shared.

The result of this inequity in most families is tremendous responsibility and stress for the man, not enough responsibility for the woman. He may be ambivalent about the results, however gratifying they are to his sense of masculinity and power. He may want or need some time off from the treadmill. He may be envious of his wife's time for reading, for museum-going, or for children. He may resent how she uses "his" money—as if she earned no part of her own maintenance, in baby-sitting, cleaning, cooking and shopping. He may actually feel that *he* works, and she spends. But he may also prefer to have it that way because he is thereby superior and she knows it.

Better arrangements can be made. If we define husband-and-wife as an equal partnership, then both should be expected to develop to their maximal potential at work and at home. In the partnership's domicile, maintenance activity should be shared. Housekeeping activities can easily be shared by two people on the basis of taste and time. If there are children they should learn that some of the maintenance chores are theirs. They should also be systematically taught as early as possible, how to fix simple meals for themselves, shop, use the phone, use public transportation, read a map, and pay attention to written messages directed to them as well as to record messages for other members of the family. In other words, they should be taught whatever adult competence they can learn.

Child care arrangements are far from ideal now, but Margaret Mead suggested many years ago that children raised with more than one adult reference point and with less tight one-to-one relationships with their parents tended to be less neurotic. Recent research by Stolz reported in *Child Development* magazine showed that children of employed mothers were likely to be neurotic only *one-third as often* as children of non-working mothers. The children in both studies were from intact homes. (Other studies have included the children of broken homes whose mothers were employed. The broken-home syndrome was a major factor in the report of neurosis in children of working mothers.)

It will take more than an equal assumption of responsibility by women to make a salutary change in working arrangements, as well as in economics and politics, but the assumption of decision-making power by women is indispensable to serious change.

It has been pointed out rather frequently in the past twenty years that industrial organization no longer requires the presence of large numbers of people in the same place at the same time. This was certainly the case in the primitive factories of the nineteenth century with their steam-powered machinery. With other sources of power such as electricity that are relatively easily disseminated, only certain process industries require centralization; others can be decentralized.

It is also the case that there is no particular rationale for a seven- or eight-hour day. Businesses and industries that arrange part-time schedules for their workers have found that they get *more* work per hour from part-timers, whose satisfactions in doing the job well are not dissipated by the requirement of spending the best part of their day on the spot. An examination of most jobs makes it clear that they are poorly planned on a management level, that most of them could be accomplished in less time. Part of the reason is that human energy and interest flag after a few hours, and the rest of the time on the job is devoted to fiddle-faddle for which the employer is paying. A rational working world would have people working on schedules they could choose for themselves in some measure, with employers paying for the fraction of the usual eight-hour day's work actually done in that period. Everyone would come out ahead—employer and employee—in terms of freedom, flexibility, and increased production.

This type of work scheduling, with increased sensitivity to human capacity, is something women understand very well. Attentiveness to human working rhythms could generate much greater productivity. I have had employees who could not get up in the morning, but could do a great job on a noon to 7 p.m. schedule. One young man worked best from midnight till 6 a.m. Why not?

With both members of the husband-and-wife team working sensible hours, neither of them need suffer the syndrome of being trapped in an economic rat race. Both could enjoy the freedom of thinking, reading, esthetic experiences, continuing education, and regular exercise. The tight family structure and land misuse that characterize the suburbs would go, in favor of more rational living arrangements near work (or more work at home) and better use of open land.

With equal partnership arrangements in families, another blow could be dealt to the rigid hierarchies that pass for organizational structure in most working places. Instead of bureaucratic pyramids with people walled into boxes in an organization chart, ad hoc structures could be developed for finite periods of time to do specific jobs. The resulting working flexibility and openness to new questions, problems, and activities would keep all human beings developing as individuals all their lives, making maximum personal and social use of potentials they scarcely know exist now.

Notes

1. B. Berelson and G. A. Steiner, *Human Behavior: An Inventory of Scientific Findings* (New York: Harcourt, Brace and World, 1964); M. F. Ashley-Montagu, *The Natural Superiority of Women* (New York: Macmillan, 1953).
2. J. J. Gallagher, "Sex Differences in Expressive Thought of Gifted Children," *Personnel and Guidance Journal* 140 (November 1966).

Psychological Androgyny and Positive Mental Health: A Biosocial Perspective

Jeanne Marecek

The re-examination of sex-role ideology has been a major focus of the Women's Liberation Movement. Our traditional concepts of masculinity and femininity have been sharply polarized, prescriptive, and highly differentiated. Feminists assert that such sex-role conceptions are limiting and potentially destructive. They argue instead for androgyny—an integration of masculine and feminine characteristics within each individual, coupled with an ideology that encourages the expression of both masculine and feminine behaviors, regardless of the sex of the individual actor. The purpose of this paper is to extend the inquiry into sex-role ideology by examining androgyny in light of the ongoing social-structural and biological changes in American society. Unlike other discussions of androgyny in the feminist literature, this one will be limited to the pragmatic: Does androgyny work? Do androgynous individuals benefit from their role orientation?

Traditional sex roles do not provide women and men with the optimal behavior repertoires for adapting to recent biosocial changes. Androgynous self-concepts are more suited to the life styles that Americans are now adopting and will continue to hold in the future. If this is the case, androgyny is an aspect of positive mental health and is an appropriate goal of psychotherapy.

The argument can be summarized as follows: (a) Androgynous individuals have a greater capacity for behaving in non-sex-typed, flexible, and situationally appropriate ways than do sex-typed individuals. (b) Current shifts in life expectancy, marriage and family

---

Presented in the symposium Applications of Androgyny to the Theory and Practice of Psychotherapy, American Psychological Association convention, Washington, D.C., September 1976. Used with permission of the author.

structures, and women's work involvement require individuals to be flexible, situationally adaptable, and non-sex-typed. (c) Therefore, androgynous individuals will adapt to contemporary life-style changes more successfully than sex-typed individuals.

This paper is organized to follow the line of reasoning outlined above. First, the theory of psychological androgyny and relevant research data will be reviewed. Evidence that androgynous individuals have broader behavioral repertoires than sex-typed individuals and data suggesting that androgynous individuals experience less conflict about the appropriateness of counter-stereotypic behavior will be presented, showing that we might expect androgynous individuals to adapt more successfully to new roles and to make transitions between roles with less accompanying stress. The second section will consider the biosocial changes that are altering the structure of contemporary American society, describe the role adaptations required by these changes, and speculate on the types of behaviors involved in these new roles and their relationship to psychological androgyny. Psychological androgyny will be presented as a possible necessary adaptation to the emerging social reality. The last section of the paper will draw the implications of this argument for psychotherapists.

PSYCHOLOGICAL ANDROGYNY

Traditional conceptions of ideal human beings draw a sharp dichotomy between male and female. Traits and behaviors deemed "masculine" are thought to be inappropriate or even pathological for women, and "feminine" qualities are regarded similarly for men. However, our everyday experiences belie this dichotomy. Even the most stereotypically feminine roles (e.g., child-caretaker, housewife) require liberal doses of such "masculine" traits as managerial abilities, initiative, assertion, and instrumentality. Stereotypically masculine roles such as scientist or executive are performed best by individuals who combine masculine qualities with grace and sensitivity in relating to others; who express emotions rather than suppressing them; and who are open to intuition as well as to analytical thought. Moreover, many individuals play a number of different roles in their adult lifetimes—roles that require a range of stereotypic and counterstereotypic traits. In addition, increasing numbers of individuals—especially women—hold roles that run directly counter to stereotypic role orientations.

Spokespersons for the Women's Movement have asserted that our traditional system of sex-role differentiation is outmoded and destructive; sex-typing is seen as preventing women and men from reaching their potential to be full human beings. In place of sex-differentiated conceptions of human nature, the Movement advocates "androgyny," the combination and integration of masculine and feminine modes of behaving and experiencing.

Androgynous individuals hold self-concepts that are independent of stereotypic concepts of maleness and femaleness. Their behavior reflects their openness to all elements of the human personality, regardless of whether they are conventionally viewed as same-sex or cross-sex (Bem, in press).

Research on the implications of psychological androgyny for individual behavior is in its infancy. The work of Bem and her colleagues (Bem, 1974) suggested that roughly one-third of college undergraduates score in the "androgynous" range of the Bem Sex-Role Inventory (reprinted in the Instruments section of this text). Further research demonstrated that androgynous individuals were less likely to avoid cross-sex behaviors than were sex-typed individuals; when required to perform cross-sex behaviors, the androgynous individuals did so with greater equanimity.

The most thorough of Bem's explorations into androgyny were made in the domains of nurturance and independence. By confronting subjects with targets selected to produce nurturance (e.g., a kitten, a baby, a miserable fellow undergraduate), the amount of nurturant behavior elicited could be observed. By placing individuals in situations resembling the Asch conformity paradigm, the frequency of responding counter to group norms could be measured. The results of these studies suggested that the androgynous individuals had the fewest behavioral inhibitions, with the sex-typed males second, and the sex-typed females making the poorest showing. The masculine-typed subjects were inhibited in their expressions of nurturance and emotional support, while the feminine-typed subjects were inhibited in their ability to stand firm in their opinions. In summary, the culturally-imposed definitions of masculinity and femininity carry the price of limiting individuals' behavior repertoires and of producing feelings of discomfort and conspicuousness when cross-sex behaviors are performed.

If research on androgyny and behavior is in its infancy, then research on androgyny and mental health is in utero or, possibly, not yet conceived. Yet, we might note that both masculine and feminine sex types, when carried to extremes, limit the individual's range of coping mechanisms and interfere with his or her ability to respond with flexibility to emerging situations. The "feminine" triad of passivity, dependency, and docility, when carried to an extreme, resembles the clinical syndromes of depression or passive personality disorders. The ego-centered, impulsive, aggressive masculine stereotype resembles the psychopath or sociopath.

BIOSOCIAL CHANGE

It is a well-worn cliché that the past decades have been years of extraordinary change. Like most clichés, it is true. Changes have occurred in technological development, in cultural values, in social institutions, and in individual behavior. Some of the changes that have a direct impact on the roles that women and men play and the behavioral options they have in playing those roles are covered in this section.

It might be helpful at the outset to remind ourselves of two attributes of the changes to be described. First, change is ongoing; we live in a dynamic society, not a static one, which means that we cannot predict with certainty what situations will be prevalent in the future. Although we can analyze trends and thus make educated guesses about the direction of change in the future, we cannot foretell when trends will level off or reverse themselves.[1] Second, the changes mentioned here are already taking place. The situations that we describe already exist and the life styles they entail are already embraced by many individuals.

Life Spans and Life Cycles

Perhaps the most fundamental change in recent decades is the gradual extension of the average life span and the shifts in the lengths of various stages in the life cycle. The average life expectancy in the United States is currently seventy-six years for women and sixty-eight years for men—half again as many years as the average life expectancy at the turn of the century.

 This decline in mortality has implications for many of our major social institutions. For example, it is now the norm for women to spend the latter years of their lives as widows, for individuals to have several years of life remaining after their children have departed from the household, and for men and women to survive beyond the

---

[1]Of course, the effects of certain trends may persist for a generation or more and can be predicted. For example, the "baby boom" of the mid-forties has (predictably) led to a disproportionate abundance of people in their thirties at the present time and will produce a swell in the ranks of the aged in the early years of the next century.

period of productive employment and to spend a number of years in retirement. Each of these changes must be addressed on an institutional level and on a personal level. It is important to have legislation ensuring that widows will have adequate old-age incomes, allocating community resources for the purposes of enriching the retirement period, and providing housing suitable for childless couples. It is also important that individuals themselves adapt their behavior and attitudes to these life circumstances. Changes in sex-role orientation are one kind of adaptation. Let us now consider the sex-role orientations that seem most compatible with life circumstances in contemporary U.S. society.

The "Empty Nest"

First, feminine sex-role orientations that focus on homemaking and child rearing exclusively are too narrow for the modern woman, who will have between twenty and thirty years of life after her offspring have left the household. Bart's studies of women suffering from depressive disorders suggest that women who have singlemindedly pursued a home-and-child-centered life style risk apathy, feelings of inadequacy and worthlessness, and depression when their children move into adulthood (Bart, 1971). At the present time, the majority of women obtain paid employment during this period of the life cycle and their work involvement may protect them from feelings of uselessness, loss, and emptiness. It seems that an androgynous sex-role orientation would better suit this life pattern than a stereotyped sex-role orientation. The androgynous woman would have the flexibility to make the transition from a home-centered life style to a work-centered life style. Her value orientation would allow her occupational involvement to be meaningful and self-satisfying. The departure of her children would not signify the loss of her own raison d'etre.

Widowhood

Few women contemplate widowhood before it happens, and even fewer choose to actively prepare for it while their spouses are alive and healthy. Nonetheless, the number of women who will experience widowhood is overwhelming and remarriage is not always desired or easily accomplished. The sources of psychological stress on widows are numerous. Widows have been overlooked by social planners, legislators, and mental-health caregivers. Hence, the personal stresses of bereavement are compounded by social and economic stresses.

Sex-typed self-conceptions can also jeopardize women's ability to adapt to widowhood. Women who have histories of roles completely complementary to their husbands will find the loss of their spouses difficult to cope with on pragmatic as well as emotional levels. Women who are inhibited in performing nonstereotypic behaviors will have to break down those inhibitions before they can function adequately as single persons. On the other hand, women with androgynous sex-role orientations may accommodate to the role of widow with greater ease. Although the pain of the loss of a spouse will be no less intense, androgynous women may have fewer behavioral adjustments to make in order to carry on a single life style. The stresses of modifying the self-concept and learning new and uncomfortable behaviors will not be added to the grief of losing a spouse.

Retirement

Increased longevity has made retirement a significant life stage. Greater numbers of individuals live to enjoy retirement and also spend more years as retirees; a disproportionately large segment of the population will be retired in the early years of the next century. Decreased mortality is not the only factor influencing retirement. Shifts in the economy and the size of the labor pool are placing downward pressures on the age of retirement. Some of us may have the option of retiring, with full benefits, as young as fifty-five.

In theory, retirement is a reward for years of employment, a reprieve from the responsibilities of parenthood and a period to indulge in interests and activities precluded by previous life styles. However, theory is not necessarily reality. Retired men often report difficulties in shifting from a competitive, hard-driving, high-pressured life style to a relaxed, pleasure-centered life style. Some women find it difficult to make the transition from preoccupation with the family's needs and wishes to a focus on themselves without experiencing guilt and feelings of worthlessness. Because men commonly are married to women somewhat younger than they are, there is often a discrepancy in the time of retirement. This may mean that the husband postpones his retirement plans while the wife continues working, an arrangement which can be a source of stress for their marriage.

Many of the problems of retirement are enmeshed in a larger matrix of cultural values regarding work, self-sacrifice, and so on. However, the fact that men and women struggle over different issues in adapting to retirement suggests that sex-role beliefs are also relevant. Do androgynous individuals face retirement with greater equanimity than sex-typed individuals? There is no empirical evidence on this question. However, androgynous men who are more open to the pleasures of such "feminine" interests as caring for grandchildren, participating in culture and the arts, and enjoying close personal relationships in addition to more conventionally "masculine" activities may find retirement more stimulating than stereotypically "masculine" men. Similarly, if androgynous women enjoy such "masculine" activities as competitive athletics in addition to their "feminine" interests, they may spend their retirement years in a more diversified and stimulating way than sex-typed women do.

Labor-Force Participation

Even more dramatic than the changes in life span are the shifts in women's labor-force participation since World War II. The number of mothers in the United States who also hold paid jobs outside the home has more than doubled in the past two decades. If the present trend continues, by 1980 the majority of mothers will hold outside jobs in addition to their family responsibilities. As women accept this dual role responsibility, there are adjustments to be made by members of their families. Their husbands will be required to share more equitably in the responsibilities of child care and housework.[2] We might also expect that women who work will exert more bargaining power within their marriages than their unemployed counterparts do. For many women, entry into the labor force means that some of the household and child-care functions previously in their purview are now purchased from nonfamily members (or assigned to extended-family members).

The reorganization of the household that has accompanied women's entry into the labor force had already engendered shifts away from traditional sex-role conceptions. When both wife and husband participate in paid work and home responsibilities, the polarities on which traditional sex-role conceptions rest are minimized. In addition, power in the marriage tends to be distributed more equally, with husbands relinquishing some control and

---

[2]Evidence to date suggests that this reallocation of labor has not yet taken place. Women in the labor force continue to shoulder most home responsibilities. However, as dual roles for women become more prevalent and socially acceptable, wives may begin pressuring their husbands for redistribution of home responsibilities. At the present time, residual guilt and the weight of family traditions have slowed the inevitable changes in family structure.

primacy within the home and wives gaining some. Finally, the very fact of a woman's paid employment challenges the traditional sex-role dichotomy. The view of husbands as protectors and providers of the household loses credence when wives share in providing income and support for their families. The traditional view of wives is belied by the working wife who has nonfamily commitments, has her own schedules, and draws personal gratification from her work as well as her family. Androgyny—a state in which the individual feels free to develop and express both cross-sex and same-sex potential—is a byproduct of these changes in women's labor-force participation.

Marriage, Divorce, and Fertility

A third set of demographic facts can be brought to bear on the question of androgyny. These concern the rates and timing of marriages, childbirth, and divorce in the United States. Unfortunately, demographic statistics are often reported in aggregate forms that can obscure patterns of individual behavior. For example, reports of overall trends may be misleading because the trends are composites of several age cohorts and socioeconomic groups that exhibit divergent patterns of behavior. Nonetheless, some general inferences can be drawn from the statistics.

Let us consider marriage statistics first. In recent years, the average age of brides marrying for the first time has been rising slightly. Although the rise itself is inconsequential, it is interesting to consider some of the factors associated with the rise. First, women quite frequently postpone marriage until their education is completed. Recent years have seen a great rise in the number of women going to college and beyond. We might surmise that women who have completed college prior to marrying will be more committed to working while married and more likely to take an active role in planning and limiting their families. A second recent trend is the dramatic increase in the number of never-married women in their late twenties and early thirties. In general, these women are well educated and working in professional occupations. A third relevant trend is that the number of women who live "on their own" (that is, not in their parents' house) prior to marrying has also climbed rapidly in recent years.

These trends suggest that certain groups of women will have been exposed to the liberalizing influences of education and an independent life style prior to getting married. In addition, these women may have a stronger sense of their identity as individuals—an identity that will be maintained throughout their marriages. Experience in the labor force or in higher education tends to discourage exaggerated femininity and encourage androgyny. Carrying out the role of employee or student requires intellectual discipline, initiative, assertion, and other qualities conventionally regarded as masculine. Thus, by postponing marriage in favor of employment or education, young women are likely to develop more androgynous self-concepts and behavior repertoires. In addition, they are likely to establish self-identities that are compatible with androgynous role choices throughout their adult lives.

Very little needs to be said about the recent precipitous decline in birth rates in the United States. All social scientists are aware of it, and there are as many explanations for it as there are demographers. Fortunately, we do not need to be concerned about its causes, which in any event are probably numerous. Its effects interact with other social changes taking place. For instance, the fewer children a woman has, the shorter will be the time period in which child care is a major focus in her life. Although the necessity of developing child-care skills remains important, the necessity of developing other skills to be used in other pursuits is of parallel importance. A college-educated woman who bears two children prior to age thirty may well return to the labor force by the time she reaches her late thirties; she can look forward to twenty to twenty-five years of paid employment.

As family size shrinks, the role of child rearing in women's lives becomes correspondingly more limited. This means that a self-conception centered around motherhood will be discordant with women's actual life styles. An androgynous self-conception, in which child raising is one of a number of things a woman does—rather than a definition of who she is—is more in keeping with current preferences for family size.

A final demographic trend that is quite distinct in the United States is the rise in the rate of divorce. In 1964, the ratio of divorces to new marriages was one to four; in 1974, the rate was one divorce for every 2.3 marriages. Some theorists (Bernard, 1972) predict that the divorce trend will continue to rise to a point where half of U.S. marriages end in divorce. Persons at added risk for divorce are members of low socioeconomic groups, couples who married young, and individuals with previous divorce histories.

One of the most important repercussions of rising divorce rates is the rise in the number of single parents. Currently, the vast majority of single parents are women, although this may not remain true in the future. The single individual who raises children, manages a household, and bears the burden of financial support for the family is forced by circumstance into an androgynous role. She must singly carry out the responsibilities normally fulfilled by a husband-wife team.[3]

The stresses of being a single parent can be severe. Sheer lack of financial resources and adjusting to the radical changes in life style brought on by the abrupt financial reversal, as well as conflict and guilt brought on by role incompatibility, are sources of great stress. There may be no stress-free way in which a single individual can fulfill the roles that society normally allocates to two individuals without developing alternative social structures and support networks. However, the individual who is androgynous will have a better basis for meeting the demands of both masculine and feminine roles than will the individual who is sex typed. Although it may always require a balancing act to juggle the many demands of the single-parent role, the balancing act will be more successful if the actor has the personal capacity to play each of the roles involved without engendering anxiety, excessive self-doubt, or discomfort.

Summary

Several important demographic trends in U.S. society have been described. We have been concerned with their net effect on the distribution of roles and behaviors between women and men. Taken as a whole, these trends seem to portend two changes in sex roles: (1) the roles that women and men play will be less rigidly determined by their sex than they once were; and (2) individuals—both women and men—can be expected to hold more roles and a greater diversity of roles than was previously the case. Both these factors argue in favor of androgyny.

PSYCHOLOGICAL ANDROGYNY, MENTAL HEALTH, AND PSYCHOTHERAPY

Still to be discussed are the connection between androgyny and mental health and the implications of this connection for psychotherapy.

It is notoriously difficult to formulate definitions of positive mental health that transcend one's cultural background and values. However, Western conceptions of mental health commonly include such qualities as flexibility and the ability to accept change; personal

---

[3]Statistics on the number of men who regularly make child-support payments to their ex-wives show that this is not a responsibility that is faithfully fulfilled.

integration and balance; the absence of extreme behavior or rigidity; a self-conception that is in accord with the reality of one's behavior and the environment; and the ability to adapt to a variety of circumstances.

Any model of mental health must be interpreted according to the social conditions at the time. I have tried to show that contemporary U.S. social conditions favor androgyny. Sex roles have become much less polarized than conventional stereotypes would have them. The life events that both men and women are likely to face require a more androgynous perspective than the life events of the past. Many of the recent sociocultural changes require flexibility and adaptiveness in sex-role behavior. What was once regarded as appropriate behavior for men and women is no longer best suited to the reality of their lives. Thus, sex-role flexibility, a balanced self-conception integrating both the "masculine" and "feminine" aspects of the self and an openness to the reality of sex-role diversity are qualities of positive mental health in today's society.

Models of mental health bear directly on therapists' work with clients. Notions about what people ought to be like—both notions that are articulated and those that are not—shape therapists' interventions with clients, their judgments about clients, and their recommendations for treatment. A therapist whose definition of mental health embodies different qualities for men and for women may be operating in terms of a social reality that no longer exists. Much of the current wave of dissatisfaction with psychotherapy revolves around this issue. For example, women clients complain that therapists label counterstereotypic behaviors as regressive or immature; that their therapists seem disinterested in everyday problems, preferring to focus on childhood experiences; and that therapists seem more concerned about the happiness and satisfaction of the client's husband or boyfriend than those of the client herself. The rapidity of social change regarding sex roles seems to have temporarily surpassed some therapists' ability to modify their attitudes and therapeutic practices.

Androgynous models of mental health reflect the social changes that are taking place and the social reality of many clients' lives. However, individuals who hold androgynous self-conceptions will also impel further changes in our definitions of male and female and our allocation of roles to women and men. Thus, the therapist who uses an androgynous model of mental health is, effectively, an agent of social change. Clients who formulate androgynous self-conceptions can become agents of social change in their families and their social environments. It has been argued that therapists should steer clear of sociopolitical stances in the process of doing therapy. However, I would argue that the therapeutic role cannot be carried out in a neutral, value-free way, because it always involves making judgments about another person's behavior. Seen in this perspective, the therapist is a change agent, whether he or she espouses an androgynous model of mental health or a sex-typed one. Change in the direction of androgyny may be seen as a positive, future-oriented, and humanistic goal of psychotherapy.

REFERENCES

Bart, P. B. Depression in middle-aged women. In V. Gornick & B. K. Moran (Eds.), *Woman in sexist society*. New York: Basic, 1971.

Bem, S. L. The measurement of psychological androgyny. *Journal of Consulting and Clinical Psychology*, 1974, *24*(2), 155-162.

Bem, S. L. Beyond androgyny: Some presumptuous prescriptions for a liberated sexual identity. In J. Sherman & F. Denmark (Eds.), *Psychology of women: Future directions of research*. New York: Psychological Dimensions, in press.

Bernard, J. *The future of marriage*. New York: World, 1972.

Beyond Androgyny:
Some Presumptuous Prescriptions for a Liberated Sexual Identity[1]

Sandra Lipsitz Bem

This article attempts to develop a conception of mental health which is free from culturally imposed definitions of masculinity and femininity. Bem's recent research on psychological androgyny is discussed in detail, and serious questions are raised about the traditional conception of sexual identity and its centrality in the definition of the healthy personality.

Traditionally, the ideal or healthy personality has included a concept of sexual identity with three basic components: (1) a sexual preference for members of the opposite sex; (2) a sex-role identity as either masculine or feminine, depending upon one's gender; and (3) a gender identity, a secure sense of one's maleness or femaleness. In this article, each of these components is discussed in turn, and particular emphasis is placed on the concept of sex-role identity. With respect to the first component, that of sexual orientation, it is argued that one's sexual preferences ought ultimately to be considered orthogonal to any concept of mental health or ideal personality. With respect to the second component, that of sex-role identity, it is argued that masculinity and femininity represent complementary domains of positive traits and behaviors, and that it is therefore possible, in principle, for an individual to be both masculine and feminine, both instrumental and expressive, both agentic and communal, depending upon the situational appropriateness of these various modalities. Moreover, it is argued that for fully effective and healthy human functioning, masculinity and femininity must each be tempered by the other,

---

[1]The research described in this article was supported by National Institute of Mental Health Grant 5 RO1MH 21735 to Sandra L. Bem.

Keynote Address for APA-NIMH Conference on the Research Needs of Women, Madison, Wisconsin, May 31, 1975. Reprinted from an earlier draft written for Julia A. Sherman and Florence L. Denmark, editors, THE PSYCHOLOGY OF WOMEN: FUTURE DIRECTIONS IN RESEARCH, Psychological Dimensions, Inc., 1977. A much abbreviated version of this paper was presented at APA in Chicago, 1975, under the title "Androgyny and Mental Health." Used with permission of the publisher, author, and American Psychological Association.

and the two must be integrated into a more balanced, a more fully human, a truly androgynous personality. Finally, with respect to the third component, that of gender identity, it is argued that a healthy sense of maleness or femaleness becomes possible precisely when the artificial constraints of gender are eliminated and when one is finally free to be one's own unique blend of temperament and behavior.

I consider myself an empirical scientist, and yet my interest in sex roles is and has always been frankly political. My hypotheses have derived from no formal theory, but rather from a set of strong intuitions about the debilitating effects of sex-role stereotyping, and my major purpose has always been a feminist one: to help free the human personality from the restricting prison of sex-role stereotyping and to develop a conception of mental health which is free from culturally imposed definitions of masculinity and femininity.

But political passion does not persuade and, unless one is a novelist or a poet, one's intuitions are not typically compelling to others. Thus, because I *am* an empirical scientist, I have chosen to utilize the only legitimated medium of persuasion which is available to me: the medium of empirical data. What I should like to do in this paper is to summarize the data on psychological androgyny that we have collected over the last four years, and, in addition, to utilize the congenial setting of this conference to raise even deeper questions about the traditional conception of sexual identity and its centrality in the definition of the healthy personality, questions which go well beyond my current data.

The ideal or healthy personality has traditionally included a concept of sexual identity with three basic components: (1) a sexual preference for members of the opposite sex; (2) a sex-role identity as either masculine or feminine, depending upon one's gender; and (3) a gender identity, i.e., a secure sense of one's maleness or femaleness (c.f., Green, 1974). I should like to comment in this paper on each of these three components in turn.

SEXUAL PREFERENCE

With respect to the first component, that of sexual preference, my remarks can be brief. Let me simply assert, along with the proponents of gay liberation and the recently enlightened American Psychiatric Association, that one's sexual preferences ought ultimately to be considered orthogonal to any concept of mental health or ideal personality. Let us begin to use the terms "homosexual" and "heterosexual" to describe acts rather than persons and to entertain the possibility that compulsive exclusivity in one's sexual responsiveness, whether homosexual or heterosexual, may be the product of a repressive society which forces us to label ourselves as one or the other.

SEX-ROLE IDENTITY

I turn now to the concept of sex-role identity, a concept which has traditionally been conceptualized in terms of masculinity and femininity. Both historically and cross-culturally, masculinity and femininity have represented complementary domains of positive traits and behaviors. Different theorists have different labels for these domains. According to Parsons (Parsons & Bales, 1955), masculinity has been associated with an instrumental orientation, a cognitive focus on getting the job done or the problem solved, whereas femininity has been associated with an expressive orientation, an affective concern for the welfare of others and the harmony of the group. Similarly, Bakan (1966) has suggested that masculinity is associated with an "agentic" orientation, a concern for oneself as an individual, whereas femininity is associated with a "communal" orientation, a concern for the relationship between oneself and others. Finally, Erikson's (1964) anatomical distinction between "inner" (female) and "outer" (male) space represents an analogue to a quite similar psychological distinction between a masculine "fondness for what works and for what man can make, whether it helps to build or to destroy" and a more "ethical" feminine commitment to "resourcefulness in peacekeeping and devotion in healing."

My own research has focused on the concept of psychological androgyny. As such, it has been predicated on the assumption that it is possible, in principle, for an individual to be both masculine and feminine, both instrumental and expressive, both agentic and communal, depending upon the situational appropriateness of these various modalities; and even for an individual to blend these complementary modalities in a single act, being able, for example, to fire an employee if the circumstances warrant it, but to do so with sensitivity for the human emotion that such an act inevitably produces.

The possibility that a single individual can embody both masculinity and femininity has, of course, been expressed by others as well. Jung (1953) described the anima and animus which he believed to be present in us all, and more recently, Bakan (1966) has argued that viability—both for the individual and for society—depends on the successful integration of both agency and communion. Moreover, the concept of androgyny itself can now be found not only in the psychological literature (e.g., Berzins & Welling, 1974; Block, 1973; Pleck, 1975; Spence, Helmreich, & Stapp, 1975), but in the literature of other disciplines as well (e.g., Bazin & Freeman, 1974; Gelpi, 1974; Harris, 1974; Heilbrun, 1964; Secor, 1974; Stimpson, 1974).

And yet, although I believe that it is *possible* for people to be both masculine and feminine, I also believe that traditional sex roles prevent this possibility from ever becoming a reality for many individuals. Over the last few years, the Women's Liberation Movement has made us all aware of the many ways that we, both men and women, have become locked into our respective sex roles. As women, we have become aware of the fact that we are afraid to express our anger, to assert our preferences, to trust our own judgment, to take control of situations. As men, we have become aware of the fact that we are afraid to cry, to touch one another, to own up to our fears and weaknesses.

But there have been very little data within psychology to give legitimacy to these experiential truths. In many ways, my goal over the last few years has been to gather some of that legitimizing data, to try to demonstrate that traditional sex roles do restrict behavior in important human ways.

Although there is no previous research which bears on this hypothesis directly, a review of the relevant literature nevertheless corroborates our underlying assumption that a high level of sex-typing may not be desirable. For example, high femininity in females has consistently been correlated with high anxiety, low self-esteem, and low social acceptance (e.g., Cosentino & Heilbrun, 1964; Gall, 1969; Gray, 1957; Sears, 1970; Webb, 1963); and, although high masculinity in males has been correlated during adolescence with better psychological adjustment (Mussen, 1961), it has been correlated during adulthood with high anxiety, high neuroticism, and low self-acceptance (Hartford et al., 1967; Mussen, 1962). In addition, greater intellectual development has been correlated quite consistently with cross sex-typing, i.e., with masculinity in girls and with femininity in boys. Boys and girls who are more sex-typed have been found to have lower overall intelligence, lower spatial ability, and lower creativity (Maccoby, 1966).

The point, of course, is that the two domains of masculinity and femininity are both fundamental. In a modern complex society like ours, an adult clearly has to be able to look out for himself and to get things done. But an adult also has to be able to relate to other human beings as people, to be sensitive to their needs and to be concerned about their welfare, as well as to be able to depend on them for emotional support. Limiting a person's ability to respond in one or the other of these two complementary domains thus seems tragically and unnecessarily destructive of human potential.

In addition, it would also seem to be the case that masculinity and femininity may each become negative and even destructive when they are represented in extreme and unadulterated form. Thus, extreme femininity, untempered by a sufficient concern for one's own needs as an individual, may produce dependency and self-denial, just as extreme masculinity, untempered by a sufficient concern for the needs of others, may produce arrogance and exploitation. As Bakan (1966) has put it, the fundamental task of every organism is to "try to mitigate agency with communion." Thus, for fully effective and healthy human functioning, both masculinity and femininity must each be tempered by the other, and the two must be integrated into a more balanced, a more fully human, a truly androgynous personality. An androgynous personality would thus represent the very best of what masculinity and femininity have each come to represent, and the more negative exaggerations of masculinity and femininity would tend to be cancelled out.

The Bem Sex-Role Inventory

With this model of perfection in mind, I then moved to the more mundane task of trying to bring the concept of androgyny down to empirical reality. I began by constructing the Bem Sex-Role Inventory (or BSRI), a paper-and-pencil instrument which permits us to distinguish androgynous individuals from those with more sex-typed self concepts.

Unlike most previous masculinity-femininity scales, the BSRI treats masculinity and femininity as two orthogonal dimensions rather than as two ends of a single dimension (see Constantinople, 1974, for a critique of previous sex-role inventories). Moreover, masculinity and femininity each represent *positive* domains of behavior. Too often femininity has been defined simply as the absence of masculinity rather than as a positive dimension in its own right, a practice which may itself be partially responsible for the negative picture of the feminine woman which emerges in the psychological literature. For once, I wanted to give the feminine woman an equal chance to be no "sicker" than anyone else.

Specifically, the BSRI consists of twenty masculine personality characteristics (e.g., ambitious, self-reliant, independent, assertive) and twenty feminine personality characteristics (e.g., affectionate, gentle, understanding, sensitive to the needs of others). I chose the particular characteristics that I did because they were all rated by both males and females as being significantly more desirable in American society for one sex than for the other. The BSRI also contains twenty neutral characteristics (e.g., truthful, happy, conceited, unsystematic) which serve as filler items. All sixty characteristics are shown in Table 1.[2]

When taking the BSRI, a person is asked to indicate on a scale from 1 ("Never or almost never true") to 7 ("Always or almost always true") how well each characteristic describes himself or herself. The degree of sex-role stereotyping in the person's self concept is then defined as Student's t-ratio for the difference between the total points assigned to the feminine and masculine attributes, respectively. We use the t-ratio rather than a simple difference score primarily because it allows us to ask whether a person's masculinity and femininity scores differ significantly from one another, and if they do ($t \geq 2.025$, $p < .05$), to characterize that person as significantly sex-typed or sex-reversed. Thus, if a person's masculinity score is significantly higher than his or her femininity score, that person is said to have a masculine sex role, and if a person's femininity score is significantly higher than his or her masculinity score, that person is said to have a feminine sex role. In contrast, if a person's masculinity and femininity scores are approximately equal ($t \leq 1$, n.s.), that person is said to have an androgynous sex role. An androgynous sex role thus represents the equal endorsement of both masculine and feminine personality characteristics, a balance, as it were, between masculinity and femininity. Normative data on a sample of over 2000 undergraduates from both a university and a community college indicate that approximately one-third of both popu-

---

[2]In attempting to balance the overall social desirability of the masculine and feminine adjectives, I was surprised to discover that many feminine adjectives were judged to be more socially desirable "for a woman" than were any masculine adjectives "for a man." This would seem to contradict the frequently reported finding in the literature that masculine attributes are more socially desirable than feminine ones. It should be noted, however, that my judges rated the social desirability of each adjective as it applied to a particular sex. In the absence of such specification, perhaps judges implicitly picture a male and make their judgments accordingly, thereby lowering the desirability of all feminine attributes. In order to equate the overall social desirability of the feminine and masculine adjectives, I was therefore forced to include a few feminine adjectives which were somewhat lower in social desirability (e.g., gullible), and thereby to increase somewhat the variance of the social desirability ratings within the set of feminine adjectives.

lations can be classified as significantly sex-typed, and another third as androgynous. Fewer than 10% can be classified as sex-reversed.[3]

Psychometric analyses on the BSRI indicate that it is quite satisfactory as a measuring instrument (Bem, 1974). As anticipated, the Masculinity and Femininity scores turned out to be empirically as well as conceptually independent (average $r = -.03$), thereby vindicating our decision to design an inventory that would not treat masculinity and femininity as two ends of a single dimension. Moreover, the t-ratio itself is internally consistent (average $\alpha = .86$), reliable over a four-week interval (average $r = .93$), and uncorrelated with the tendency to describe oneself in a socially desirable direction (average $r = -.06$).

The Avoidance of Cross-Sex Behavior

Once the BSRI was in hand, we were then in a position to ask whether traditional sex roles actually do lead some people to restrict their behavior in accordance with sex-role stereotypes. Specifically, do masculine men and feminine women actively avoid activities just because those activities happen to be stereotyped as more appropriate for the other sex; and, if they have to perform cross-sex activity for some reason, does it cause them discomfort to do so? In other

---

[3] As Spence, Helmreich, and Stapp (1975) and Strahan (1975) have pointed out, this definition of androgyny serves to obscure what could be a potentially important distinction between those individuals who score high in both masculinity and femininity, and those individuals who score low in both. Accordingly, Spence, Helmreich, and Stapp (1975) recommend dividing subjects at the median on both the masculinity and the femininity scales and then deriving a *fourfold* classification of subjects as either masculine (high masculine-low feminine), feminine (high feminine-low masculine), androgynous (high masculine-high feminine), or undifferentiated (low masculine-low feminine). In an attempt to clarify whether one or the other of these two definitions of psychological androgyny was likely to have greater utility for future research, we administered the BSRI along with a variety of other paper-and-pencil questionnaires, and we also reanalyzed the results of our laboratory studies with the low-low scorers separated out. On the basis of the available evidence, I now believe that a distinction between high-high and low-low scorers does seem to be warranted, that the term "androgynous" ought to be reserved only for those individuals who score high in both masculinity and femininity, and that the BSRI ought henceforth to be scored so as to yield four distinct groups of masculine, feminine, androgynous, and undifferentiated subjects. See the articles by Bem (under editorial review) and Bem, Martyna, and Watson (under editorial review) for a full discussion of this issue. It should be noted, however, that this change in scoring only serves to strengthen the findings reported in this article.

words, is cross-sex behavior motivationally problematic for the sex-typed individual, or would he or she be perfectly willing to engage in such behavior if the situation were structured to encourage it?

In order to find out, Ellen Lenney and I designed a study in which many of the more obvious external barriers to cross-sex behavior had been removed (Bem & Lenney, in press). Thus, both masculine and feminine activities were explicitly available to all the subjects; it was made clear that we did not care how well they could

---

Table 1. The Masculine, Feminine, and Neutral Items on the BSRI

Masculine items	Feminine items	Neutral items
49. Acts as a leader	11. Affectionate	51. Adaptable
46. Aggressive	5. Cheerful	36. Conceited
58. Ambitious	50. Childlike	9. Conscientious
22. Analytical	32. Compassionate	60. Conventional
13. Assertive	53. Does not use harsh language	45. Friendly
10. Athletic	35. Eager to soothe hurt feelings	15. Happy
55. Competitive	20. Feminine	3. Helpful
4. Defends own beliefs	14. Flatterable	48. Inefficient
37. Dominant	59. Gentle	24. Jealous
19. Forceful	47. Gullible	39. Likable
25. Has leadership abilities	56. Loves children	6. Moody
7. Independent	17. Loyal	21. Reliable
52. Individualistic	26. Sensitive to the needs of others	30. Secretive
31. Makes decisions easily	8. Shy	33. Sincere
40. Masculine	38. Soft spoken	42. Solemn
1. Self-reliant	23. Sympathetic	57. Tactful
34. Self-sufficient	44. Tender	12. Theatrical
16. Strong personality	29. Understanding	27. Truthful
43. Willing to take a stand	41. Warm	18. Unpredictable
28. Willing to take risks	2. Yielding	54. Unsystematic

Note: The number preceding each item reflects the position of each adjective as it actually appears on the Inventory. A subject indicates how well each item describes himself or herself on the following scale: (1) Never or almost never true; (2) Usually not true; (3) Sometimes but infrequently true; (4) Occasionally true; (5) Often true; (6) Usually true; (7) Always or almost always true.

do each activity or, indeed, if they had ever done the activity before; and the less sex-appropriate activities were always the more highly rewarded.

Subjects were told that we were preparing to do a study to find out whether people make different personality judgments about an individual as a function of the particular activity that he or she happens to be seen performing, and that we therefore needed pictures of the same person performing many different activities. The activities were arranged in pairs, and subjects were asked to select the one activity from each pair that they would prefer to perform during the photography session which was to follow. For example, one pair asked female subjects whether they would rather "prepare a baby bottle by mixing powdered formula with milk" for 2¢, or "oil squeaky hinges on a metal box" for 4¢. Although it was not made explicit, twenty of the activities were stereotypically masculine (e.g., "Nail two boards together"; "Attach artificial bait to a fishing hook"), twenty were stereotypically feminine (e.g., "Iron cloth napkins"; "Wind a package of yarn into a ball"), and twenty were stereotypically neutral (e.g., "Play with a yo-yo"; "Peel oranges").

Of the thirty pairs, fifteen required the subject to choose between activities which differed in their sex-role connotations. Of these, five pitted neutral activities against masculine ones, five pitted neutral activities against feminine ones, and five pitted masculine and feminine activities against each other. In all of the sex-role conflict pairs, however, it was the less sex-appropriate activity which always paid more. In the remaining fifteen pairs, both activities were either masculine, feminine, or neutral, and one activity was arbitrarily assigned to be the higher paying. These control pairs served primarily as a baseline measure of each subject's responsiveness to the differences in payment, and they also guaranteed that a minimum number of masculine, feminine, and neutral activities would be chosen by every subject.

In an attempt to get the purest possible measure of preference, unconfounded by the effects of competence at or familiarity with the various activities, great care was taken to assure the subjects that we were not at all interested in how well they could perform each activity or, indeed, if they had ever done the activity before. For example, they were explicitly told that they would be given only one or two minutes for each activity, not necessarily enough time for the activity to be completed, and that all we really wanted was for them to become sufficiently involved in each activity for a convincing photograph to be taken. They were also assured that simple written instructions would be available for each of the activities that they selected. In addition, in order to prevent subjects from becoming overly self-conscious about how their pictures would look, they were also assured that the later study would be done at a different university and that no one they knew would ever be likely to see their pictures. Finally, no emphasis whatever was placed on having the pictures reflect the "true" personality of the individual subject. If anything, what was implied was that we needed each subject to perform as wide a variety of different kinds of activities as possible.

As anticipated, the results indicated that sex-typed subjects were significantly more stereotyped in their choices than androgynous or sex-reversed subjects, who did not differ significantly from one another. In other words, the masculine man and the feminine woman were significantly more likely to select their own sex's activities and to reject the other sex's activities, even though such choices cost them money and even though we tried to make it as easy as we could for the subject to select cross-sex activity.

In order to find out whether sex-typed subjects would also experience greater discomfort if they had no choice but to perform cross-sex activity, the subjects then proceeded to perform three masculine, three feminine, and three neutral activities while the experimenter pretended to photograph them, and they indicated how they felt after each activity on a series of rating scales. Specifically, subjects indicated on a seven-point scale how "masculine" (for males) or "feminine" (for females), how "attractive," how "likeable," how "nervous," and how "peculiar" they had felt while performing each activity. They also indicated how much they had enjoyed each activity.

The results indicated that sex-typed subjects felt significantly worse than androgynous or sex-reversed subjects who, again, did not differ significantly from one another. That is, it was the masculine men and the feminine women who experienced the most discomfort and who felt the worst about themselves after performing cross-sex activities. Thus, it would appear that cross-sex activity is problematic for sex-typed individuals, and that traditional sex roles do produce an unnecessary and perhaps even dysfunctional pattern of avoidance for many people.

Armed with this demonstration that sex-role stereotyping restricts simple, everyday behaviors, we can now inquire into whether such stereotyping also constricts the individual in more profound domains as well. Is the masculine male low in expressiveness and communion? Is the feminine female low in instrumentality and agency? It is to these broader questions that the bulk of my research has been addressed, and it is to these that we now turn.

Independence and Nurturance

We began by designing a pair of studies on independence and nurturance (Bem, 1975). The first was designed to tap the "masculine" domain of independence. It utilized a standard conformity paradigm to test the hypothesis that masculine and androgynous subjects would both remain more independent from social pressure than feminine subjects. The second study was designed to tap the "feminine" domain of nurturance. By offering subjects the opportunity to interact with a tiny kitten, it tested the hypothesis that feminine and androgynous subjects would both be more nurturant or playful than masculine subjects. Taken together, these two studies offer one test of the hypothesis that non-androgynous subjects would "do well" only when the situation calls for behavior which is congruent with their self-definition as masculine or feminine, whereas androgynous subjects would "do well" regardless of the sex-role stereotype of the particular behavior in question. That is, they would perform as high as masculine subjects on the masculine task, and they would perform as high as feminine subjects on the feminine task.

In the study of independence, which Karen Rook and Robyn Stickney helped to design, we brought four males or four females into the laboratory for what they thought was an experiment on humor. We placed the subjects into individual booths equipped with microphones and earphones, and showed them a series of cartoons which we asked them to rate for funniness. The cartoons used in this study had been previously rated by a set of independent judges, with half of them judged to be very funny and half judged to be very unfunny.

As each new cartoon appeared on the screen, the subjects heard the experimenter call on each person in turn for his or her rating. Although the subjects believed that they were hearing each others' voices, in fact, what they were actually hearing was a tape recording. In order to induce conformity, the tape included 36 trials during which all three taped voices gave false responses, agreeing that a particular cartoon was funny when it wasn't, and vice versa. We gave subjects this somewhat subjective task of judging cartoons for funniness—rather than length of lines or the like—so that false norms might impose pressure to conform without appearing to be bizarre.

As expected, the masculine and androgynous subjects did not differ significantly from one another, and both were significantly more independent than the feminine subjects. This was true for both males and females.

In the study of nurturance, which Jenny Jacobs helped me to design, subjects came to the laboratory individually for an experiment described as a study of mood. The subjects were informed that we wanted to know how different activities would affect their mood, and that we would therefore ask them to perform a number of different activities and to rate their mood after each.

For one of the activities, we brought a kitten into the room and asked the subjects to interact with it in any way that they wished. We placed the kitten into a child's playpen which had been completely enclosed by chicken wire, and we showed the subjects how to open the playpen so that they could take the kitten out if they wanted to. The room also contained various toys that a kitten might enjoy, for example, a pencil, a ball of yarn, etc. The subject was left alone in the room with the kitten for five minutes while we observed from behind a one-way mirror. The main behavior that we measured in this situation was how much the subject *touched* the kitten. At the end of the five-minute period, we also asked the subject to indicate how much he or she had enjoyed playing with the kitten.

Later in the experiment, we again placed the kitten into its playpen, and we gave subjects ten minutes to do anything in the room that they wished. They could play with the kitten, or they could read magazines, work puzzles, play with a three-dimensional tilting maze, or whatever. Once again, we observed them from behind the one-way mirror to see how much they played with the kitten when they didn't have to.

As expected, the feminine and androgynous men did not differ significantly from one another, and both were significantly more responsive to the kitten than the masculine men. Thus, the male data confirmed our hypothesis. But the female data did not. As expected, the androgynous women, like the androgynous men, were quite responsive to the kitten, but the feminine women were significantly less responsive, and the masculine women fell ambiguously in-between.

Considering these two studies together, we see that, as predicted, only the androgynous subjects, both male and female, displayed a high level of masculine independence when under pressure to conform, as well as a high level of feminine playfulness or nurturance when given the opportunity to interact with a tiny kitten. Thus, only the androgynous subjects were *both* masculine and feminine.

In contrast, the non-androgynous subjects all seemed to be low in one or the other of these two behaviors. For example, non-androgynous males "did well" only when the behavior was congruent with their self-definition as masculine or feminine. Thus, the masculine males were low in feminine nurturance and the feminine males were low in masculine independence.

Interestingly, the results for the non-androgynous females were more complex. As we had anticipated, the masculine women were quite independent, but they were not significantly less responsive to the kitten than the androgynous women. Hence, we cannot conclude that the masculine woman is low in her expressive functioning. Rather, it is the feminine woman who, at this juncture, appears to be the most restricted. Thus, not only was she low in independence, but she was also low in her nurturance toward the kitten. Of course, it is possible that feminine women might simply find animals unappealing for some reason and that they could therefore be expected to display much greater nurturance if they were given the opportunity to interact with another human being rather than with a kitten. But the possibility must also be considered that feminine women may simply be more constricted than we had initially anticipated, and that their constriction may extend beyond the instrumental domain.

Further Explorations of the Expressive Domain

Why were the feminine woman so unresponsive to the kitten? Do they simply find animals unappealing for some reason? Was there some other feature of the situation which inhibited them? Or, contrary to conventional wisdom, are they simply not competent in the expressive domain?

In order to give the feminine women a fairer test of their expressive functioning, we carried out two additional studies. Because we wished to clarify whether the feminine women's low level of nurturance was unique to their interaction with animals, both of these studies were designed to be genuinely interpersonal situations where the subject's nurturant sympathies would be more likely to be aroused. In addition, because it also seemed possible that feminine women might be insufficiently assertive to act out their nurturant feelings if the situation required that they take responsibility for initiating the interaction with their partner, the second study was designed not only to be genuinely interpersonal, but also to place the subject into a more passive role which would require very little initiative or improvisation and where there would be virtually no ambiguity about what a subject *ought* to do if he or she wished to be nurturant. Accordingly, the first study gave the subject the opportunity to interact with a human baby, and the second required the subject to listen to a fellow student who openly shared some of his or her unhappy emotions (Bem, Martyna, & Watson, under editorial review).

In the baby study, which Carol Watson and Bart Astor helped me to design, each subject was left alone with a five-month-old baby for a period of ten minutes with the understanding that we would be observing the infant's reactions to a stranger through the one-way mirror. In fact, we were measuring the subject's responsiveness to the baby. Using time sampling procedures, we measured how much the subject smiled at the baby, how much the subject talked to the baby, how much the subject held the baby, how much the subject kissed or nuzzled the baby,and how much the subject played with the baby in a way that involved touching (e.g., tickling, patting, stretching). We then derived a global measure of the subject's overall responsiveness to the baby by adding together all of these various behaviors.

Parenthetically, I would like to note that this study involved fourteen different babies. That way, no baby was required to be "mauled" by more than six undergraduates, and most parents were eager to have their children participate and to join us behind the one-way mirror to watch the interaction. Naturally, great care was taken to protect the health and well-being of the babies who participated. For example, all subjects were urged to cancel their appointments if they felt the slightest bit ill; all of the toys and lab coats were thoroughly washed before every session; and the baby's mother or father was explicitly instructed to ask that the session be terminated if the baby ever seemed to be particularly distressed. In addition, each baby was "interviewed" before the study began to make certain that he or she was not yet afraid of strangers.

Happily, the results of the baby study supported our initial hypothesis. That is to say, feminine and androgynous subjects did not differ significantly from one another, and both were significantly more nurturant toward the baby than masculine subjects. Moreover, the results did not differ significantly for men and women. Thus, the baby study conceptually replicated our earlier finding that masculine men were low in nurturance toward a kitten and, even more importantly, it indicated that the low nurturance of the feminine woman does not extend to her interaction with humans.

As indicated earlier, however, we did still another study to clarify further whether the low nurturance of the feminine woman was situation specific. Because it seemed possible that feminine women might be most able to act out all of their nurturant feelings in a situation where they did not have to take responsibility for initiating and sustaining the interaction, as they did to some degree with both the kitten and the baby, the situation in this study was designed not only to be genuinely interpersonal, but also to place the subject into a more passive or responsive role. More specifically, this study was designed to evoke sympathetic and supportive listening on the part of the subject, but without at the same time requiring the subject to play an active or initiating role in the interaction.

In this study, which Wendy Martyna and Dorothy Ginsberg helped to design, two same-sex subjects (one of whom was actually an experimental assistant) participated in a study of "the acquaintance process." They appeared to draw lots to determine which of the two would take the role of "talker" and which the role of "listener," but in fact, the experimental assistant always served as the talker and the subject always served as the listener.

The talker began with some relatively impersonal background information, e.g., hometown, number of siblings, etc. But he or she soon became more personal. In general, the talker described himself or herself as a recent and rather lonely transfer student to Stanford. He or she talked about missing old friends, about how difficult it was to make new friends now that cliques had already become established, and about spending much more time alone than he or she really wanted to. In short, the talker described feelings common to many new transfer students. The talker did not seem neurotic, just somewhat isolated, and rather pleased to have this opportunity to share some of his or her feelings with another person. In contrast, the subject—as listener—was allowed to ask questions and to make comments, but was instructed never to shift the focus of the conversation to himself or herself.

We observed the conversation from behind a one-way mirror and recorded a number of the subjects' behaviors, such as how much responsiveness they showed in their facial expression, how many times they nodded, how many comments they made, and how positively they reacted to the talker's implicit request for further contact. After the conversation, we also asked both the talker and the experimenter to rate how nurturant the subject had seemed to them. We then derived a global responsiveness score for each subject by averaging together these various measures.

As in the baby study, the results confirmed our initial hypothesis once again. Thus, feminine and androgynous subjects did not differ significantly from one another, and both were significantly more nurturant toward the lonely student than masculine subjects. Moreover, the results did not differ significantly for males and females. These results conceptually replicate the low nurturance of the masculine male for the third time, and they demonstrate for the second time that the low nurturance of the feminine woman was situation specific and does not generalize to her interaction with humans.

Summing Up

I believe that we are now in a position to state some of the things we have learned about androgyny and sex-typing. I shall begin with the men because they're easy. Consider, first, the androgynous male. He performs spectacularly. He shuns no behavior just because our culture happens to label it as female, and his competence crosses both the instrumental and the expressive domains. Thus, he stands firm in his opinions, he cuddles kittens and bounces babies, and he has a sympathetic ear for someone in distress. Clearly he is a liberated companion for the most feminist among us.

In contrast, the feminine male is low in the instrumental domain, and the masculine male is low in the expressive domain. Because at least one-third of college-age males would be classified as masculine under our definition, it is particularly distressing that the masculine males were less responsive in all of the diverse situations that we designed to evoke their more tender emotions, to tug, if only a little, on their heartstrings. I do not know, of course, whether the masculine men were simply unwilling to act out any tender emotions that they might have been experiencing, or whether their emotionality is sufficiently inhibited so that they did not readily experience the emotions we sought to tap. But in either case, their partners in the interaction received less emotional sustenance than they would have otherwise.

We cannot conclude, or course, that masculinity inhibits all tender emotionality in the masculine male. Obviously, none of the laboratory situations that we devised was as powerful as, say, having a child who becomes ill or a friend who seems about to have a nervous breakdown. We can conclude, however, that their thresholds for tender emotionality are higher than all the other men and women we have observed. And that, I believe, is sufficient cause for concern.

Let us turn now to the somewhat more complex pattern of results shown by the women. Like their male counterparts, androgynous women also fare well in our studies. They, too, willingly perform behaviors which our culture has labeled as unsuitable for their sex and they, too, function effectively in both the instrumental and the expressive domains.

In contrast, the masculine woman is low in the expressive domain, and the feminine woman is low in the instrumental domain. Thus, for both men and women, sex-typing does function to restrict behavior. Masculine individuals of both sexes are high in independence but low in nurturance, and feminine individuals of both sexes are high in nurturance but low in independence.

In addition, however, it will be recalled that feminine women were not consistently high even in nurturance. That is to say, they were more nurturant toward the lonely student and the baby than they were toward the kitten, and there was even some evidence that they were more nurturant toward the lonely student than toward the baby (Bem, Martyna, & Watson, under editorial review).

What is the source of this variability? Although there is some evidence that the lonely student may have been especially able to arouse the nurturant sympathies of the feminine women (Bem, Martyna, & Watson, under editorial review), it seems noteworthy that feminine women were the most nurturant in that one situation where the subject was required, as a listener, to play a relatively passive or responsive role with no need to take any responsibility whatever for initiating or even sustaining the interaction. In contrast, it seems noteworthy that feminine women were the least nurturant in that one situation where the subject was actually required to remove a kitten from its cage personally and spontaneously in order to be nurturant toward it. This leads me to speculate that femininity may be what produces nurturant feelings in women, but that at least a threshold level of masculinity is required to provide the initiative and perhaps even the daring to translate those nurturant feelings into action.

These speculations about the feminine woman conclude what I think I have learned up to this point about the evils of sex-typing and the potential promise of androgyny. As I stated earlier, however, the major purpose of my research has always been a political one: to help free the human personality from the restricting prison of sex-role stereotyping and to develop a conception of mental health which is free from culturally imposed definitions of masculinity and femininity.

Certainly androgyny seems to represent the fulfillment of this goal. For if there is a moral to the concept of psychological androgyny, it is that *behavior* should have no gender. But there is an irony here, for the concept of androgyny contains an inner contradiction and hence the seeds of its own destruction. Thus, as the etymology of the word implies, the concept of androgyny necessarily presupposes that the concepts of masculinity and femininity themselves have distinct and substantive content. But to the extent that the androgynous message is absorbed by the culture, the concepts of masculinity and femininity will cease to have such content and the distinctions to which they refer will blur into invisibility. Thus, when androgyny becomes a reality, the *concept* of androgyny will have been transcended. (See Rebecca, Hefner, & Oleshansky, in press, and Hefner, Rebecca, & Oleshansky, in press, for a discussion of the concept of sex-role transcendence.)

GENDER IDENTITY

As I noted in the introduction to this paper, the ideal or healthy personality has traditionally included a concept of sexual identity with three basic components: (1) a sexual preference for members of the opposite sex; (2) a sex-role identity as either masculine or feminine, depending upon one's gender; and (3) a gender identity, i.e., a secure sense of one's maleness or femaleness.

In discussing the first two of these components, it is clear that my contribution has been largely iconoclastic. Thus, I have proposed that we reject sexual preference as relevant to anything other than the individual's own love or pleasure. And I have all but said that the best sex-role identity is no sex-role identity. I think I am prepared to be somewhat less cavalier with the concept of gender identity.

For even if people were all to become psychologically androgynous, the world would continue to consist of two sexes, male and female would continue to be one of the first and most basic dichotomies that young children would learn, and no one would grow up ignorant of or even indifferent to his or her gender. After all, even if one is psychologically androgynous, one's gender continues to have certain profound physical implications.

Thus, being a female typically means that you have a female body build; that you have female genitalia; that you have breasts; that you menstruate; that you can become pregnant and give birth; and that you can nurse a child. Similarly, being a male typically means that you have a male body build; that you have male genitalia; that you have beard growth; that you have erections; that you ejaculate; and that you can impregnate a woman and thereby father a child. No matter how psychologically androgynous you may be, you typically "inherit" one or the other of these two sets of biological givens, and you do not get to choose which of the two sets you would prefer.

Precisely because these are biological givens which cannot be avoided or escaped, except perhaps by means of a very radical and mutilating surgery, it seems to me that psychological health must necessarily include having a healthy sense of one's maleness or femaleness, a "gender identity" if you like. But I would argue that a healthy sense of maleness or femaleness involves little more than being able to look into the mirror and to be perfectly comfortable with the body that one sees there. One's gender does dictate the nature of one's body, after all, and hence one ought to be able to take one's body very much for granted, to feel comfortable with it, and perhaps even to like it.

But beyond being comfortable with one's body, one's gender need have no other influence on one's behavior or on one's life style. Thus, although I would suggest that a woman ought to feel comfortable about the fact that she can bear children if she wants to, this does not imply that she ought to want to bear children, nor that she ought to stay home with any children that she does bear. Similarly, although I would suggest that a man ought to feel perfectly comfortable about the fact that he has a penis which can become erect, this in no way implies that a man ought to take the more active role during sexual intercourse, nor even that his sexual partners ought all to be female.

Finally, I would argue that a healthy sense of one's maleness or femaleness becomes all the more possible precisely when the artificial constraints of gender are eliminated and when one is finally free to be one's own unique blend of temperament and behavior. When gender no longer functions as a prison, then and only then will we be able to accept as given the fact that we are male or female in exactly the same sense that we accept as given the fact that we are human. Then and only then will we be able to consider the fact of our maleness or femaleness to be so self-evident and nonproblematic that it rarely ever occurs to us to think about it, to assert that it is true, to fear that it might be in jeopardy, or to wish that it were otherwise.

Let me conclude, then, with my personal set of prescriptions for a liberated sexual identity:

Let sexual preference be ignored;
Let sex roles be abolished; and
Let gender move from figure to ground.

REFERENCES

Bakan, D. *The duality of human existence*. Chicago: Rand McNally, 1966.

Bazin, N. T., & Freeman, A. The androgynous vision. *Women's Studies*, 1974, *2*, 185-215.

Bem, S. L. The measurement of psychological androgyny. *Journal of Consulting and Clinical Psychology*, 1974, *42*, 155-162.

Bem, S. L. Sex-role adaptability: One consequence of psychological androgyny. *Journal of Personality and Social Psychology*, 1975, *31*, 634-643.

Bem, S. L. On the utility of alternative procedures for assessing psychological androgyny. Under editorial review.

Bem, S. L., & Lenney, E. Sex-typing and the avoidance of cross-sex behavior. *Journal of Personality and Social Psychology*, in press.

Bem, S. L., Martyna, W., & Watson, C. Sex-typing and androgyny: Further explorations of the expressive domain. Under editorial review.

Berzins, J. I., & Welling, M. A. The PRF ANDRO Scale: A measure of psychological androgyny derived from the Personality Research Form. Unpublished manuscript, University of Kentucky, 1974.

Block, J. H. Conceptions of sex role: Some cross-cultural and longitudinal perspectives. *American Psychologist*, 1973, *28*, 512-526.

Constantinople, A. Masculinity-femininity: An exception to a famous dictum. *Psychological Bulletin*, 1974, *80*, 389-407.

Cosentino, F., & Heilbrun, A. B. Anxiety correlates of sex-role identity in college students. *Psychological Reports*, 1964, *14*, 729-730.

Erikson, E. Inner and outer space: Reflections on womanhood. In R. J. Lifton (Ed.), *The woman in America*. New York: Houghton Mifflin, 1964.

Gall, M. D. The relationship between masculinity-femininity and manifest anxiety. *Journal of Clinical Psychology*, 1969, *25*, 294-295.

Gelpi, B. C. The politics of androgyny. *Women's Studies*, 1974, *2*, 151-160.

Gray, S. W. Masculinity-femininity in relation to anxiety and social acceptance. *Child Development*, 1957, *28*, 203-214.

Green, R. *Sexual identity conflict in children and adults*. New York: Basic Books, 1974.

Harford, T. C., Willis, C. H., & Deabler, H. L. Personality correlates of masculinity-femininity. *Psychological Reports*, 1967, *21*, 881-884.

Harris, D. A. Androgyny: The sexist myth in disguise. *Women's Studies*, 1974, *2*, 171-184.

Hefner, R., Rebecca, M., & Oleshansky, B. Development of sex role transcendence. *Human Development*, in press.

Heilbrun, C. G. *Toward a recognition of androgyny*. New York: Alfred A. Knopf, 1973.

Jung, C. G. Anima and animus. In *Two essays on analytical psychology: Collected works of C. G. Jung*. (Vol. 7.) Bollinger Foundation, 1953. Pp. 186-209.

Maccoby, E. E. Sex differences in intellectual functioning. In E. E. Maccoby (Ed.), *The development of sex differences*. Stanford, Ca.: Stanford University Press, 1966. Pp. 25-55.

Mussen, P. H. Some antecedents and consequents of masculine sex-typing in adolescent boys. *Psychological Monographs*, 1961, *75*, No. 506.

Mussen, P. H. Long-term consequents of masculinity of interests in adolescence. *Journal of Consulting Psychology*, 1962, *26*, 435-440.

Parsons, T., & Bales, R. F. *Family, socialization and interaction process*. New York: Free Press, 1955.

Pleck, J. H. Masculinity-femininity: Current and alternative paradigms. *Sex Roles*, 1975, *1*, 161-178.

Rebecca, M., Hefner, R., & Oleshansky, B. A model of sex-role transcendence. *Journal of Social Issues*, in press.

Sears, R. R. Relation of early socialization experiences to self-concepts and gender role in middle childhood. *Child Development*, 1970, *41*, 267-289.

Secor, C. Androgyny: An early reappraisal. *Women's Studies*, 1974, *2*, 161-169.

Spence, J. T., Helmreich, R., & Stapp, J. Ratings of self and peers on sex-role attributes and their relation to self-esteem and conceptions of masculinity and femininity. *Journal of Personality and Social Psychology*, 1975, *32*, 29-39.

Stimpson, C. R. The androgyne and the homosexual. *Women's Studies*, 1974, *2*, 237-248.

Strahan, F. Remarks on Bem's measurement of psychological androgyny: Alternatives, methods and a supplementary analysis. *Journal of Consulting and Clinical Psychology*, 1975, *43*, 568-571.

Webb, A. P. Sex-role preferences and adjustment in early adolescents. *Child Development*, 1963, *34*, 609-618.

Surviving Sexism:
Strategies and Consequences

Alice Jeghelian

The *American Heritage Dictionary* defines sexism as "discrimination by members of one sex against the other, especially by males against females based on the assumption that one sex is superior." I prefer to define sexism as "prejudicial attitudes and patterns of behavior toward either sex, based on cultural stereotypes or myths pertaining to that sex." For women in particular, sexism is a victimizing experience that severely limits their options. To compound the matter, in our institutions such victimizing behaviors are so common and customary that they are often unrecognized even by the victims themselves.

Thus sexism is a rather formidable external (and internal) obstacle to women's work success. How some women confront sexism is the topic of this article. My remarks are drawn from my clinical observations as a psychologist and from my experience as an affirmative action officer for an institution. I comment briefly on sexism in institutions and some general responses to it, focus on the problems experienced by those women who choose to confront sexism, and then describe some of the strategies and supports necessary for combating and surviving sexism.

Obviously, sexism exists in our society and in all our social institutions, beginning with the nuclear family. One such institution is the employing institution, whether it is a factory, an insurance company, a hospital, or a school. So far our equal employment opportunity laws have been of little use in eliminating sexism in employing institutions. They do help protect women and minorities against overt acts of exclusion and discrimination; sexism, however, is what Wells (1973) has called "covert discrimination." It is nurtured under a veneer of tradition supported by both the self-concept of the working woman and the organizational power structure. According to Wells, "Present patterns of management provide such a powerful, pervasive, familiar picture that we hardly notice what is missing" (p. 56). Whenever women experience overt sex discrimination, they can seek assistance from the administrators of federal regulations. But what does a woman do when sexism in her institution persists in denying her equal treatment not by outright exclusion but by subtle and not-so-subtle oversights engendered by traditional practices and time-honored customs? This fight is often individual. It is lonely. And its sources of assistance are few.

WOMEN'S RESPONSES TO SEXISM

Women in general, as a result of the women's movement and the civil rights movement, are becoming increasingly aware of their secondary status in our society and increasingly sensitive to the conditions that prevent them from enjoying their rights more fully, not only as workers but also as persons. Most women know about the Civil Rights Act, for example. And most women have heard about "women's liberation," even if not all of them understand it completely. And more and more women—albeit with humor and a little self-consciousness—are displaying some of the signs of social awareness, even if it is only by wearing a pin that says "Uppity Women Unite."

Although on the one hand more women are aware of their low status, few women actually see themselves as victims. In discussing the reactions of the "traditional woman" to unjust discrimination, Torrey (1973) has described various psychological factors that dispose such women to be indifferent to or unaware of discrimination. Among these factors is the reluctance to perceive self as victim: "Nobody enjoys being told that she might have been happier, richer or more successful if it weren't for some injustice" (p. 32). Torrey further states, "The woman who toils daily at dull and ill-paid or unpaid work and who sees no means of changing it has a strong motive to think that it is inevitable or only fair or even virtuous" (p. 32).

Thus, women seem to fall into four groups in terms of their responses to sexism: (a) those who deliberately take some action regarding a victimizing experience due to sex discrimination; (b) those who, for reasons important to them, choose not to act at this time or are constrained in some way from acting at this time, not necessarily by choice; (c) those who are intellectually aware of the problem of sexism but somehow feel that it has not affected their lives; and (d) those who do not understand or acknowledge it in any way. Clearly, those who confront sexism are still a small minority. For most women it appears that the psychological defense mechanisms of avoidance and denial successfully protect them from even considering such a confrontation.

WOMEN WHO CONFRONT SEXISM

The first group—those who decide to do something about their grievances, those who confront sexism—are the focus of this article. These women are in fact emerging as a potential client population for counselors and therapists. They seem to have a common symptomatology. In feeling aggrieved and acting on their grievances by seeking help, they are acting differently from other women, and in so doing they experience new and painful kinds of stress (for which new coping mechanisms must be learned). All express tremendous anxiety and conflict about seeking assistance. All feel that "taking some action" is like going to the U.S. Supreme Court. They are hurt and angry. But many are also afraid or reluctant to do anything about the perceived injustice. Most of them secretly hope that, when they seek help, the helper will go out and somehow set things straight without getting them personally involved. The conflict is a classic one: deciding which is worse—to let the status quo continue or to fight it.

In a very real as well as a figurative sense, these women are caught in the same dilemma Hamlet describes in his famous soliloquy: "To be, or not to be: that is the question: / Whether 'tis nobler in the mind to suffer / The slings and arrows of outrageous fortune, / Or to take arms against a sea of troubles, / And by opposing end them." But for these women, "to take arms against a sea of troubles" does not necessarily end them. Instead it may produce additional stress from threats of reprisal and may even result in outright punishment (Bird 1973; Torrey 1973). In fact, Rossi (1974) has found that punishment is a common response to professional women who simply aspire to careers in "masculine turf." She says that ambitious women "must have thick skins and the utmost inner security to withstand what they so often experience, subtle and overt forms of punishment rather than encouragement and support" (p. 369). Obviously, when a woman dares to complain about an injustice in addition to everything else, the reprisal reactions will be even greater.

THE CASE OF MARY

There are, of course, many variations of grievance problems and their presenting symptoms, but let me describe Mary, a composite case illustrating some of the complaints presented by women in this group.

Mary was a secretary in an educational institution. She worked for a male administrator, Dean Jones, who was very appreciative of her services over the years and customarily delegated a great deal of responsibility to her—not by official assignment but rather by default: "Take care of this for me, Mary. . . ." "Set it up for me, Mary. . . ." Gradually Mary came to take over completely the operation of several important functions of the dean's office. It was her quiet hope that when she received her bachelor's degree from the evening program, the recognition in status and pay, which belonged to the functions she was performing, would also be hers. Certainly, from the praise she'd always received from the dean she felt encouraged to hope for such a promotion, although it was never explicitly discussed and she had never asked about it outright. When she finally received her degree, therefore, she looked forward to some exciting new development. But nothing happened. The dean would have forgotten the occasion altogether had she not asked him for the day off in order to attend her commencement. Mary was hurt but didn't let herself dwell on it; and the dean later presented her with a pen-and-pencil set.

Very shortly after that Mary learned indirectly that a new position was being created: that of an administrative assistant to the dean, responsible for many of the functions she was presently performing. It was just the promotion she had been hoping for! But as applicants began pouring in, Dean Jones never suggested to her, nor did she ask, that she also be considered a candidate. She surmised that she wasn't good enough, that somehow she had failed to make the grade. And it just hurt too much to ask why. So she suffered her mortification in silence. Her boss never knew about it. Instead he hired someone else as his assistant, a young man with a newly minted master's degree from a neighboring institution (one of those elite universities that other schools always feel inferior to). He was two years younger than Mary and had never been employed full-time before, but he had been president of the student government association of his undergraduate institution and had an easy assurance about him. Mary spent the next six months training the new assistant, showing him how to do all the things she had been doing. He learned quickly that she already was managing things superbly and, like the dean before him, began to leave all the details to her.

A year later this young man was promoted to a junior deanship, and Dean Jones was once again looking for an administrative assistant. This time Mary worked up the courage to suggest herself as a candidate, only to be totally rebuffed by his shocked response: "And lose you as my secretary? I should think not!" It was at this point that Mary picked up the phone and called for an appointment with the affirmative action counselor.

PRE-GRIEVANCE COUNSELING

Mary's behavior during her initial appointment can perhaps best be described as furtive. She apologized for taking the counselor's time. She seemed uneasy and ambivalent about being there. "I don't know what to do, but I don't know if I want you to do anything either. . . ." After the counselor—a woman—assured Mary that she had no plans to do anything but listen, Mary went on to tell her story, describing how her disappointment and hurt had gradually begun to outweigh her loyalty to her boss, who continued to gloat over her like one of his prized possessions. She said she found herself getting easily upset over little things, feeling frustrated and acting short-tempered with colleagues, nagging at her boss, frequently wanting to cry and not knowing why, feeling low and sometimes altogether miserable. She said she wanted help but didn't want to cause any trouble. Maybe there was something wrong with her after all, she thought. In seeking help, then, Mary had not really acknowledged to herself that she might have an employment grievance. Her case is typical of those seen in a pre-grievance counseling context.

The goal of the helper in pre-grievance counseling is first to enable an individual to recognize and separate "fact" from "fuming" and then to assist that individual in coming to some decision regarding a planned course of action, providing backup and support during such action. In pre-grievance counseling with women like Mary, and there are a surprising number of them, the helper cannot focus immediately on the grievance. In fact, like Mary, the individual may not even have identified her problem as a "grievance." Typically, the client has been denying or repressing the feelings caused by the victimizing experience. When she finally does seek help, depending on where she turns, it may be just for relief of her symptoms or for some legal information or for assurance that there isn't something wrong with her, since she feels so distressed about the situation.

In my own work with such clients, I first try to provide an atmosphere of trust to help the woman get at her unexpressed feelings, to understand them and where they come from, and to accept them as legitimate. Together we examine the conditions that have aroused the reactions in her, and very cautiously we evaluate them—in terms of fairness as perceived by her and in terms of what we know about her rights under the law. I show her my concern and my positive regard for her as an individual. And I give her the necessary information with which to make a sound decision for herself.

In the case of Mary, the affirmative action counselor from the start demonstrated her complete understanding and respect for Mary's feelings and her long loyalty to the dean. She also helped Mary see that she had a right to be angry and that her anger was legitimate. She pointed out that the situation, however, might not be legitimate. The counselor helped Mary separate the two and look at them objectively. For Mary, it was a relief at first just to be able to talk with someone about her problem. But she also needed to know what, if anything, she could do about it. The counselor pointed out that essentially she had five options: (a) stay on the job and say nothing; (b) quit; (c) confront her boss; (d) complain through internal channels; or (e) complain through external channels, that is, file a discrimination suit. Like most women seen in a pre-grievance counseling context, Mary chose the middle course: to confront her boss and try to work things out for herself at that level. She rejected doing anything as drastic as filing a suit against the institution. (All the same, it seemed to strengthen her to know that she had that choice.)

Many of the reactions experienced by women seen in a pre-grievance counseling context are like those described by Peterson and Spooner (1975) in their article on the career crises of certain health professionals. They have compared the reactions of professionals to the five psychological response stages of terminally ill patients depicted by Kubler-Ross (1969). When we apply the same theoretical formulation to women victims of sex discrimination, we find a similar configuration of responses, namely: (a) denial, or a tendency to ignore the crisis or hurt; (b) anger, or the experience of rage and resentment, which may be either externally or internally directed (usually internally, with women like Mary); (c) initiation of some action, or an attempt to negotiate assistance (such as seeking help from an affirmative action counselor); (d) depression—or despair and even hopelessness as a reaction to increased stress, especially if no assistance or support is available; (e) acceptance of reality—and the return of belief in oneself and the strengthening of resolve to undertake some affirmative action in one's own behalf.

CONFRONTATION AND ITS CONSEQUENCES

In order to confront Dean Jones, Mary now needed help in planning strategies: deciding on ways of approaching the dean, rehearsing what she would say and how she would say it, building up her confidence, developing a repertoire of assertive responses and behaviors for the interview, and so forth. (During this stage of counseling, I usually try to be as concrete as possible in the kinds of suggestions I offer. It is also important during this stage to prepare the woman for the very real possibility that she will not be successful in this approach and remind her that she has the option of using the internal complaint procedure.)

The counselor reassured Mary that she could handle the confrontation. And she did. The dean was a bit taken aback, but he said that of course he would consider her for the assistant's job, "even though you have no master's degree." Meanwhile, interviews were being held, but Mary was not offered one. When she spoke up a second time, she was granted an interview by the dean, but it was postponed several times because there was always some important letter to be typed or some important meeting to be attended. Rather than react emotionally to each new slight, Mary now had the know-how to build on the experience, to note it down, to document it, and to study more objectively what really seemed to be going on. Perhaps most important, she had someone to consult with as she went along.

Soon Mary began to notice changes in the behavior of the two male deans. She found she was being excluded from all but the most routine office information. Correspondence and other communications that had always gone across her desk were somehow finding their way past her. The men developed the habit of meeting over coffee in the faculty dining room. The dean began making his own appointments. The junior dean began doing some of his own work. Staff meetings were called without Mary's prior knowledge. Candidate resumés were whisked away from her. In short, Mary was made to feel like an outsider, isolated from the vital information that keeps an office ticking. All of her original symptoms now returned, this time in multiple proportions. The stress she had felt earlier had had an internal source; the renewed stress came from an external source, particularly Dean Jones' changed behavior toward her.

Thus, as a result of acquiring new personal coping mechanisms and using them to pursue an appropriate professional goal, a woman may be subject to increased stress, increased frustration, isolation, and even outright harassment. (This is contrary to the usual mental health paradigm!) Mary did not get the promotion. But rather than suffer silently, as she had done in the past, she quickly decided to take her case to the internal complaint mechanism of the university. She was now ready to focus on grievance.

In filing a sex discrimination complaint, some women, of course, do not require pre-grievance counseling. They are quick to perceive a violation of their rights and quick to challenge the action. When they seek advice, they are ready to lodge a complaint and just want information as to where and how. Invariably, they have already attempted a solution on their own through the channels available to them, and they have failed—usually spectacularly. It has been my experience that these women, and women like Mary, now face the prospect of even greater tension and stress. For in filing a complaint, even though it is only via the internal grievance route, a woman is challenging the organizational system itself; and institutional integrity is at stake.

INSTITUTIONAL REACTIONS

The organizational system can handle almost any complaint better than a complaint charging sex discrimination. Why? Because sexism is ingrained and sexist behavior so automatic that it seems to have a force of its own, separate from conscious or voluntary control. So when a woman charges sex discrimination, the institutional reaction is one of shock and righteous indignation. Discrimination is an ugly word. The system genuinely deplores it. The system says it does not tolerate discrimination of any kind, and I think it means it. But what the institution recognizes and prohibits is discrimination of the most obvious and blatant sort, the sort that hardly exists any more. Far more subtle and therefore more dangerous is the kind of discrimination resulting from the sexism in the normal, acceptable, everyday routine of the institution.

According to a survey conducted by a Philadelphia consulting firm called Options for Women ("Isolation" 1974), women in administration report knowing little about what is happening in their companies (i.e., they are not part of the information grapevine, formal or informal). They tend not to be told about the opportunities for professional development or the criteria for promotion. Women who are promoted are usually isolated from other women down the line. Normal contacts with men in the organization are also limited because of male discomfort in dealing with women on the job, at meetings, or even at lunch. Other common obstacles faced by women, according to the survey report, include: lack of encouragement to apply for certain kinds of jobs: insufficient support when promoted to a "nontraditional" job; and, as in the case of Mary, denial of the salary and title that should go with actual responsibility. It is easy to see why an institution is hard put to call such "normal" behavior discriminatory! So far most organizational systems have not been able to control sexism of this type. And the institution's grievance mechanism usually has few norms or case precedents by which to judge such complaints. These are just a few of the reasons that a sex discrimination complaint is so difficult for an institution to handle.

In order to be heard by the institution, then, a sex discrimination charge requires a very forceful approach. The complainant has to show that she knows her rights, has access to legal counsel, and is willing to take her complaint outside the institution for settlement if necessary. In other words, in filing a complaint internally, a woman is wise to let some of her heavier artillery be seen right from the start. She has to be sure of herself and of her ground, and, above all, she has to be firm. The more documentation she can provide supporting her charge, the better (letters, memos, notes on conversations, meetings, phone calls, etc.—with dates, times, places, and witnesses).

Discrimination is hard to prove, even harder to disprove. Sexism is controversial as a charge, embarrassing as a finding. In most court cases, however, complaints have been won on procedural flaws in the institution, flaws that have left open the possibility that the subjective factors of sexism or racism might have entered into an action. Institutional management has been sloppy: Policies and procedures have not been made explicit; supervisors have not been trained properly; information regarding promotional paths and salary scales has not been freely disseminated. Affirmative action plans, if any exist, have been inadequate or have failed to serve as evidence of good faith on the part of the institution. And so, many complaints have won their cases.

Mary succeeded in hers. She was promoted to the assistant's position and given the appropriate salary increase on the basis that (a) she had all the necessary qualifications, (b) possession of a master's degree was not a bona fide occupational qualification, (c) she had already demonstrated the ability to perform the work, and (d) she merited a promotion. I should add that she also could have claimed that she was unjustly overlooked for promotion the previous year, but since she herself had not inquired about the possibility then, she did not push for back pay consideration in her appeal.

POST-COMPLAINT FALLOUT

When a woman wins her case, whether through personal confrontation, internal grievance procedures, or external suit, in all probability she will continue to encounter institutional sexism in various guises (Bird 1973; Torrey 1973; Wells 1973). She must learn how to recognize these guises and how to deal with them as well. Institutional environments do not change easily. They do, however, continue to react. One characteristic reaction, at least in the beginning, is for the environment to shrink or recede. Co-workers avoid the woman, especially if the final decision in her complaint case has not yet been reached. It is as if she has something contagious. Contact with her becomes minimal. It is hoped that by this time she can handle her feelings of isolation.

Other common problems experienced at this stage may have to do with office space and location, support staff services, mail delivery, telephone extensions, dull assignments (or no assignments), inclusion at meetings, exclusion from the lunch circuit, and what to do when the men are playing squash. The woman may find that her program ideas are not sought, or if sought not implemented, or if implemented not credited. And she reflects her situation like a tennis ball, with frequent downs, constant back-and-forths, and highs that are heady but of short duration. Thus, even though she has won a skirmish, the guerrilla warfare is still going on, and she has to keep her artillery in good repair and stored within sight. In other words, there is a post-complaint fallout period in which the emotional tensions of the past continue and are in fact frequently exacerbated.

CONCLUSIONS

What can we conclude about dealing with sexism in institutions? First, sexism in institutions is a reality, and correcting its discriminatory effects can be costly to an institution in terms of dollars and reputation. Second, fighting sexism is extremely difficult, and winning a case can be psychologically costly to the woman in terms of the tremendous emotional and physical stress she must endure in order to prevail. Third, the process of fighting sexism involves recognition of a grievance, an informed decision to act on it, and the determination to see it through to a satisfactory resolution. Fourth, in each stage of this process the aggrieved woman requires a different type of assistance and information. Initially some women, like our composite, Mary, may require emotional support to enable them to get their own feelings together. From that point on, the woman complainant additionally needs help in understanding her rights under the law, developing greater sensitivity to the signs of institutional sexism, deciding what actions to take, and then sticking to her goal. Fifth, if she has sought professional help, the helper does not necessarily have to be an affirmative action counselor or someone versed in the law. The helper should, however, know at least something about the equal opportunity statutes that protect a woman's rights to employment and education. And finally, the counselor should be able to suggest strategies for responding to the institutional sexism that often camouflages a violation of those statutes.

REFERENCES

Bird, C. *Everything a woman needs to know to get paid what she's worth.* New York: McKay, 1973.

Isolation is major problem for women in business. *Women Today*, December 9, 1974, pp. 160-161.

Kubler-Ross, E. *On death and dying.* New York: Macmillan, 1969.

Peterson, W. D., & Spooner, S. E. Career crises for helping professionals: Who counsels the counselor in crisis? *Journal of College Student Personnel*, 1975, *16*, 80-84.

Rossi, A. Discrimination and demography restrict opportunities for academic women. In J. Stacey, S.Béraud, & J. Daniels (Eds.), *And Jill came tumbling after: Sexism in American education.* New York: Dell, 1974.

Torrey, J. W. A psychologist's look at women. *Journal of Contemporary Business*, 1973, *2*, 25-40.

Wells, T. The covert power of gender in organizations. *Journal of Contemporary Business*, 1973, *2*, 53-68.

Power, Collusion, Intimacy-Sexuality, Support: Breaking the Sex-Role Stereotypes in Social and Organizational Settings

Barbara Benedict Bunker[1][2]

Edith Whitfield Seashore

Women are moving into new roles in their personal and organizational relationships. In organizations, they are moving into executive roles in which rational decision making and the exercise of power and authority are required. Personally they are experimenting with new forms of social relationships—for example, the dual-career family with a redistribution of the traditional sex-role behaviors (Rapoport, 1971)—or new living structures like communes, with roles redistributed in a variety of patterns (Kantor, 1972). These new roles call for new behaviors which may not be tied to the traditional female role. The focus of this paper is on the issues raised for the woman herself, and for the other men and women who relate to her, by her assumption of new behaviors.

The values surrounding sex-role behavior in our culture are such that women are more likely to be disapproved of if they adopt masculine behaviors than men are if they adopt feminine behaviors (Broverman, Vogel, Broverman, Clarkson, & Rosenkrantz, 1972). Women's increasing awareness of these overt and covert forms of discrimination has energized them to expand the roles they can occupy and the behaviors which are seen as acceptable in any role.

During the last several years these changes have received widespread attention both in the public press and in the informal conversations of men and women. As we, the authors, have worked within

[1]The authors are named alphabetically and no seniority is intended in the order.

[2]The authors are grateful to Lee Bolman, Douglas Bunker, and Charles Seashore for comments on an earlier version of this article.

Reprinted from *Beyond Sex Roles*, A. G. Sargent (Ed.). St. Paul, Minn.: West Publishing Co., 1977, pp. 356-370. Used with permission of publisher.

organizations and in training settings, issues which arise from the loosening of the grip of sex-role stereotypes, particularly on women's behavior, have confronted us constantly. This paper is a starting point for conceptualizing what men and women are experiencing as they rearrange their relationships in response to this new situation. The issues which we have designated as power, collusion, intimacy-sexuality, and support are ones which in our experience were omnipresent in a wide variety of settings and are major sources of anxiety and confusion to those who are dealing with them.

As women move into new roles in organizations they are confronted with two tasks. First they have to be able to do a new job; this, as we have said, may require new behaviors. Second, they have to deal with the effects of the behaviors on their relationships. In this process several things happen. Their initial attempts at behavior change may be awkward. Others' reactions to the change may be partly due to that awkwardness and partly to the unexpectedness of the behavior. The previously quiet and responsive woman who becomes assertive, for example, may feel uncomfortable with her new behavior and may be responded to in that way. This situation increases the potential for confusion in existing relationships as well as for the development of productive new kinds of relationships.

To make an informed choice, however, one must understand the situation in which the choice is being made. The four issues, which we believe are crucial in this period when traditional sex-role behavior is open to negotiation, encourage the exploration of four questions. In the section on power we shall ask: What are the effects on men, women and institutions of women assuming positions of influence previously reserved for men? In discussing collusion we inquire: By what process do we become conscious of and begin to change the effects of sex-role socialization? Under intimacy-sexuality the question is: How do attraction and friendship, the personal relationships of men and women, intersect the work setting? Finally, in a section on support we explore ways in which women can share common issues and help each other understand and deal with either personal or externally caused dilemmas. Our major attention in all four sections will be devoted to women under the assumption that if women understand these issues, they are better able to engage in re-educative relationships.

POWER

We want to discuss two types of power, role power and personal power. The power that comes from occupying a particular role, that is acquired when one takes a position, has been called role power or legitimate power (French & Raven, 1959). It has traditionally been associated with men. The other type, personal power or influence power, is informal; that is, it is tied to the person and not to role. It has traditionally been associated with women. As more and more women acquire legitimate power through occupying roles which previously were denied them, they move into a world for which they were not socialized, a world that is hardly prepared to receive them.

The exercise of legitimate power requires behaviors that may not be well practiced by some women. It requires clear decision making, assertiveness, and accountability. It is sometimes a lonely task. Becoming more assertive, expressing her own views first rather than soliciting others', being pro-active rather than re-active, indicating clearly the degree to which she is willing to share power, being decisive, all these behaviors are less a part of the socialization of women than of men. For this reason women who are moving into executive positions often feel awkward. It may take a while to enjoy the pleasure of being assertive if earlier training labeled that behavior as unfeminine.

Some women have contained and overcontrolled their natural assertiveness. When at last it is let loose, those who are the recipients of the assertiveness find her to be aggressive, pushy. However, her intention may have been assertive but not aggressive. She may not have learned how to manage the expression of her assertiveness in a graduated manner. We have had similar experiences with both men and women who are newly in touch with anger which has long gone unexpressed. Time and practice are needed to be able to use this anger constructively. It is also important to differentiate the aggressiveness which is really an assertiveness management problem from the angry aggressiveness of women who are newly conscious of societal restrictions and are in a period of generalized anger. Though the behaviors may be indistinguishable, the motivation must be clarified and understood before the anger can have a productive outcome. A woman who has practice, the concern of others, and informative feedback can shape her aggressive-assertive behavior into highly effective functioning.

The assertive woman who knows her own mind and direction is so different from the female stereotype that a man may label her "unfeminine." Unfortunately, other women who are not conscious themselves of the effects of sex-role socialization may join in this reaction. Only a clear understanding of the sex-role stereotypes which we all share will prevent their being doled out as punishments in this period of renegotiation of male and female roles. Meanwhile, women who are testing out their own assertiveness need the support of other women who have been through the process and who can provide feedback on behavior as well as help to sift others' reactions. We will return to this notion of support systems later.

A second important issue for women with newly acquired role power is the climate in which that power is exercised. In our culture, the power of roles is usually played out in a competitive environment. Young men are early socialized to win, to be best, to compete. Young women are expected to do well until their adolescence when the socialization process reverses and we find them calibrating their achievements relative to males (Horner, 1969). Competition with men is not encouraged for young women; being desirable, receptive, and chosen is encouraged. When a woman passes from such an adolescence to the position of corporation executive, she walks a tightrope of ambivalence. Women who have "made it" against the grain of the dominant socialization pattern in our culture have done so in the very competitive world of men.

Although competition is energizing, it has been repeatedly demonstrated that it does not always lead to the most efficient and productive problem-solving process (Deutsch, 1973). Moreover, shifting a normatively competitive work climate into a more collaborative one is not a one-person job, it involves the sustained work of most of the members of the organizational team. Many women experience great frustration when trying to participate in a very competitive climate; they need to understand why.

During their socialization, men usually acquire a whole range of behaviors which permit them to compete at moderate levels through banter, "zinging" each other, the repartée in which they take each other's measure. Women not only lack such behaviors, but they may have had experiences in which attempts to develop them were sanctioned as "unfeminine." To participate is often to collude in a content and context which are sexist. When most of the daily interchange of an organization is conducted in a competitive mode, women often feel ignored, invisible, and/or excluded (especially when they do not have the behaviors to participate). As they become frustrated and angry, they may explode into tears or show some other form of frustration-releasing behavior. Men are often incredulous at this situation. "No one was preventing this woman from participating, so why on earth is she blowing up like this?" He may feel guilty (did he do something?), angry (what's her problem?) or puzzled, depending on the way he handles inexplicable emotion.

Since women are socialized not to show anger openly, both men and women should realize that tears are more often manifestations of anger and frustration than of hurt. Many men, in our experience, translate a woman's tears into, "I have hurt her. What did I do? I didn't do anything! So what the hell is she crying about? I can't understand women." When the correct translation is more often, "She's crying, I wonder what that's about. Maybe she's mad or frustrated about something and can't express it. I guess I'll try to find out what she's feeling."

We are not suggesting that women are the only ones who may want to elaborate their behavioral repertoire. While competitive behavior or having a comfortable attitude in the presence of conflict will help women in many work settings, our experience in training managers and business executives is that men are also dissatisfied with their competitive job climate. When pressed, they express dissatisfaction with the grinding competition that cannot give way to other forms of interpersonal collaboration. Many feel trapped in known behavior patterns and dissatisfied with the relationships these patterns produce. Women learn useful skills as part of their socialization: how to express feelings and how to develop relationships which can contribute to reshaping the work climate. The dilemma for women is how to adapt to the present situation as well as to change it. At this point men and women have a great deal to offer to each other in the molding of new work climates.

Let us now turn to the second type of power, personal power. French and Raven (1959) have described five bases of power which people use to influence others. In addition to *legitimate* power, already discussed, there is *reward* and *coercive* power. This is the sort of influence a person wields who is able to supply resources or to apply sanctions or punishments. *Expert* power comes from an influential person's special skills or competencies, while *referent* power comes from the identification of the influence with the powerful person. As we consider these bases for power, it seems clear that all can be used in conjunction with role power to strengthen it. At the same time a most important power base, personal power, seems entirely missing. Perhaps this is because personal power, though acknowledged by organizational theorists as important, has not been studied systematically or thoroughly. We suggest that this is the kind of power that women use best.

Personal power is acquired from capacities which the person embodies. Without trying to be exhaustive we will suggest a few of the sources of personal power. Influence based on a collaborative relationship where trust and mutual respect are present is one aspect of personal power. In most organizational settings women have not had the formal role but they have had the ear of men in those roles, hence, "the power behind the throne," "leading from behind" and other expressions characterize this unofficial but real kind of influence. Executive secretaries to influential persons in an organization often maintain an informal communication network which has great influence on their bosses and their decisions. The basis of this influence is partly informational and partly relational, that is, the person is experienced as insightful, trustworthy, of good judgment and permitted to have influence. Collaboration and trust, both relational qualities, are two aspects of personal power.

A second source of personal power is the capacity to generate good solutions to difficult problems. It may involve the creative capacity to think outside the givens of a situation. It may mean being able to think into the future before others have made those projections. It can be experienced either in work settings or in personal relationships. A model for the latter is Mary Poppins, that magical lady who always has just what you need in her carpetbag and whose medicine bottle dispenses your prescription in a flavor you adore. Mary Poppins stands for the intuitive quality of seeing what someone else wants or needs and working to make it happen. In reality as in fantasy, a finely tuned perceptiveness of others' needs can be the basis of great personal influence.

Charisma is the word currently in vogue to describe personal power. Since power is more often associated with men, it is easier to identify and describe charismatic men, such as, the Kennedy men, Leonard Bernstein, than charismatic women. Charisma is a combination of personal attractiveness which compels attention and liking, and a style of self-presentation in which affect and intellect combine to make the person difficult to ignore. Charisma in men is often associated with highly controlling assertive behavior (Lieberman, Yalom, & Miles, 1973), as well as strength, humor, energy, warmth, and articulateness. But what of female charisma? We suspect that for a woman to be responded to as charismatic, she must combine personal attractiveness, strength and energy; sensitivity, warmth and humor; being "together" and self-aware in a way which is perceived as feminine—in other words, she does not defy the female sex-role stereotype. Perhaps as women enlarge their roles, new models of charisma in women will emerge.

A final source of personal power is that of a good idea presented at the right time. This is not the same thing as the problem-solving capacity previously described. Here, the idea itself is so compelling and inherently cogent that it is powerful and independent of its source. As a result, the one who is its source is experienced as powerful. Our view is that men and women are equal candidates for this type of power but that in settings where women are not listened to, they may have difficulty exercising this type of personal power.

Many well-known powerful women today have gained their power by associating with men who have real role power. Eleanor Roosevelt is an example of a woman who enlarged her role as first lady, which was without official power, and used it to extend her own influence into all kinds of important affairs. Her relationship to real power plus her capacity to use her own influence made her a formidable woman.

Ken Kesey has presented a model of negative personal power in Nurse Ratchett in his novel *One Flew Over the Cuckoo's Nest*. Miss Ratchett is a tyrant with low role power who works her tyranny on others through the passive acquiescence of the ward doctor whom she influences to sanction her decisions officially. Miss Ratchett, who appears, on first impression, pleasant and helpful, is, on further inspection, manipulative and castrating, everyman's nightmare of the negative use of personal power. What we need in both literature and public life are women who can be positive models of role and personal power.

COLLUSION

Another issue which confronts men and women who are trying to re-examine the sex-role stereotypes into which they have been socialized is collusion. Collusion, as we define it, means that an individual acts in order to fulfill others' expectations rather than from his or her own needs. We will limit our discussion to situations where collusion occurs around sex roles. One of the authors, for example, lived for years in the firm belief that all things mechanical, including changing light bulbs, were not within her capacity. Since her husband traveled a lot, her view caused her no little inconvenience. As she came to recognize the collusion (women can't do mechanical tasks), she found herself able to do a number of mechanical jobs much to her own and her husband's satisfaction.

Since much of our early training teaches us how males and females behave, there is bound to be confusion when these patterns are questioned. Who opens doors? Who goes in and out of elevators first? Who swears in front of whom? Because of role-expected behaviors, the world is a place where men and women can interact predictably. We are not suggesting that all behavior which meets sex-role expectations is collusive. However, our experience is that many women, and probably men, too, act *before* they ask themselves the question, "Do I really want to do this?", "Is this really the way I feel I want to continue to behave?", and only later realize that they did something not because it was appropriate but because they should, "because I am a woman." For example, a husband says to his wife, "Hey, why didn't you call me and let me carry in those grocery packages?" This man is indicating he is willing and able to carry in the packages; but his wife may be asking herself "Is he telling me that a man *should* carry in the packages? I'd better go get him to carry them in so he won't feel less manly." Suppose the wife is having these thoughts. If the relationship is collusive, she won't question her husband's need to carry the packages, she'll go get him. If the wife is conscious of herself, she may think, "Well, how do I feel about carrying packages? Sure it's nice to have help with a big load. But it isn't, so I'll do it myself."

Most men and women have been socialized to sex-role response without thinking through whether their real feelings match social expectations. The first step in beginning to examine collusive patterns is awareness. Growth in awareness of collusions proceeds by a series of steps. First, you see others acting in ways which are not collusive and you question your own behavior. For example, you may notice that a friend does not stop and wait for a man to open a door but opens it herself. You wonder, "Why do I wait? Do I want to wait?" Or, in another case, the only woman manager in a four-person management team is included with the women assistants in her office on the schedule of daily coffee making assignments while the three male managers are not. She does not protest. You wonder, "How would I handle that situation?"

The second step is often the discovery after the fact that you have been engaged in a collusion you did not like. For example, the owner of a shop you frequent makes a sexist comment to you and you laugh with him. As you leave the shop, you become conscious of what you did and become angry at him and at yourself. Our experience is that this "after-the-fact consciousness" is a common stepping-stone to awareness in the collusive situation itself. Gradually, as you become increasingly conscious of your feelings, you are able to experience them more and more within the situation that creates them. This process is a hanging on or a slowing down of the immediate sex-role response to others in order to give yourself time to figure out what you want to do. Talking about situations with others of the same sex who have had similar experiences is another means of bringing yourself into better touch with your feelings.

You may be aware that your behavior is collusive and want to change it, but you may not have the resources to do so. For example, you may have to let someone else change the porch light until you can learn how it is done. You might maintain collusion in order to keep a relationship going. For example, early in dating relationships the women may be hesitant to put forth their own ideas or wishes before hearing from the man. "If he doesn't like my ideas he may not want to continue to see me." Here is another example. Recently we have been experimenting with paying for the lunch of male colleagues who often pay for ours. We say as we reach for the check, "It's my turn this time." If this is a first attempt to pick up the check, the lunch partner, registering sheer horror, says, "No, I asked you." We may respond with anything from "Well then, let the drinks be on me this time," to "Well, I would really like to treat you. So if not this time, then let's agree that next time it's my check." All of these are ways of letting the other person know that the relationship is not entirely satisfactory and that you are committed to figuring out a way to change it. You are saying, in effect, "I will agree to colluding this time only if we agree jointly to begin to change."

Some anxiety will undoubtedly be experienced in the breaking of old collusions. Men, particularly, may experience a woman's new capacity to be "for herself" as somehow "against him." Suppose, for example, the old pattern has been that in matters of recreation the woman usually went along with what the man suggested. One day she asserts herself and chooses a different recreation from the one he has suggested. He may feel not only that she is asserting herself, but that this assertion is a challenge to him. It is urgently important when changing old patterns to discuss and thus clarify the intentions that are the unspoken part of the behavior. They need to be brought out into the open and shared so that in the face of new behavior, the other person will not assign wrong motives.

We can identify two types of collusive behavior. The first type, collusion with others' expectations, we have just been discussing. A secretary dusts her boss's office and brings coffee, not because it is part of her job, but because she thinks he expects it of her. The female graduate student laughs at a male faculty member's sly references to her body, not because she enjoys his appreciation, but because he would be offended if she expressed annoyance. This type of collusion is often conceptualized as a demand a woman feels that others are making on her. But she has not checked to see what the feelings of the others really are. Women whose self-esteem is primarily dependent on being useful to men may resist a close examination of collusive behavior because it would deprive them of the reinforcement that behavior brings.

The second type of collusion is equally interesting but more subtle; it is collusion with one's own internalized sex-role stereotypes. A prime example occurs when one of the authors finds herself dashing home to get dinner for her family with little attention to her own work or recreation. Her need to fulfill her own image of good mother and wife (Supermom) supercedes her need to have time for herself and the development of strategies for meeting both sets of needs.

Giving up collusion and really acting for oneself is a sweet freedom, but it is not won easily. Many women who put themselves first ask themselves (or others ask them) "Aren't you being selfish?" This fear is understandable and stems from their early training. Women are taught to put others' needs first and to get self-esteem from being rewarded by others. If women stop putting others first, there is the anxious question "Will anyone love me for myself? They love me now for being so sensitive to their needs."

It is easy to confuse knowing what you feel and what you want, with having to get what you want. The two are separable. It is quite possible to want very much to take a vacation alone with your husband, but to decide that particular needs of the children are urgent and that you will not take that vacation. Knowing your own needs means that even if you choose to suspend them, you do not pretend they do not exist and thus prevent yourself from seeking alternate ways of dealing with them. The capacity to feel strong needs and also to know that you can honor them or put them aside if necessary is very reassuring. It increases feelings of identity.

Seduction, the use of ritualized sexual behaviors to get what you want, can be a special case of collusion. Seductive messages are usually verbal or nonverbal cues inserted into another message that stands by itself. The person being addressed has to interpret the double message. The woman, for example, who asks her boss for a day off, eyelids aflutter, standing closer to him than usual, is trying to persuade at several levels. If he says "yes" because of her attractiveness when he really feels he should say "no," he has been part of a seductive collusion. The "sandwich" technique is another form of seduction. A man may open a conversation with a compliment to his female colleague about her appearance, make an unwelcome request for extra work, and then, squeezing her arm warmly, congratulate her on her excellent performance rating. If she accepts the extra work because of the compliments and his warmth, she has colluded. When one understands how seduction is used, it is possible to "play the game," that is, enjoy the seductive repartee, without letting it affect the decisions to be made.

INTIMACY-SEXUALITY

Two linked issues which raise anxieties as more and more women join the work force are intimacy and sexuality, the characteristics of personal relationships between men and women. Friendship does not mean the same thing to men as to women. Women are raised to cultivate close personal relationships with others, particularly men and often women. Men have no such training, so that the characteristics of what men and women refer to as "close friendships" are often quite different. For many men, friendships mean sports or recreational activities, having a good time with cronies, but no necessary self-disclosure or personal mutual exploration. Women, on the other hand seldom refer to anyone as "close" if they do not know a considerable amount about their thoughts and feelings at a quite personal level. Some if not many men make such self-revelations only to their wife or girlfriend.

Thus, personal closeness is linked in male experience with sexuality, physical intimacy. For women, there is no necessary link between personal closeness and sexuality; in some relationships it is present, in many it is not. Some women can move into a relationship and permit it to become close without feeling that sex is a necessary consequence. For men whose relationships do not usually separate intimacy and sexuality, the entrance of many women into the work world increases the potential for relationships which may involve closeness and thus lead to a sexual exchange. This is a source of anxiety for some, a threat and perhaps a promise. The anxiety about intimacy-sexuality is present in working men as well as their wives. Because of it, many resist the idea of women entering work settings where they are not currently employed.

When there are only a few women in an organization and they are in lower status positions, it is not uncommon to find that sex is the wampum being exchanged for advancement. Sex in this domain is power; the message is "If you sleep with me, I'll see that you are considered for the special opening . . ." Since women have been lower in status, it is women who have traditionally been exploited by the aggressive use of sex. What they have not been able to do until recently is get together and discuss their situation so that they could take action. In one company we worked with, women who had been divided by jealousy and competition with each other (and divided up by the men in the company), finally got together and as a group began to challenge the system. They were able to do it successfully through the support they gave each other and by sharing information. Men have traditionally discussed their female conquests, but when women began to discuss the behavior of male coworkers, there were surprising revelations. The women discovered that what they had thought were "private relationships" were widely shared by coworkers. They decided that if they all refused to buy into the system, it could not survive.

Not all men are seeking sexual conquest, of course. There are usually a group of men in organizations who are actively testing the women's sexual availability and a group who are not. If there is a small number of women and a large male work force, the number of men who test their availability may become an irritating problem to the women. Men who are not seeking sexual relationships may be prone to deny that the issue exists because they are not receiving continual interaction as are the women. These men, who might be supportive, may be totally unaware of the situation in which the women find themselves.

Another issue for women is how to interact with the man who first evaluates her attractiveness. If he does not find her physically appealing, he discounts her and she may have difficulty being heard or accepted for her competence in role. If he finds her attractive, he may either interact with her seductively, testing to see if she will respond or he may withdraw because his sexual feelings get in the way of being able to work easily with her. Either reaction creates stress in the working relationship. An additional anxiety some men experience is to wonder whether, as women become more assertive, they will also become sexually aggressive and become the seducers.

In some sense the most acceptable relationship between men and women *is* a sexual one because it is easy to understand. In a sexual relationship, the traditional role of the male is the seducer and the role of the woman is to be seducible. The great fear of many women is that if they are not seducible, if they say no to a sexual request, then the relationship will end. For women who are not very self-confident, it may be easier to accede to a sexual request even if it does not make her happy, than risk the loss of the relationship. We are not speaking only about sexual intercourse. A great many behaviors are part of the ritual of sex and fit this pattern. At a dance, for example, the woman who regretfully refused a request to dance until she finished an interesting conversation with a woman friend would be a raving nonconformist! A request to dance has sexual overtones and insofar as the woman is oriented toward being chosen by men it supercedes other involvements. The collusion around sexuality has been challenged in the physical sphere (Masters and Johnson, 1966) but less articulately in the area of the rituals of seduction which lead to that final activity. It is these rituals which are most apt to be a problem in the work setting.

As the numbers of women in organizations increase there is great potential for moving beyond present anxieties into satisfying professional and personal relationships. The resistance of many men has dissolved after one good working relationship with a woman peer which was personal but not sexual. The man who has never had to relate to women except as wife, lover, or family member may attempt to recreate the traditional role relationships with women colleagues unless he has experienced a peer relationship. Men often focus on fears of what they will lose! They won't feel comfortable, be able to swear or tell off-color stories, and so on. When women are part of the work setting, these fears can be tested in reality. Until that happens, they only breed resistance.

Lest we be misunderstood, let us make clear that we are not trying to reduce relationships between men and women in work settings to totally neutral ones. Our differences can be the source of much energy and enjoyment. Sexual attraction and the deeply internalized rituals surrounding it make personal relationships on the job or in the community sufficiently complicated that being able to face and discuss these issues openly is critical.

SUPPORT

In order to do what they want to do, most people need to be in an environment of supportive relationships. This is particularly true for women moving into a position of responsibility in an institution where they have not traditionally carried these roles. When companies begin to promote women, they need more than a token woman. They need to promote enough women so that these women can form support groups for each other. Why do women need support? Not because they are extra fragile, but because they are outside of the male apprentice and support network. In most organizations, the more established officers of the company keep a sharp eye on, and encourage younger men of promise. Frequently, they advise with them, take them in as proteges and use influence to make possible their advancement. This is infrequently true of women. Therefore, if they are to realize their potential, women need other women to make the climate one in which they too feel supported.

As women try out new sensations and behaviors, they feel powerful and excited, but they also may experience some deprivation—a feeling that a familiar part of them has been lost and that their newly acquired behavior has made them very vulnerable. As a result of this feeling of deprivation, women often return to old sex-role stereo-types to escape for a while from the unfamiliarity and vulnerability of the new roles.

There are a number of ways in which women can be supportive of each other as they experiment with new roles. They can seek ways to share common dilemmas; they can support each other's exper-imental behaviors and learn from each other's experiences.

In organizations, two special groupings of women must learn the rewards of mutual support—those in peer groups and those in superior/subordinate relationships. For a while, women in key man-agerial positions will have few female peers. So women throughout an organization will have to seek each other out and build their own referent-group support system. Partially because of their greater numbers, men can more easily provide each other with a continuing support system.

All women who move up in an organization will undoubtedly share similar experiences, for example, how to feel comfortable in previously all-male staff meetings. Most women were taught early to orient to men; these patterns are carried into adulthood. An analysis of group interaction demonstrates what even a casual observation of groups will quickly reveal. In mixed-sex groups, most conversation is oriented toward men. Women's comments are most often inter-rupted, overlooked, or unheard because men are not used to paying attention to what women are saying. Women have colluded with this pattern, and they ignore other women too. One way to break this collusion is for women to support other women by paying special attention to what they are saying (regardless of whether or not it is agreeable to them) and reinforcing them so that they will be heard and dealt with. This can be a very simple and powerful process once you begin to work with it. One example: after a woman begins to speak, another woman can watch the group carefully. If the speaker has been interrupted the other woman can remark, "I think we only heard half of your thought, what was the rest of it?" and help her to finish. Or if a woman who spoke was ignored, another woman can reinforce her statement with: "Barbara really had an interesting comment on what we were discussing" or "I would like to hear what Edie had to say again; I'm not sure it was clearly understood." In any group, women must not permit other women's ideas to be dropped.

During crises, support will also be greatly needed. Crises may range from the difficulty of entering into "Man's World," to encoun-tering major problems on the job, to integrating home priorities with job priorities. Women can understand and support with much more empathy than men; they must be available to each other when critical situations arise.

In the superior/subordinate relationship, there are many opportunities for mutual support, and often these are totally missed or misused. Women in key positions can become important models for those who are striving, and for whom there are so few women models. They can become model androgynous women who have moved upward and retained their female attributes while at the same time incorporating more "masculine" characteristics (Bem, 1974). Women superiors can become respected colleagues, friends, "bosses."

Women subordinates are often jealous of the success of their superiors; they are not used to being responsible to, working for, and being rewarded by a woman. Often, they continue to respond to women in sex-role stereotypes, such as: women can type their own material, handle their own travel arrangements; their work has lower priority than a man's because it is not as important. These problems in the relationship must be confronted and the relationship redirected into ways in which superiors and superordinates can begin to support each other. Men often rely on sexuality in male/female superior/subordinate relationships to maintain human connectedness. Women must rely on mutual respect and competence for this kind of human connection with other women. If these ingredients are present in the relationship it becomes one of enormous support.

Women who try new ways of mutual support find it very satisfying. It is essential that organizations recognize this satisfaction, understand its potency, and encourage women to continue to build support systems for their survival and their productivity.

CONCLUSION

The issues we have discussed: power, collusion, intimacy-sexuality, and support are crucial in this period when old sex-role stereotypes are giving way to more androgynous roles for men and for women. As women move into these new roles they feel anxious, angry, confused, curious, delighted, and liberated. As men experiment with enlarging the boundaries of the traditional male role, they will experience these same feelings. Our intent has been to help women understand the internal and external sources for these feelings.

What is happening to women has implications for both personal relationships and for the organizations in which they work. Men need to be ready to engage in a re-education process around their relationships if they are to navigate this period of transition successfully. Organizations must be willing to re-examine the assumptions on which much organizational behavior is based. Most important, however, is the continued articulation of issues such as the ones raised in the paper and their discussion between the sexes in both personal and institutional conflicts. We can expect changes both in the climate of institutions and in the relationships of men and women as they head in the direction of increased authenticity and mutuality.

REFERENCES

Bem, S. L. Sex-role adaptability: One consequence of psychological androgyny. *Journal of Personal and Social Psychology*, 1975, *31* (4), 634-643.

Bem, S. L. The measurement of psychological androgyny. *Journal of Consulting and Clinical Psychology*, 1974, *42* (2), 155-162.

Broverman, I. K., Vogel, S. R., Broverman, D. M., Clarkson, F. E., & Rosenkrantz, P. S. Sex-role stereotypes: A current appraisal. *Journal of Social Issues*, 1972, *28*, 59-78.

Deutsch, M. *The resolution of conflict: Constructive and destructive processes.* New Haven: Yale University Press, 1973.

French, J. R. P., & Raven, B. The bases of social power. In D. Cartwright (Ed.), *Studies in social power.* Ann Arbor, Mich.: Institute for Social Research, 1959.

Horner, M. S. Fail: Bright women. *Psychology Today*, November 1969, *3*.

Kantor, R. M. *Commitment and community: Communes and utopias in sociological perspective.* Cambridge, Mass.: Harvard University Press, 1972.

Lieberman, M. A., Yalom, I. D., & Miles, M. B. *Encounter groups: First facts.* New York: Basic Books, 1973.

Masters, W. H., & Johnson, V. E. *Human sexual response.* Boston: Little, Brown, 1966.

Rapoport, R., & Rapoport, R. N. *Dual-career families.* Middlesex, England: Penguin, 1971.

How Developmental Theory Can Assist Facilitators to Select and Design Structured Experiences

Carole Widick   Michael Cowan

In recent years, interest and participation in small-group experiences of various kinds have grown phenomenally. Counseling centers, schools, and community agencies routinely use T-groups, encounter groups, value-clarification methods, and other structured group activities. In addition to providing help for more than one person at a time, structured group approaches provide a more focused, less threatening approach to self-exploration than traditional group-counseling approaches. Typically, structured group activities center attention on a particular topic and offer creative and organized ways for an individual to examine his or her beliefs and behaviors; some offer approaches to attitudinal and/or behavioral change. The purpose of the activities in this book, for example, is to allow individuals to explore the extent to which their attitudes and behaviors reflect stereotyped sex-role assumptions.

SELECTION AND DESIGN OF ACTIVITIES

Too often, group activities are selected on the basis of availability, facilitator preference, or current fads. We would like to suggest that the group or workshop leader select and design structured experiences only after a thoughtful and systematic consideration of the needs of the client group and the leader's own available knowledge.

One such systematic way of selecting or designing structured learning activities for particular client groups makes use of the famous Lewinian equation, "Behavior is a function of the interaction of

---

Carole Widick is assistant professor in the College of Education, The Ohio State University, Columbus, Ohio, and Michael Cowan is director of the Center for Student Development, St. John's University, Collegeville, Minn.

person and environment" [B=f (P×E)]. This means that three elements need to be considered in planning structured experiences: (1) the desired outcome (B)—What clients should do, feel, or know as a result of the learning experience; (2) the person (P)—What we need to know about a particular client group in order to plan appropriate and meaningful learning experiences for them; (3) the learning environment (E)—What elements should be included in the selection or design of a structured experience to promote particular outcomes for specific individuals.

In the context of this book, the desired outcome (B) of the activities is an enhanced awareness of the limiting effects of sex-role stereotypes on people's behavior. This paper offers a detailed consideration from a developmental perspective of the person variable (P) in the equation. The specific activities and learning strategies in this book can be thought of as potential learning environments (E) that can help clients attain certain desired goals.

The "interactionist" perspective of the B-P-E model is widely acknowledged and accepted by those involved in group work, but those planning workshops often assume that the person in the equation has universal characteristics. At a philosophic level, that may make sense; however, in laboratory education important individual differences may exist that need to be recognized and included as a part of the actual design of the experience.

Imagine if you will a scenario in which you, a facilitator, have been asked to conduct a series of workshops for the appropriately vague purpose of "helping people clarify their values about sexuality and sex-role behavior." With a zest and courage born of hours in the arena as a group facilitator, you accept the assignment.

If the group consisted of fifteen young people, both male and female, ranging in age from seventeen to twenty, you might overhear the following comments during an introductory activity:

"I'm going to college this fall and I'm going to be living in a coed hall. I'm not sure if I'll be able to handle it—you know, guys around all the time."

"I just read this really neat book by Susan Brownmiller about rape. It's really made me see how oppressed women are. I really want to talk about that."

"My girlfriend often accuses me of being chauvinistic. I really don't think I am. I think of her as a person, not a chick or anything like that. But it's hard to know what to do; sometimes she likes it when I open doors for her; then other times she gets mad. How are you supposed to treat girls, anyway?"

In a different group of fifteen women between the ages of thirty-five and fifty, you might overhear these comments:

"I feel like I've spent ten years being a mother. Now I want to be something more, or at least different. I know that I'm changing, and my husband tries to encourage me, but he is apprehensive."

"I find myself wanting everything—a perfect family life, a tastefully decorated home with a creative flair, a career at which I am superb, success, peace of mind, excitement, calm; yet, all I ever seem to do is think about all the possibilities. Doing the things I want seems impossible."

"I've never been married and never want to be. In this society, marriage is a burden for a woman and a free ride for a man."

These two groups may be similar in some ways, but in many others they are quite different. If we take Lewin's suggestion seriously, the design of a workshop on sexuality can be tailored to fit the differences as well as the similarities. How does one go about such a task?

The starting point is the participants: what differences among them need to be taken into account? Obviously, a multitude of individual differences exist (sex, age, race) that might be of importance. If the workshops are designed with developmental goals in mind, such as resolving personal conflicts or understanding societal forces, then developmental differences among participants must be considered. A participant's developmental place in the world determines his or her interests and preferences, concerns and problems, the form and style of relationships, and, to an extent, the way that person learns and changes. Simply stated, people who are at different places developmentally are quite different people with different needs. Group activities can be designed to acknowledge and respond to those differences.

THE PERSON: A DEVELOPMENTAL PERSPECTIVE

Developmental theories may be defined as psychological models that focus on changes in the individual over his or her life span. Two different types of developmental theories will be considered here. *Psychosocial* developmental theorists (Erikson, 1968; Chickering, 1969) focus on the sequence of tasks or demands with which the individual must cope. *Cognitive* developmental theorists (Perry, 1970; Kohlberg, 1969) stress the stages through which individuals move in the integration of their thinking about their experiences. Psychosocial theorists stress changes in *what people deal with* as they develop; cognitive stage theorists stress changes in *how people think* about their experiences as they develop.

Psychosocial Development

Erikson (1968) suggested that psychosocial development occurs in eight major stages. Each stage poses a developmental task and a crisis point at which time the task must be resolved in some fashion. For example, during the *identity* stage, or adolescence, the task of establishing one's identity looms when physical and sexual maturity is being attained, when the ability and skill for thinking about complex, abstract questions such as "Who am I?" are being developed, and when societal institutions (family, school, government) demand a series of decisions—particularly about one's career and one's values. Havighurst (1953) and Blocher (1974), among others, have suggested that there are coping skills associated with each stage that are important when completing the tasks of that stage.

Erikson's four developmental stages from adolescence through the life span are:

1. *Identity* vs. *Identity Confusion* (adolescence). Integrating an identity and making those commitments that express that identity.
2. *Intimacy* vs. *Isolation* (young adulthood). Developing and committing oneself to close, reciprocal, loving relationships.
3. *Generativity* vs. *Stagnation*. Creating, giving, nurturing, teaching, and accepting responsibility for the future of society.
4. *Integrity* vs. *Despair*. Finding meaning and value in life as one faces diminishing powers and death.

Individuals who are at different life stages are probably concerned about different issues, experiencing somewhat different pressures, and needing different skills for resolving their particular developmental dilemmas. Both of the groups described earlier may be quite concerned about sex-role issues, but for the seventeen- to twenty-year-old group, the issues may revolve around identity and intimacy: Who am I? Specifically, what sort of man or woman can I be? What sort of man or woman can I love? What sort of relationship can I invest in? For the thirty-five- to fifty-year-old group, identity is no longer a potential but a fact; change and growth must be built on the history of individual commitments. For these people, the issues may revolve around the tasks of the generativity stage: What am I producing? Do I contribute? Who/what has defined me to this point? How can I use and integrate all my interests, given the realities of my life?

Interestingly, Sheehy's interviews with adults extend our understanding of the generativity stage (Sheehy, 1976). Many people in their late thirties or early forties appear to confront a crisis that Sheehy calls "Mid-life Transition"—a point at which one perceives a narrowness in his or her life and feels the urge to broaden, to branch out, and to explore new turf. Typically in our culture, this transition conforms to sex-role patterns. For men, the transition may involve a turning from career involvement to expression of feelings, introspection, and seeking a closeness with others. For women, who have usually invested in relationships and the nurturing of families, the middle years seem to invoke a desire for a different kind of productivity—an investment in ideas and concrete products—those tangibles and intangibles associated with a "career."

Implications of Psychosocial Development for Workshop Design

Involvement will be more meaningful for most participants if the activities are selected and designed to correspond with their developmental concerns and if those activities help the participants gain needed coping skills. Two ways to determine what concerns are most salient for a particular group are the following:

1. *Inquiry.* It is good practice for group leaders to elicit a list of immediate concerns from participants either prior to the scheduled activity or in an initial data-gathering session at the beginning of the structured experience. For example, a standard brainstorming procedure can yield a list of concerns that can be used as topics for value-clarification activities, or "developmental" issues can be used as a framework within which concerns can be identified.

2. *Psychosocial Developmental Theory.* On the basis of theoretical and empirical knowledge, a facilitator can make some a priori assumptions about what issues people will be facing, depending on their different life stages. Knowledge of this sort can give a group leader some preliminary guidelines that can be used to select and create activities.

For the seventeen- to twenty-year-old group, relevant content is likely to focus on issues of stabilizing personal identity, tentative commitments to career possibilities, and initial decisions about the place of intimacy in one's life. The key issues, in other words, are likely to be the typically important concerns of the young adult.

For the thirty-five- to fifty-year-old group, psychosocial theory suggests that relevant concerns are likely to revolve around whether or not the individual perceives him- or herself to be contributing to the welfare of others in a significant way. At this stage in the life span, concerns tend to center on evaluating the results of commitments made in young adulthood. After making this type of evaluation, some people continue on their present courses, some make modifications consisting largely of shifting emphases (e.g., career to family or vice versa), while others make radical changes in their life styles.

Psychosocial development theories remind us that people do in fact have different concerns at different phases of their lives. Further, they help us to anticipate what these concerns are likely to be for different client groups. With this information, selection and design of structured experiences can be accomplished in a way that may enhance the relevance of the experiences for group participants.

For example, a typical technique for many group experiences is force-field analysis. An individual is asked to set a goal and then to analyze internal and outside forces that help or hinder attainment of that goal. Psychosocial developmental theory suggests some factors to be considered when using force-field analysis. For a seventeen- to twenty-year-old group, made up of individuals who are still contemplating their first major commitments, the activity should be useful as a way of teaching decision-making skills and looking at current issues. The force-field approach is a good method of achieving closure in a workshop. On the other hand, for the mid-life transition group, the idea of making changes, with the range and variety of forces both impelling and restraining change, can be a powerful and emotion-laden task. If this is the case, the activity can be scheduled in the middle of a workshop, designed to help individuals spell out and rank the varieties of forces. Follow-up activities can be provided that concentrate on (1) self-directed change and (2) what happens in one's immediate family or work environment when one is making changes.

Cognitive Stage Development

The work of Perry (1970), Loevinger and Wessel (1970), and Kohlberg (1969) has attracted attention recently. In general, all postulate development as a process of growth through stages of reasoning. That is, individuals at different stages of development perceive and organize certain issues or experiences in different ways and as a result tend to behave differently. Perry's model of development is useful to bring the idea of cognitive-stage development into focus and to suggest important individual differences that may need to be considered in workshop design.

In general, Perry describes development as a pattern of changes in reasoning about the nature of the world or subparts of that world (the nature of man or woman). He identifies three orientations that an individual passes through sequentially: dualism, relativism, and commitment. In abbreviated form, these orientations are described here:

Dualism

Dualistic thinkers perceive a two-category world: good/bad, right/wrong. All knowledge, including ideas and values, can be considered either right or wrong. The facilitator's role is to be an authority and provide the correct answers—in this case to specify the right (appropriate) sex-role behavior and attitudes to hold.

Possible Dilemmas

This individual expects to be given, or at the very least to find, answers, hence can be quite troubled by ambiguity.

Relativism

Relativistic thinkers perceive a world of many legitimate and complex alternatives. The facilitator's role is to act as a resource or as a guide through the complexity—to help the individual examine various points of view about sex roles and sort out fact, opinion, and values.

Possible Dilemmas

This individual may be overrun and at times overwhelmed by complexity and yet may fear the task of deciding on a stance and may want to avoid making decisions.

Commitment

Committed individuals perceive a world of alternatives but choose a set of values—a course of action on which to proceed. The facilitator can serve as a model and support for the individual in taking a stand.

Possible Dilemmas

This individual may be jolted by the challenges to commitment and may need encouragement.

It seems logical to assume that most people travel from dualism to commitment many times in their lives as they confront new experiences. For each area, they seem to have to let go of "Truth," wander in the wilderness of many equally valid, yet conflicting answers, and eventually choose a path through which to define their identities. For the seventeen- to twenty-year-olds, sex-role behavior may be strictly prescriptive ("A man who likes to take care of children is not a man") or extensively relativistic ("A man can be anything—a dancer, football player, teacher, doctor, nurse, lumberjack, homemaker, strong, weak, active, passive"). The same is true of the thirty-five- to fifty-year-old group, who may represent the whole range of orientations to sex roles and their situations, from "Marriage is an instrument of oppression for women in this society" to "Marriage is an institution that is sometimes unfair to both men and women, but in some instances it can be a very positive force for the growth of both partners" to "I believe that, for me, a rather traditional marriage is of major importance. I have come to the belief that I need a stable, loving relationship, and I think a monogamous marriage relationship is the place where I can best find that." Interestingly, even in the area of sex-role behavior, individuals probably think in different ways along the developmental continuum; for example, one person may be quite relativistic, even committed, in ways of thinking about men and women and marriage—yet, as a new parent, that same person may be starting with some rather dualistic assumptions. Thus, in a workshop group, the facilitator may have many individuals at different places in their thinking about various issues.

Implications of Cognitive Development Theory for Workshop Design

Goals. Different developmental orientations suggest different workshop goals. Individuals who view sex-role behavior in a dualistic fashion need to look at other points of view and allow themselves to entertain a multitude of perspectives. In essence, the goals can be seen as a kind of opening up—a person cannot make mature, thoughtful decisions about his or her own life without having encountered the options available. Therefore, a facilitator can select activities that ask the participants to generate as many alternatives as possible (e.g., make a list of as many characteristics of man/woman as possible; discuss an issue with someone who has a different point of view; and present and argue a point of view that he or she does not agree with—e.g., many role-reversal activities).

In the processing of any activity, a facilitator can focus on alternate perspectives by highlighting the different experiences, perceptions, and outcomes rather than seeking a common conclusion.

For example, a sex-role exploration activity could be looked at in terms of diversity of perceptions and could be processed to emphasize that aspect.

If an individual views sex-role behavior relativistically, it may be appropriate for that person to prepare to make commitments and take action. Making commitments requires the capacity to narrow and adopt a sustained and sustaining focus. This seems to involve the clarifying of values—the capacity to sort out that which is centrally important—and the learning of decision-making skills.

For this purpose, a facilitator can select activities that ask participants to rank order or choose among a series of alternatives (e.g., value-clarification strategies); discuss an issue with someone who has a different point of view and reach consensus; and take a stand and generate a supported argument to justify that position (e.g., an internal dialogue).

The diagram below shows this design process based on cognitive-stage theory:

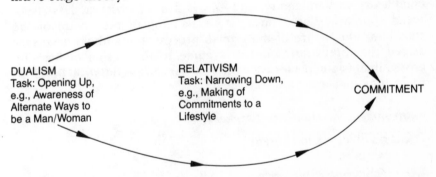

DUALISM
Task: Opening Up,
e.g., Awareness of
Alternate Ways to
be a Man/Woman

RELATIVISM
Task: Narrowing Down,
e.g., Making of
Commitments to a
Lifestyle

COMMITMENT

Workshop Processes. Cognitive-stage theorists also suggest that individuals at different stages of development have quite different characteristics, which may be very important in planning the process of a workshop.

Theorists suggest that individuals at the "beginning" stages of development tend to be characterized by cognitive simplicity, absolute thinking, concrete thinking, externally guided behavior, dependence on authority figures, and egocentrism in viewing others and self.

Those at more advanced developmental levels tend to be more cognitively complex, relativistic in thinking, abstract in thought, internally guided in behavior (intrinsically motivated), interdependent in relationships, and allocentric and empathic in ways of viewing others.

During a discussion of sex roles, those individuals with the first set of characteristics would be expected to have very different opinions from those of the second group. Hunt (1970) has suggested that individuals at different developmental stages need different learning or group environments in which to learn, grow, and feel comfortable. Widick, Knefelkamp, and Parker (1975) have explored the value of designing environments matched to developmental level. Thus far, their work suggests that individuals who are more dualistic in their thinking need support at a time when they are being pressed to look at an issue from various points of view. This support can be provided by creating a climate of trust among participants. However, attending to interpersonal climate is not sufficient; the dualistic thinker expects answers and hence needs a highly structured, highly concrete process in order to cope with the ambiguity of relativistic ideas. For the relativistic thinker, support can be provided by an interpersonal climate of trust. The individual who is relativistic thinks abstractly, tends to be comfortable with complexity and ambiguity, and enjoys a more abstract, less structured approach. Based on an understanding of the nature of the stages and the nature of the growth process, the authors have suggested the following model as a guide to the design of learning environments for persons at different levels of cognitive development:

Environment for Dualistic Thinkers

Focus on diversity in content
    (awareness)
Direct, concrete experience
    emphasized
High degree of structure
Personal atmosphere

Environment for Relativistic Thinkers

Focus on choice among alternatives
    (decision-making)
Vicarious experience emphasized

Low degree of structure
Personal atmosphere

In practice, this means that leaders may want to modify particular activities to conform with the general developmental level of the client group. For a more dualistic group, a discussion of sex-role stereotypes would need to be structured by use of specific questions, concrete dilemmas (What would you do if a male and a female, equally qualified, applied for the same job?), explicit modeling by the facilitator, and a structured format for reaching closure. For a more relativistic group, the facilitator would need only to provide a useful stimulus question and help individuals focus on the implications of the discussion for their own lives. Perhaps, more pertinent yet, the facilitator needs to be able to "read" the developmental level of individuals and respond to each in terms of his or her needs. During a value-clarification activity, a more dualistic thinker may need the support of some concrete examples; a more relativistic thinker may need help in moving toward a value decision.

DEVELOPMENTAL THEORY AND WORKSHOP DESIGN

After looking in some detail at the person variable in the $B=f(P \times E)$ equation, we return to the question with which we began this article: How can developmental theory help the facilitator select and design structured experiences?

We will attempt to answer the question by providing a systematic procedure for the selection or design of such experiences. We believe this design procedure to be applicable to brief workshops, extended small-group experiences, and classroom instruction.

Behavior (B)

I. What are the desired outcomes of the experience?

A. *Behavioral.* What should people be able to do?

B. *Affective.* What should people be able to feel?

C. *Cognitive.* What should people be able to know?

A specific consideration of desired goals is the necessary first step in the selection or design of structured experiences. These goals determine what is to follow in the planning process.

Person (P)

II. What is the developmental status of the persons who will be participating in the experience?

A. *Psychosocial development.*

1. What developmental tasks or crises are these individuals

probably being confronted with, given their current positions in the life span?

2. What skills are they likely to feel a need for in dealing with these developmental tasks?

B. *Cognitive stage development.*

1. How do the participants reason abut their own experiences? Where do their current ways of understanding themselves and others fall on the cognitive simplicity-complexity continuum?

2. Can the learning experience be planned in such a way as to challenge the individual to reason and problem solve at the next higher developmental level? What is necessary for the individual to feel comfortable and secure enough to become involved?

Environment (E)

III. Having established goals and apprised ourselves of the developmental status of our participants, what needs to be taken into account in the selection or design of developmental structured learning experiences?

A. *The task.* What will participants be asked to do? Is the content of the task relevant to the members' issues? Have cognitive stage considerations been taken into account? How concrete or abstract should the task be? How much structure should be provided in instruction?

B. *The interaction of participants.* How should the participants deal with each other? Do participants need to encounter those who think/feel differently? Do participants need the support of others struggling with the same issues? Is feedback between participants appropriate?

C. *The role of the leader.* Is the leader a directive "structurer" or a nondirective facilitator? How are people at different developmental levels likely to react to authority? How involved should the leader become in the activity itself?

D. *The process perspective.* How do people think about the activities they have experienced? Can alternative ways of looking at the event be designed (e.g., round-robin sharing of participants' reactions)? Can the processing be used to examine how persons' choices/commitments affect their ways of viewing things? Who would structure the processing? (The leader? The participants themselves?)

We have attempted to pose a number of specific questions for the selection or design of structured learning experiences using the B-P-E equation as a framework. It is our belief that the initial answer to each of the above questions is "that depends." No absolute answer—no favorite activity—is likely to adequately reflect the complexity of the persons with whom we deal. In our own work, the answers to the questions we have articulated above and to the many others that could be added do in fact depend on our goals, and especially on the current developmental status of our clients.

Although this approach to selection and design is somewhat complex, it also is a systematic and theory-based way to proceed. Anyone who is interested in pursuing developmental theories and their implications for the selection and design of structured learning experiences will, we hope, find a good beginning in the bibliography.

BIBLIOGRAPHY

Blocher, D. H. *Developmental counseling.* New York: Ronald Press, 1966, 1974.

Chickering, A. *Education and identity.* San Francisco: Jossey Bass, 1969.

Erikson, E. *Identity: Youth and crisis.* New York: W. W. Norton, 1968.

Harvey, O. J., Hunt, D. E., & Schroder, H. M. *Conceptual systems and personality organization.* New York: John Wiley, 1961.

Havighurst, R. J., & Blocher, D. H. *Human development and education.* New York: Longmans Green, 1953.

Hunt, D. E. A conceptual level matching model for coordinating learner characteristics with educational approaches. *Interchange,* 1970, *1,* 68-72.

Hunt, D. E. A conceptual systems change model and its application to education. In O. J. Harvey (Ed.), *Experience, structure, and adaptability.* New York: Springer, 1966.

Hunt, D. E. Matching models for teacher training. In B. Joyce & M. Weil (Eds.), *Perspectives for reform in teacher education.* Englewood Cliffs, N.J.: Prentice-Hall, 1972.

Knefelkamp, L. L. Developmental instruction: Fostering intellectual and personal growth. Unpublished dissertation, University of Minnesota, 1974.

Kohlberg, L. Stage and sequence: The cognitive-developmental approach to socialization. In D. A. Goslin (Ed.), *Handbook of socialization theory and research.* Chicago: Rand McNally, 1969.

Kohlberg, L., & Mayer, R. Development as the aim of education. *Harvard Educational Review,* 1972, *42,* 449-495.

Kohlberg, L., & Turiel, E. Moral development and moral education. In G. Lesser (Ed.), *Psychology and educational practice.* Chicago: Scott Foresman, 1971.

Loevinger, J., & Wessel, R. *Measuring ego development* (Vols. I & II). San Francisco: Jossey Bass, 1970.

Perry, W., Jr. *Intellectual and ethical development in the college years.* New York: Holt, Rinehart and Winston, 1970.

Sheehy, G. *Passages.* New York: Dutton, 1976.

Sprinthall, N. A curriculum for schools: Counselors as teachers for psychological growth. *The School Counselor,* May 1973, 361-369.

Widick, C. An evaluation of developmental instruction in a university setting. Unpublished dissertation, University of Minnesota, 1975.

Widick, C., Knefelkamp, L. L., & Parker, C. The counselor as a developmental instructor. *Counselor Education and Supervision,* June 1975.

For a discussion of training style and sex roles, see M. S. Sprague & A. Sargent, Toward androgynous trainers. In J. E. Jones & J. W. Pfeiffer (Eds.), *The 1977 Annual Handbook for Group Facilitators.* La Jolla, Calif.: University Associates, 1977, pp. 147-153.

APPENDIX

Exploring Sex-Role Concepts:
Guidelines for Participants*

These guidelines are to let you know what to expect in the group situation. Please read the following comments and suggestions carefully before you participate in a structured group experience.

GOALS

The three major goals of the group session are to help you:

(1) increase your awareness of how your perception of your sex role (i.e., styles, habits, anticipations, and feelings toward male-female relationships) affects your interactions with others.

(2) broaden your perceptions of how others feel.

(3) modify or direct your growth in an area related to male-female relationships that is important to you.

FACILITATORS

Group facilitators are not *leaders* in the traditional sense of the term. Perhaps the best way to view them is as resource persons. That is,

---

Adapted from *Encounter: Group Processes for Interpersonal Growth* by G. Egan. Copyright 1970 by Wadsworth Publishing Company, Inc. Used by permission of the publisher, Brooks/Cole Publishing Company, Monterey, California.

*Discussions of group guidelines and contracts are available in G. Egan, Contracts in Encounter Groups. In J. W. Pfeiffer & J. E. Jones (Eds.), *The 1972 Annual Handbook for Group Facilitators*. La Jolla, Calif.: University Associates, 1972, pp. 185-196. See also J. W. Pfeiffer & J. E. Jones, Design Considerations in Laboratory Education. In J. E. Jones, & J. W. Pfeiffer (Eds.), *The 1973 Annual Handbook for Group Facilitators*. La Jolla, Calif.: University Associates, 1973, pp. 177-194.

through their interactions with participants, the structure of the group, and the group activities, the facilitators will attempt to help you gain some new insights into female-male relationships. However, they are in the group also because they are interested in growing interpersonally.

NATURE OF THE EXPERIENCE

The group session is most meaningful for those who are open to new experiences and who do not have specific expectations for what will happen to them or how they will feel. You have the option of not participating in any activity. The group experience is based on the following principles:

(1) *Learning by Doing.* You will learn some ways that your sex-role attitudes affect your behavior toward others through your involvement in small-group learning activities and discussion of your experience in these and in related out-of-class activities.

(2) *An Openness to Experimentation.* You will be asked to experiment with your own behavior by attempting to relate to members of the other sex in new ways. This means that you will try to deal with group members by using behavior you might not ordinarily use. For example, if you are usually quiet and reserved in dealing with the other sex, you may experiment with various styles of assertive behavior.

(3) *Not Prejudging the Experiment.* The person who comes to a group convinced that the experiment will not work usually leaves it feeling the same way. The prophecy is self-fulfilling. You are asked to reserve your judgment. The only way to know whether the experiment works is to open yourself to it as completely as possible.

(4) *Feedback.* Your own behavior is a major input in the workshop, and it is important to see how this behavior affects others. You are asked not only to react naturally to others but to tell others how you feel about their behavior. You, too, will receive feedback from other participants, and by means of such feedback you may be able to come to a better understanding of how your sex-role attitudes and behaviors facilitate or hinder your interpersonal relationships.

A CLIMATE OF EXPERIMENTAL LEARNING

If the group experience is to have a facilitative effect on your understanding of yourself and others, certain points must be kept in mind. These are:

(1) *Remember the Importance of Sex Role.* For the purposes of this workshop, you are to assume that all your feelings, attitudes, and behaviors in some way reflect your view of what a man or woman *ought* to be or do.

(2) *Focus on the Here-and-Now.* When you talk about events that have happened or are happening outside of the workshop, do so in such a way as to make them relevant to what is happening in the group. You will be asked to deal with your experiences as they occur in the session itself rather than in your past; your interactions with other group members are an integral part of the experience.

(3) *Avoid Generalities.* Words addressed to everyone tend to be addressed to no one. As a group member, try to speak in concrete and specific terms. For instance, when speaking about yourself, use "I" instead of "you," "one," "we," "people," "men," and the like. Do not say, "Most of the people in this group think I'm aggressive." Indicate who you are referring to and what specifically that person is doing that makes you feel the way you do. An example: "When Mary doesn't voice her reactions to what I say, she gives me the impression that she thinks I'm too pushy and is afraid to speak up to me."

(4) *Be Open to Self-Disclosure.* Be open about yourself and your functioning in the workshop activities. Talk about yourself in an honest and direct manner. Facts about yourself are not important, but through telling others about yourself you translate yourself for them. You are not asked to reveal your past or your darkest secrets. You are important as you are *now*. What you say about yourself and what you experience should encourage others to know you more completely. Your openness can constitute an invitation to others to involve themselves with you in a way that helps you develop a better understanding of yourself.

(5) *Practice Active Listening.* Examine your ability to listen to and really hear others. *Active listening* is not just hearing words and sentences and understanding their meaning; it is an awareness that another person's feelings, as well as his

ideas, are important to your understanding of him or her. Learning to pick up both verbal and nonverbal cues is a part of active listening.

(6) *Confront Others.* Sometimes you will find it impossible to agree with what another person is saying or doing. If this is true, tell him or her so as honestly as you can, and say why. Confrontation is basically an invitation to another to examine or reflect upon his or her behavior and how it may interfere with forming more meaningful and productive interpersonal relationships. The *way* you confront is very important. Confrontation is not just irresponsibly "telling a person off." Responsible confrontation is an invitation to self-examination. It should focus on a specific form of behavior that the person *can* change if he or she desires to do so.

People learn best when they are made aware of both positive and negative aspects of their behavior. Too much of either positive or negative feedback (or confrontation) generally hinders a person's general growth. For example, a person who heard only negative comments about him- or herself would not become aware of the positive ways in which he or she affects others. Therefore, it is important to remember that confrontation is but one part of the two-part process that helps people understand their effect on others. You can confront best by letting the person know both the things that interfere with that person's relationships in the group and the things that facilitate those relationships.

(7) *Respond to Confrontation and Feedback.* If confrontation and feedback are used responsibly—that is, as invitations to self-examination—then the best response *is* self-examination. However, when we are confronted or offered feedback, even by someone who is concerned for us and wants to involve him- or herself with us, our instinctive response is to defend ourselves and to attack the confronter. We respond to the punitive side effects (or at least we may interpret them that way) of the confrontation instead of the confrontation itself. Because confrontation is an invitation for self-exploration and learning, try to listen to what other people are saying and not to the feelings they evoke in you.

BIBLIOGRAPHY

Astin, H. S., Parelman, A., & Fisher, A. *Sex roles: A research bibliography*. Rockville, Md.: National Institutes of Mental Health, 1975.

Bach, G. R., & Deutsch, R. M. *Pairing*. New York: Avon, 1970.

Bach, G. R., & Wyden, P. *The intimate enemy*. New York: Avon, 1968.

Bernard, J. *The sex game*. New York: Atheneum, 1972.

Bird, J., & Bird, L. *Marriage is for grownups*. New York: Image Books, 1971.

Carter, D., & Rawlings, L. (Eds.). *Psychotherapy for women: Treatment for equality*. Springfield, Ill.: Charles Thomas, 1976.

Chester, P. *Women and madness*. New York: Doubleday, 1972.

Clinebell, H. J., & Clinebell, C. H. *The intimate marriage*. New York: Harper & Row, 1970.

DeBeauvoir, S. *The second sex*. New York: Bantam Books, 1961.

DeLora, J., & DeLora, J. *Intimate lifestyles: Marriage and its alternatives*. Pacific Palisades, Calif.: Goodyear, 1972.

Education for survival (Final Report, Sex Role Stereotypes Project. USOE-D-72-2507). Washington, D.C.: National Education Association, July 1973.

Ellis, A. *The American sexual tragedy*. New York: Grove Press, 1962.

Farrell, W. *The liberated man*. New York: Random House, 1974.

Fitzgerald, L., & Harman, L. (Eds.). Counseling women. *The Counseling Psychologist*, 1973, *4*(1), 2-101.

Fox, R., Lippett, R., & Schindler-Rainman, E. *Towards a human society—Images of potentiality*. La Jolla, Calif.: NTL Learning Resources Corp., 1973.

Friedan, B. *The feminine mystique*. New York: Dell, 1964.

Hobbs, L. *Love and liberation*. New York: McGraw-Hill, 1971.

Huber, J. (Ed.). *Changing women in a changing society*. Chicago: University of Chicago Press, 1973.

Kirkendall, L. A., & Whitehurst, R. N. *The new sexual revolution*. New York: Brown, 1971.

Lederer, W. J., & Jackson, D. D. *The mirages of marriage*. New York: Norton, 1968.

Maccoby, E., & Jacklin, C. N. (Eds.). *The development of sex differences*. Palo Alto, Calif.: Stanford University Press, 1974.

Mead, M. *Male and female*. New York: Dell, 1955.

Money, J., & Ehrhardt, A. A. *Man and woman, boy and girl: Differentiation and dimorphism of gender identity*. Baltimore: Johns Hopkins, 1972.

Morgan, R. (Ed.). *Sisterhood is powerful*. New York: Vintage Books, 1970.

Nichols, J. *Men's liberation: A new definition of masculinity*. New York: Penguin, 1975.

O'Neill, N., & O'Neill, G. *Open marriage*. New York: Avon, 1973.

Osipow, S. H. *Emerging woman: Career analysis and outlook*. Columbus, Ohio: Charles E. Merrill, 1975.

Otto, H. (Ed.). *The family in search of a future*. New York: Appleton-Century-Crofts, 1970.

Packard, V. *The sexual wilderness*. New York: Pocket Books, 1968.

Pleck, J., & Sawyer, J. *Men and masculinity*. New York: Prentice-Hall, 1974.

Project on sex equality and guidance opportunities: Resource for counselors, teachers and administrators (Rev. Ed.). Washington, D.C.: SEGO Project, American Personnel and Guidance Association.

Rogers, C. *Becoming partners: Marriage and its alternatives*. New York: Delacorte Press, 1972.

Rosenberg, M. B., & Bergstrom, L. V. *Women and society: A critical review of the literature with a selected annotated bibliography*. Beverly Hills, Calif.: Sage, 1973.

Roszak, B., & Roszak, T. (Eds.). *Masculine/feminine: Readings in sexual mythology and the liberation of women*. New York: Harper & Row, 1969.

Sargent, A. G. (Ed.). *Beyond sex role stereotypes*. St. Paul, Minn.: West Publishing, 1975.

Sheehy, G. The mentor connection: The secret link in the successful woman's life. *New York*, April 5, 1975, 20ff.

Sheehy, G. *Passages: Predictable crises of adult life*. New York: Dutton, 1976.

Veblen, T. *The theory of the leisure class*. New York: Menton, 1953.

Vilar, E. *The manipulated man*. New York: Farrar, Strauss, and Giroux, 1972.

Yorburg, B. *Sexual identity: Sex roles and social change*. New York: John Wiley, 1974.

Zuckerman, E. L. (Ed.). *Women and men: Roles, attitudes and power relationships*. New York: Radcliffe Club of New York, 1975.

DATE DUE

7.31 '80	
12.04 '80	
1 01 '81	
5.21 '81	
8.06 '81	
DEC 15 1986	
JUN 15 1987	
7.01 '87	
11.18 '87	
11.23 '88	
MAY 6 '92	
MAY 6 '92	

BRODART, INC.   Cat. No. 23-221